# Women in East Asian Cinema

# Women in East Asian Cinema

Gender Representations, Creative Labour and Global Histories

Felicia Chan, Fraser Elliott and Andy Willis

EDINBURGH
University Press

Edinburgh University Press is one of the leading university presses in the UK. We publish academic books and journals in our selected subject areas across the humanities and social sciences, combining cutting-edge scholarship with high editorial and production values to produce academic works of lasting importance. For more information visit our website: edinburghuniversitypress.com

© editorial matter and organisation Felicia Chan, Fraser Elliott and
　Andy Willis, 2024, 2025
©the chapters their several authors 2024, 2025

Grateful acknowledgement is made to the sources listed in the List of Illustrations for permission to reproduce material previously published elsewhere. Every effort has been made to trace the copyright holders, but if any have been inadvertently overlooked, the publisher will be pleased to make the necessary arrangements at the first opportunity.

Edinburgh University Press Ltd
13 Infirmary Street,
Edinburgh, EH1 1LT

First published in hardback by Edinburgh University Press 2024

Typeset in 10.5/13 Adobe Sabon
by Manila Typesetting Company

A CIP record for this book is available from the British Library

ISBN 978 1 3995 0492 8 (hardback)
ISBN 978 1 3995 0493 5 (paperback)
ISBN 978 1 3995 0494 2 (webready PDF)
ISBN 978 1 3995 0495 9 (epub)

The right of Felicia Chan, Fraser Elliott and Andy Willis to be identified as the editor of this work has been asserted in accordance with the Copyright, Designs and Patents Act 1988, and the Copyright and Related Rights Regulations 2003 (SI No. 2498).

# Contents

| | |
|---|---|
| List of Illustrations | vii |
| Acknowledgements | viii |
| Contributors | ix |
| Foreword | xiii |

Introduction: Women in East Asian Cinema: Gender
Representations, Creative Labour and Global Histories     1
*Felicia Chan, Fraser Elliott and Andy Willis*

## Part I: Gender Representations

1 A Cinema of Pleasure: He Xiaopei's Home Video Aesthetics
    and Queer Feminist Politics     13
    *Hongwei Bao*
2 Work Ethic(s) of Being a Woman: Images of Female Labour
    in Hong Kong Cinema (1950s–60s)     29
    *Fiona Y. W. Law*
3 'Functioning on the Fringes': Interrogating New
    South Korean Womanhood and Millennial Trauma in
    *Microhabitat* (2017)     50
    *Dave McCaig*
4 The Female Gaze in Xu Jinglei's *Letter from an Unknown
    Woman* (2004)     66
    *Bérénice M. Reynaud*
5 *Ichi* (2008): Female Stars and Gender Representations in
    the *Zatoichi* Franchise     79
    *Jonathan Wroot*

6 Agency and Subjectivity of the Female Protagonists in
  Qiong Yao Films    93
  *Xuelin Zhou*

## Part II: Creative Labour

7 Japanese Documentary Filmmaker Haneda Sumiko:
  Authorship and Gender Perspective    107
  *Alejandra Armendáriz-Hernández,*
  *Marcos Centeno-Martin and Irene González-López*
8 A Challenge on Every Page: Female Screenwriter-Directors
  in the South Korean Film Industry    124
  *Monika Kukolova*
9 The Film Star and Her Husband: The Collaboration
  between Takamine Hideko and Matsuyama Zenzō    138
  *Till Weingärtner*
10 Angie Chen: Hong Kong Film Pioneer    153
   *Andy Willis*
11 Her Own Feminism: Authorship and Editing in Ning Ying's
   Filmmaking Practice    166
   *Francesca Young Kaufman*

## Part III: Global Histories

12 Figurations of the *Nyonya*: The Uses and Abuses of
   Peranakan Chinese Representation in Film    185
   *Felicia Chan*
13 Temporally Performing a Region: A Feminist Analysis of
   Southeast Asian Women's Filmmaking    200
   *MaoHui Deng*
14 Celebrating Women in Global Cinema: Disruptive
   Programming and East Asian Women on International Screens    216
   *Fraser Elliott*

Appendix 1    231
Index    234

# Contributors

**Alejandra Armendáriz-Hernández** is a PhD candidate at the University Rey Juan Carlos, Madrid, writing a dissertation on female authorship and representation in the films directed by Tanaka Kinuyo. Her research, teaching and publications include the study of women filmmakers in Japan, gender representations in East Asian and transnational film connections between Japan and Latin America.

**Hongwei Bao** is an Associate Professor in Media Studies at the University of Nottingham, where he also co-directs the Centre for Contemporary East Asian Cultural Studies. His research primarily focuses on queer culture, independent documentary and alternative media production in contemporary China. He is the author of *Queer comrades: Gay identity and tongzhi activism in postsocialist China* (2018), *Queer China: Lesbian and gay literature and visual culture under Postsocialism* (2020) and *Queer media in China* (2021). He has published articles in journals such as *Continuum*, *Cultural Studies*, *Culture Unbound*, *Feminist Media Studies*, *Global Media and China* and *Intervention*.

**Marcos Centeno-Martin** is Lecturer in Film and Media and Japanese Studies at the University of Valencia and Honorary Research Fellow at Birkbeck, University of London. His research interests revolve around Japanese documentary film, including film theory, memory, transnationality and film representation of the Ainu people.

**Felicia Chan** is Senior Lecturer in Screen Studies at the University of Manchester where she researches the construction of national, cultural and cosmopolitan imaginaries in film and media. She is author of *Cosmopolitan cinema: Cross cultural encounters in East Asian film*

(2017), co-editor of *Chinese cinemas: International perspectives* (2016) and founding member of the Manchester-based Chinese Film Forum UK.

**MaoHui Deng** is Lecturer in Film Studies at the University of Manchester. He is the author of *Ageing, dementia and time in film: Temporal performances* (2023), which puts forward the first sustained analysis of films about dementia from a temporal viewpoint. He has also published chapters on films about dementia in *The Routledge Companion to European Cinema* (2021), *Contemporary narratives of ageing, illness, care* (2021) and *The politics of dementia* (2021).

**Fraser Elliott** is Lecturer of Film, Exhibition and Curation at the University of Edinburgh and a member of the Chinese Film Forum UK. His research specialises in the circulation of Chinese-language film in the UK and the histories of Hong Kong Cinema. He is a member of the Chinese Film Forum UK; Festival Consultant for the Taiwan Film Festival Edinburgh; collaborator with the Hong Kong Film Festival UK; and co-editor of *Full-throttle franchise: The culture, business and politics of* Fast and Furious (2023).

**Irene González-López** is Lecturer in Japanese Studies at Birkbeck, University of London. Her research primarily focuses on postwar Japanese cinema and issues related to gender and sexuality, both in front and behind the camera. She is the co-editor of *Tanaka Kinuyo: Nation, Stardom and Female Subjectivity* (2018).

**Monika Kukolova** is Lecturer in Film Studies in the School of Arts, Media and Creative Technology at the University of Salford. Her research explores the tensions in cross-media representations of belonging, and she focuses particularly on the creative labour of women in the film industry.

**Fiona Yuk-wa Law** is a lecturer in comparative literature at the University of Hong Kong. Her research interests include film studies and animal studies in the Asian context, with particular focus on the relationship between cinematic and literary representations, healing narratives, visual cultures, animal welfare and urban culture. Her writings can be found in *Journal of Chinese Cinemas*, *Animal Studies Journal*, *A Companion to Hong Kong Cinema*, *Screening the Nonhuman: Representations of Animal Others in the Media* and *Antennae: The Journal of Nature in Visual Culture*, among others.

**Dave McCaig** is Senior Lecturer within the Lincoln School of Film and Media at the University of Lincoln. He teaches in a variety of undergraduate and postgraduate programmes within the school. These include the BA Film and Television Studies, MA Gender Studies and MA Cultural Studies programmes. He has published widely in the areas of East Asian film and culture. Current research interests include masculinity and shamanism within the modern South Korean television drama and the role and function of *ero-guro-nansensu* in 'New Generational' Japanese Horror.

**Bérénice M. Reynaud** holds a PhD in Chinese studies on Chinese women's cinema from Université Jean Moulin Lyon 3. She is an associate researcher at the IETT institute in Lyon. Her research focuses on Chinese women filmmakers, gender and feminism in contemporary Chinese Cinema. She has published in *Monde chinois – Nouvelle Asie*, *The Chinese Independent Cinema Observer*, *Annali di Ca' Foscari: Serie Orientale* and in the edited volume on art and censorship *Tactiques d'expression à l'ombre de la censure* (2023).

**Till Weingärtner** is Lecturer in Contemporary East Asian Studies (Japan) at University College Cork, Ireland.

**Andy Willis** is Professor of Film Studies at the University of Salford and Senior Visiting Curator: Film at HOME, Manchester. He is the co-editor, with Jonathan Wroot, of *Cult Media: Re-packaged, Re-released and restored* and *DVD, Blu-ray and beyond: Navigating formats and platforms within media consumption* (both 2017), with Felicia Chan, of *Chinese cinemas, international perspectives* (2016) and, with Wing Fai Leung, of *East Asian film stars* (2014). In addition, he has curated a number of seasons and programmes of East Asian films, including *CRIME: Hong Kong style* (2016) and *The original ass kickers: Hong Kong Cinema's female action heroes* (2019), and with Sarah Perks, *Made in Hong Kong* (2007) and *Visible secrets: Hong Kong's women filmmakers* (2009).

**Jonathan Wroot** is Senior Lecturer and Programme Leader for Film Studies at the University of Greenwich. He has previously published research on home media formats and Asian cinema distribution. He has recently co-edited a collection entitled *New Blood: Critical Approaches to Contemporary Horror*. He has also completed a written history of the *Zatoichi* franchise.

**Francesca Young Kaufman** is a former university lecturer in East Asian History and now an independent scholar. She completed her thesis on the politics of representation in Chinese Cinema since 1989 at the University of Edinburgh in 2017. Her work explores the intersections between visual culture, memory and protest in modern Chinese history. She also runs a specialist coaching practice supporting academics with burn-out prevention and recovery, called Beatha Coaching (beathacoaching.org).

**Xuelin Zhou** is an Associate Professor in Media and Screen at the University of Auckland, New Zealand. His research interests focus on film studies and cross-cultural studies. He has published extensively in Chinese film studies. He is the author of *Young rebels in contemporary Chinese Cinema* (2007), *Youth culture in Chinese-language film* (2016) and *Globalization and contemporary Chinese Cinema: Zhang Yimou's genre films* (2017).

# Foreword

*Valentina Vitali*

> Myth, [. . .] as a form of speech or discourse, represents the major means in which women have been used in cinema: myth transmits and transforms the ideology of sexism and renders it invisible [. . .] and therefore natural. (Claire Johnston, 'Women's cinema as counter-cinema')

The notion that until recently very few women worked behind the camera is one of cinema's most stubbornly entrenched and widespread myths. Women have been part of cinema since its beginning. They have also largely been erased from film history. Lack of evidence – another myth – has hardly been the problem. We are confronted, rather, with a self-fulfilling sexist prophecy: assuming that women in creative roles are a rarity, too few looked for evidence to the contrary. That industry awards and journalistic 'Top 100 Greatest Films of All Time' exercises should reinforce patriarchal canons is little surprise. But what of established historiography? In a prestigious university press *Directors' Cuts* series (one of many such series), of the fifty directors featured, only three are women. Of the forty-seven male directors, forty-four are white.

The year 2023 marks thirty years of the Women Film Pioneers Project (WFPP). Currently featuring 313 women in creative roles in silent cinema alone, the project has only just begun to scratch the surface of women's creative labour in Asian cinemas. Indeed, research in this area is very scarce. The field is incipient and the present anthology pioneering – a welcome and long-overdue addition to a small but growing number of recent anthologies and special journal issues that have begun to re-inscribe women in the history of filmmaking. For 313 women during the first thirty years of cinema surely begs the question: how many must there have been in the ninety years that followed, left behind by film historiography and obliterated from film history? It is a question that has far-reaching implications beyond gender or area studies. Because, while the alleged paucity of women's creative labour in cinema has produced occasional studies of a few iconic *autrices*, the somewhat hagiographic nature of these studies has made it so that the presence and operation of women in cinema is reduced to personalised accounts that block our understanding of films' relation to social change. Change, that is, of which women's work in cinema is precisely a cause and an effect.

(In)visibility remains to this day a doubly intractable problem for contemporary Asian women filmmakers. In the industry as in historiography, (in)visibility is often a matter of geographical positioning, and access to festivals a struggle for all but the best connected. But there is more to a history of women in cinema than adding a few or even many women's names to the canon. The wider critical significance of such an endeavour is less the visibility of women's work in film history as what happens to our historiographic apparatus when the mirror is cracked (Smelik, 1998). This collection should be welcome, therefore, as much as a resource to complement existing literature on Asian cinemas as a catalyst for historical re-articulation – an opportunity to rethink the historiographic model to whose inadequacy Asian women in film owe their invisibility.

The chapters that follow examine the cinemas of the region through three windows: representation, labour and circulation. Traversed by the active presence of women, these three perspectives invite us to look again at the interconnected cultural and industrial terrains within which women have shaped cinema in Asia. Amrita Chhachhi and Thanh-Dam Truong have noted that, while early feminist research highlighted the invisibility of women, a new generation of feminists has pushed forward a research agenda aimed at the reformulation of key concepts such as subjectivity and agency (Chhachhi and Truong, 2009, p. 4). Part I of this anthology responds to this shift in focus with chapters that, given the industrial and textual limits within which women have worked in East Asian cinemas, explore how they moved within those limits. They are chapters that challenge a third myth of film historiography – namely, that cinema by women is a fringe phenomenon, at worst a rarefied avant-garde niche, at best a genre 'for and about' women. It is not simply that several of the women featured in this collection as a whole worked within the industry's centre-ground – figures such as Bao Zhifang, Angie Chen or Haneda Sumiko. Some of the films examined here offer a gendered regional lens that historiography has tended to marginalise ostensibly because the films did not have a significant financial impact. More likely because, as the authors show, the objective of filmmakers such as

He Xiaopei, Xu Jinglei or Qiong Yao remains, for the industry, an intractable one: not the short-term accumulation of surplus, but the transforming of subjectivities, 'a molecular political process' that, in the long term, 'subtly creates epistemic shifts' (Chhachhi and Abeysekera, 2015, p. 571). This hardly makes their films a peripheral cinema.

In Part II, on creative labour, this anthology tackles a fourth deeply engrained film historiographic myth: that in cinema only directors input creative labour. Long discounted as anachronistic, this grossly inaccurate view of the filmmaking process persists in the proliferation of individual *auteur* – read 'film director' – studies. In reality, during the first twenty years of cinema a star had far more of a say on the shape and content of their film than anyone else on or off the set. From the 1920s onwards, with the formation of large, vertically integrated studios on the west coast of the United States, the production sector emerged as the US film industry's locomotive. But for many decades Hollywood's modus operandi remained a unique formation. In many cinemas the world over, it was the exhibition and/or distribution sectors that came to define the local industry's priorities. Take Bollywood, to name but one, where to this day the leverage of these sectors is such that most stars continue to exercise greater decisional and creative input than film directors. And yet, not one of the many female stars that graced the Indian screens was ever recognised for her creative labour. Not even the legendary Miss Gohar (aka Gohar Khayyam Mamajiwala) who, in her role of star and producer, ran India's longest-running studio, Ranjit Movietone, well into the 1950s. To think of actors or editors as creative labourers means rejecting historiographic conventions that, assuming Hollywood's industrial model as the default template, mistake production to be the driving sector of all cinemas. By broadening the scope of what we take creative labour in cinema to be, the better to explore the vital artistic input of editor Ning Ying or star Takamine Hideko, this collection invites us to question the provincial universalism that allows historians to continue measuring all cinemas against a Hollywood that no longer exists. It encourages us to investigate and write into our analysis of the films the specificity of the industrial fabric that sustains individual cinematic formations.

The anthology closes with a section on global histories that revisits the knotty issue of what may constitute a national cinema. The regional perspective adopted prompts us to let go of statist understandings of 'the national' – national culture as a neatly defined, self-enclosed and, in cinema, often mythologised object. It cautions us against the autocratic collapsing of the state, the political territory it polices and its ideological tools, with the infinitely more fluid production of cultural artefacts, their regional or global circulation and reception. At a time when nationalisms of various persuasions once again rear their ugly head, this collection reminds us of the porousness and inclusionary character of cinema as an open social process. Whether we look at Cambodia, China, Hong Kong, Indonesia, Japan, Korea, Lao, Malaysia, Myanmar, the Philippines, Singapore, Taiwan, Thailand or Vietnam, women's work in cinema has tended to be marked by the necessity to address actual communities while, at the same time, working against the imaginary coherence of both community and nation. The range of subjects addressed by the films discussed here is thus characterised by an engagement with the intersectionality of gender with other axes of difference and inequality, issues of class, labour, colonialism, urbanisation. These are films and essays that urge us to factor into our histories of individual national cinemas the resilience of the region's material culture, the continuing resonance of patriarchies and critical alliances across borders policed by the state.

Back in 2015, the arrest of five young women preparing to sticker Beijing's public transport against sexual violence – members of Young Feminist Activism, an online coalition that played cat-and-mouse with the authorities – was met with web petitions signed by over two million people (Watkins, 2018, pp. 5–6). Along with #MeToo, this was one in a string of women-centred mass events to erupt around the world since the stock market crash of 2008 – a global feminist revival that produced, among other things, a manifesto for a 'feminism of the 99 per cent' (Arruzza et al., 2019). What does cinema afford these movements? Who are the women making films in Asia now? What kind of films do they make? Is this revival of militant feminism worldwide changing the limits within which women work in cinema? Is it changing the ways in which they move within those limits? This anthology opens up the historiographic ground upon which we can begin to attend to these questions. And, through them, arrive at the theoretical frameworks and cultural practices that will enable us to better grasp and shape cinema's relation to social change today. It is only appropriate that this pioneering volume – partly the happy outcome of an innovative collaboration between curators and historiographers – should thus conclude with an examination of programming trends and the curatorial approaches that may help us scrap procrustean canons, aimed, as these are, at reducing cinema – and, with it, our worldview – to algorithmic uniformity.

## References

Arruzza, C., Bhattacharya, T., and Fraser, N. (2019). *Feminism for the 99%: A manifesto*. London: Verso.

Chhachhi, A., and Abeysekera, S. (2015). Forging a new political imaginary: Transnational Southasian feminisms. In R. Baksh and W. Harcourt (eds), *The Oxford Handbook of transnational feminist movements* (pp. 553–77). Oxford: Oxford University Press.

Chhachhi, A., and Truong, T.-D. (2009). *Gender, poverty and social justice*. The Hague: International Institute of Social Studies, Working Paper no. 482.

Johnston, C. (1973). Women's cinema as counter-cinema. In *Notes on Women's Cinema*. London: Society for Education in Film and Television, *Screen*, Pamphlet 2, pp. 24–31.

Smelik, A. (1998). *And the mirror cracked: Feminist cinema and film theory*. London and New York: Palgrave Macmillan.

Watkins, S. (2018). Which feminisms? *New Left Review II, 109* (Jan-Feb), 5–76.

# Introduction:
# Women in East Asian Cinema: Gender Representations, Creative Labour and Global Histories

*Felicia Chan, Fraser Elliott and Andy Willis*

The study of women in film lends itself to a number of productive interventions in the study of world cinema. Historically, the study of women as the object of the male gaze has engendered numerous strands of argumentation in feminist film theory, psychoanalysis and theories of stardom. In more recent years, the encounter with the female gaze, either as alternative or complementary to the male gaze, or even as a distinct epistemological framework altogether, has expanded the boundaries of film studies into addressing its own historical underpinnings. In 1987, Denise Riley addressed the 'historical formations of "women" as a category' and argued that '"women" is historically and discursively constructed, always in relation to other categories which themselves change' (p. 35). As critical debates continue in many socio-cultural fields on this subject, the focus of this volume remains on the issues of cinema and representation, both on- and off-screen, and particularly on historical absences and historiographical interventions in both the representation of women in East Asian cinema, and/or East Asian women in cinema, while at the same time exploring the usefulness of 'East Asian' as a descriptor itself.

Alongside the continued importance of debates centring on gender representation in film studies, there has been a contemporary turn towards women's contributions to filmmaking more broadly, in terms of production as well as its circulation and canonisation. Early studies of American cinema – such as Marjorie Rosen's *Popcorn Venus: Women, movies and the American dream* (1973) and Molly Haskell's *From reverence to rape: The treatment of women in movies* (1974) – explored the images of women that circulated in films, and their approach can be broadly described as socially focused. As film studies developed as an academic discipline, a more theory-based method developed, drawing on psychoanalytic models of analysis in terms of screen representations;

the psychoanalytic approach has been one of the key areas of research in film studies since Laura Mulvey's seminal essay (1975) on the male gaze in the 1970s and the development of feminist film studies that followed. During this period, writers also tended to offer feminist readings of films, whilst championing the work of women filmmakers operating outside the mainstream in the independent sector or utilising alternative film forms such as those associated with the avant-garde. A good example of this is E. Ann Kaplan's *Women and film: Both sides of the camera* (1983), which has a first section devoted to feminist readings of films such as *Blonde Venus* (dir. Josef von Sternberg, 1932) starring Marlene Dietrich, *Lady from Shanghai* (dir. Orson Welles, 1946) starring Rita Hayworth and *Looking for Mr Goodbar* (dir. Richard Brooks, 1977) starring Diane Keaton, and a second section that explores filmmakers including Marguerite Duras, Yvonne Rainer and Sara Gómez. Kaplan's book significantly ends with a chapter titled 'The future of the independent feminist film: Strategies of production, exhibition, and distribution in the USA', which shifts to a discussion of the strategies that could be employed by practitioners within the film industry.

Film studies as a discipline has long been rooted in its study of, mostly male, directors – whose classification as 'auteur' helped legitimise its academic study. Feminist film studies incorporating women as authors are working within this historical auteurist mode. Ground-breaking, and highly influential, in the early 1970s studies of women's contribution to American cinema would begin to challenge these orthodoxies. For example, in her influential 1973 piece 'Women's cinema as countercinema', Claire Johnston discussed the work of directors Dorothy Arzner and Ida Lupino, arguing that their work could be read as potentially subversive. The British Film Institute published *The works of Dorothy Arzner: Towards a feminist cinema* in 1975. This collection contained contributions from Johnston ('Dorothy Arzner: Critical strategies') and Pam Cook ('Approaching the work of Dorothy Arzner') and argued for the significance of one of the few female directors in Hollywood's 'golden age'. Today, the centrality of Arzner and Lupino in this canon of margins has been further challenged, by the recent uncovering of the contributions of Esther Eng, a queer Chinese-American woman who worked between Hong Kong and the US and whose works are contemporaneous with Arzner's (Marchetti, 2021; Wei, 2014); available records reveal that Esther Eng made five films between 1937 and 1941 (sometimes under her Chinese name Ng Kam-ha). Yet, even as film studies in the present attempt to recuperate forgotten histories, as a woman filmmaker who is also of Chinese and East Asian origin, the reinsertion of Eng's contribution to the understanding of American and global film histories remains relatively slow.

Driven by aspirations to redress problematic absences, or limitations, projects such as Christine Gledhill and Julia Knight's (2015) re-framing of 'women's film history' are working to address broader questions of canonisation and the processes by which film histories are understood. As recognition of the 'woman director' gains ground in popular writing and the cultural intermediaries of the film world, scholars – including Patricia White with her book *Women's cinema, world cinema: Projecting contemporary feminisms* (2015) – are working to interrogate what these new formulations mean for conventional ways of engaging with film. The move in some research quarters to look behind the camera at labour and other roles in the filmmaking process beyond the director has been slower to gain momentum, although it certainly has over the last two decades. Perhaps the clearest example of this is the Women Film Pioneers Project (WFPP) developed by Jane Gaines since the early 1990s and accelerated by her collaboration with the Columbia University Libraries in 2013. The WFPP (n. d.) is a vast 'digital publication and resource that advances research on the hundreds of women who worked behind the scenes during the silent film era', global in scope and free to access through its website. In a vein similar to Gaines's open-access, democratised chronicling of previously under-discussed contributions by women in the silent film era, a project led by Gina Marchetti and titled 'Hong Kong Women Filmmakers' (HKWF) has taken a similar approach to filmmakers in (and from) Hong Kong. The project's website houses a vast archive of information, alphabetised and sorted by theme, which paints a clear picture of the quantity of women's contributions to Hong Kong cinema, which goes far beyond the canon of conventional wisdom otherwise represented by the work of a handful of names – such as Ann Hui, Clara Law and Mabel Cheung – who have found relative success in the international film festival ecosystem.

In anglophone scholarship, much of the work that has been undertaken in relation to the representation of women and women film practitioners has tended to focus on American and European contexts. In terms of East Asian cinema, this work tends to be informed by national and pan-national studies with an eye to East Asian locations, broadly delineated for ease of reference as the geographical and cultural locations dominated by China, Japan and Korea. These include, for example, Lingzhen Wang's study of *Chinese women's cinema: Transnational contexts* (2011), Jennifer Coates's *Making icons: Repetition and the female image in Japanese cinema, 1945–1964* (2016) and Irene González-López and Michael Smith's edited collection, *Tanaka Kinuyo: Nation, stardom and female subjectivity* (2018). These dedicated, book-length investigations accompany a handful of individual case-studies embedded in survey handbooks such as *The Palgrave Handbook of Asian cinema* (Magnan-Park et al., 2018) and *A companion to Hong Kong cinema* (Cheung et al., 2015). Together, this growing body of literature is working to redress the legacies of male-focused scholarship and the tendencies of international film circulation to prioritise the work of male filmmakers, particularly directors. It is our hope that this edited collection moves in parallel to the work of projects such as the WFPP and HKWF in contributing to the continually expanding corpus and providing the space to discuss, as well as ways to address, these under-represented histories.

To this end, this collection places the analysis of gender representation and the politics of visibility in dialogue with histories of women's work behind the scenes, in directing, editing, writing and acting. The rationale for this volume is, then, to highlight understudied areas of women's contributions to cinema and to re-direct women's film history towards a global 'film history' more broadly, through a case-study focus on the cinema of East Asia, its diaspora and its spheres of influence. A key aim is to highlight the importance of re-historicising women's creative labour in film beyond on-screen representation, by creating opportunities for dialogue among established and emerging scholars working in different areas of East Asian film studies. As film scholars ourselves whose research is focused on historiographical perspectives and curatorial practices, we welcomed contributions that addressed issues of production, distribution and exhibition circuits, alongside textual readings of screen representations. This volume extends the collaboration that began with the formation of the Chinese Film Forum UK (CFFUK), a Manchester-based research network and film collective (see Chan and Willis, 2016, 2017). Alongside considering the international circulation of Chinese-language cinemas, a core part of the Chinese Film Forum UK's work since 2009 – curating and programming selected film seasons and hosting discussions – is to critically understand the place of Chinese cinemas in UK film culture, and some of these conversations have inevitably extended into related fields of study into Asian film as a whole (see Rawnsley, 2013). The increasingly fluid production cultures of East Asian cinemas, including regional and international co-productions, have furthermore meant that rigid definitions of the regional origin of films are increasingly difficult to apply.

Acknowledging this, *Women in East Asian Cinema* extends the exploration of 'East Asian cinema' to include readings of East Asia's influence on Southeast Asian cinema and discourses. The delineation of East Asia is usually mapped geographically and historically onto the 'greater China' region (including Taiwan and Hong Kong, each having its own cinematic and cultural histories distinct from the mainland), Japan and Korea, as well as its wider sphere of influence in Southeast Asia (Indonesia, Malaysia, the Philippines, Singapore, Thailand, Vietnam). While we acknowledge that these territorial boundaries can be contested, we employ the term 'East Asia' based on the understanding that these nation-states within the region nonetheless share certain post-war histories that have shaped their present-day formations, and that these are reflected in the films: notably, the Japanese occupation of much of East and Southeast Asia in World War II, the defeat of Japan as a military power and its rise as an economic power within the region; Cold War politics between the western allies, led by the USA, and the communist eastern bloc led by the USSR; the Asian financial crisis of 1997; and the rise of China as an economic and cultural power in the 2000s, alongside the burgeoning of the 'Korean Wave', among others. The detailed impact of these histories on the region's film cultures is addressed in studies such as Kinnia Yau's 'The early development of East Asian Cinema in a regional context' (2009) and Sangjoon Lee's *Cinema and the cultural Cold War: US diplomacy and the origins of the Asian Cinema Network* (2020). The extension into Southeast Asia in this volume is only a modest one (two chapters out of fourteen), and there are numerous studies on Southeast Asian cinemas, its regional and individual national film cultures, filmmakers and audiences that lie far beyond the scope of this volume (see, for example, Baumgärtel, 2012; Khoo et al., 2020; Lim and Yamamoto, 2012), in which these loose geographical boundaries operate as moveable placeholders, put in place to start (rather than end) a conversation. As such, the chapters in this volume are grouped under three main thematic headings: gender representations, creative labour and global histories. The chapters are brought together not with the ambition to achieve a 'comprehensive' survey of women in East Asian cinema – no such survey can ever be usefully attempted – nor as 'representatives' of any national or regional cinema. In other words, as an edited collection *Women in East Asian Cinema* is less a curatorial project than an anthology of individual snapshots of the subject in time and place. Each snapshot speaks to another, sometimes directly, but oftentimes tangentially, each implicit conversation building up a web of allusions around the idea of 'women in East Asian cinema' as a threshold concept.

As said above about the importance of labour and representation behind the screen, we acknowledge that studies of gender representation in film remain important for the ways in which they allow for broader contextual readings and framings of social and cultural practices within a given period. How women are represented on film can tell us something about the society in which such films are produced, and indeed something about the very conditions of production themselves. The chapters in Part I on 'Gender Representations' do this through a range of studies of relatively under-explored films and creative figures in anglophone writings on East Asian film. Hongwei Bao's chapter offers a reading of Chinese lesbian filmmaker He Xiaopei's autobiographical films through their home video aesthetics, both much understudied modes of filmmaking, which enable the expression of a lived experience and perspective that cannot be easily captured through readings of traditional authorial frameworks or feminist screen representations. Fiona Y. W. Law's chapter reviews the Hong Kong cinema of the 1950s and 1960s, which spanned a range of genres to articulate the experiences of a range of women across Hong Kong society in a period of rapid societal modernisation: these include landladies, domestic servants, factory workers and women who worked in the night-time economy. Law argues that, underpinning all these representations, it is the act of being a 'woman' with all its social pressures and expectations that renders it a 'job' in itself. Dave McCaig's chapter offers a close reading of a Korean film, *Microhabitat*, and the insights it offers into troubled expressions of contemporary South Korean womanhood. Bérénice M. Reynaud explores the female gaze in Xu Jinglei's *Letter from an Unknown Woman*, adapted from Stefan Zweig's 1922 novel of the same name and the remake of an earlier adaptation from 1948 by Max Ophüls, as one that does more than simply reverse the male gaze; instead, it offers insight into the multiplicities of the female perspective in ways that allow it to disrupt masculine perspectives and modes of filmmaking. Jonathan Wroot's chapter looks at the 'gender-flipped' adaptation of the *Zatoichi* franchise *Ichi* (2008) and surveys its reception and the limits of its challenge to patriarchal structures of the franchise and the genre. Xuelin Zhou's chapter closes this section by highlighting a genre of films little known in anglophone scholarship, known as 'Qiong Yao films'. Qiong Yao (sometimes romanised as Chiung Yao) is the pen name of a prolific Taiwanese novelist and film producer, Chen Che. Historically, the film adaptations of her novels, including those which she produced, have been considered excessively sentimental and rather 'slight', thus not of notable national or international interest. Zhou argues against this neglect and makes a case for how these films express the collective subjectivities of Taiwanese women between the 1960s and 1980s and speak to the changing roles of women in a time and place undergoing rapid social and political change, as Taiwan was coming to the end of nearly four decades of martial law (1949–87). Each chapter in this section offers a micro-study of lesser-known film-texts or body of works that nudges the scope of discussion on gender in film in different directions and expands on possibilities for further research.

The chapters in Part II on 'Creative Labour' cover case-studies that focus on women's labour within the industry, notably authorship, stardom and other under-researched, below-the-line work such as editing and other off-screen contributions of women across the cinemas of Japan, South Korea, Hong Kong and mainland China. The chapter by Alejandra Armendáriz-Hernández, Marcos Centeno-Martin and Irene González-López explores the pioneering documentary filmmaker Haneda Sumiko, tracing her career and interrogating an authorial style beginning with her education documentaries of the 1950s. Together they unpack Haneda's uneasy identification with the 'woman filmmaker' label amid developing discourses in film criticism and feminism in twenty-first-century Japan. This chapter is followed by Monika Kukolova's exploration of women screenwriters in South Korea, whose careers have formed new collaborations and possibilities across the country's film and television industries. In an effort to counter the auteur-led, masculine focus of international attention on South Korea's recent film trends, Kukolova suggests that greater attention paid to the labour of screenwriters can provide global viewers with a more accurate and contemporary understanding of the region's cinema. Till Weingärtner's chapter traces the star image of actor and writer Takamine Hideko across historical developments in Japan and the Japanese industry. Noting how Takamine would play active roles in shaping her directors' vision and how this collaboration was presented to the public, Weingärtner interrogates questions of agency and the relationship with her actual labour and the carefully managed representations of this work for Japanese audiences. Moving finally to studies of filmmakers across Hong Kong and mainland China, Andy Willis's chapter provides a space to detail and acknowledge the significant contributions of director Angie Chen's films to the Hong Kong film industry. Following his curatorial experience with Chen's films, Willis divides her career into three distinct periods to highlight her sophisticated representations of gender and sexuality within a controlled studio system, her ground-breaking commercial work and, finally, Chen's distinctively personal work as a documentarian. Francesca Young Kaufman brings this section to a close with a chapter analysing the feminist politics that independent Chinese documentarian Ning Ying embeds in her authorship and editing in her film *I Love Beijing* (2001). Noting the increased control that Ning Ying maintains over her films through her practice as both director and editor, Young Kaufman re-emphasises the importance of authorship for women working in non-dominant positions within China's film industry, through the filmmaker's representation of female characters and experiences.

The final part of the collection focuses on 'Global Histories'. Here, the chapters move beyond the traditional limitations of notions of East Asia and explore both films that were produced in or represent Southeast Asia and the circulation of these works internationally. Felicia Chan's chapter takes as its focus the figure of the *nyonya*, a term used to identify women of Peranakan descent in Southeast Asia, particularly in Singapore and Peninsular Malaysia. Chan explores the figurations of the *nyonya* in two ways: first, through the film characters who are identified or coded as Peranakan women, and second, through the feminisation of Peranakan representation as a whole through the *nyonya*'s mastery of the domestic space. A case-study of the film *Crazy Rich Asians* (dir. Jon M. Chu, 2018) explores these in relation to international contexts. MaoHui Deng's chapter, the penultimate one in the volume, focuses on aspects of Southeast Asian women's cinema. Here, rather than attributing a simple national label, Deng draws together films from Singapore, Malaysia and in particular the Philippines, through a reading of *Nervous Translation* (dir. Shireen Seno, 2018), to explore how works such as this adopt an aesthetic strategy that celebrates the present tense and, in turn, invite us to think of the concept of a geographical 'area' from a temporal viewpoint. As Deng puts it in his chapter, he is seeking to discover how 'Southeast Asian women's filmmaking challenges Eurocentric frameworks of national and cultural histories imposed on non-European countries by re-emphasising the interconnections of history, culture and politics in the world from a temporal framework' – thus giving voice to something that this collection also seeks to do as a whole.

One of the key areas that the editors were keen to explore was the circulation of work by women film practitioners. Indeed, some of the canon creation that critics and scholars, as well as contributors to this volume, have tried to counter can be attributed to the limited circulation of work by East Asian filmmakers. It is therefore essential that this be addressed. To that end, in the final chapter on 'Disruptive programming and East Asian women on international screens', Fraser Elliott explores the challenges that curators must confront when programming the work of women filmmakers. Through the case-study of *Celebrating Women in Global Cinema* (CWiGC), a curatorial initiative that took place at

HOME (an independent cinema and cross-art-form venue in Manchester, England) and that hosted retrospectives of work by East Asian and Southeast Asian filmmakers, he addresses the question of whether such curatorial work can effectively counter limiting representations of the contributions by women from the film industries of East Asia.

## References

Baumgärtel, T. (2012). *Southeast Asian independent cinema: Essays, documents, interviews*. Hong Kong: Hong Kong University Press.

Chan, F., and Willis, A. (Eds.) (2016). *Chinese cinemas: International perspectives*. London: Routledge.

Chan, F., and Willis, A. (2017). Interventions on cultural margins: The case of the Chinese Film Forum UK and the presence of Taiwanese cinema in the UK. In K. F. Chiu, M. Y. Rawnsley and G. Rawnsley (eds), *Taiwan cinema: International reception and social change* (pp. 80–91). London: Routledge.

Cheung, E. M. K., Marchetti, G., and Yau, C. M. E. (eds) (2015). *A companion to Hong Kong cinema*. Hoboken: Wiley Blackwell.

Coates, J. (2016). *Making icons: Repetition and the female image in Japanese cinema, 1945–1964*. Hong Kong: Hong Kong University Press.

Gledhill, C., and Knight, J. (2015). *Doing women's film history: Reframing cinemas past and future*. Champaign: University of Illinois Press.

González-López, I., and Smith, M. (2018). *Tanaka Kinuyo: Nation, stardom and female subjectivity*. Edinburgh: Edinburgh University Press.

Haskell, M. (1974). *From reverence to rape: The treatment of women in movies*. New York: Holt, Reinhart and Winston.

Hong Kong Women Filmmakers, HKWF. (n. d.). Retrieved from https://hkwomenfilmmakers.wordpress.com

Johnston, C. (1973). Women's cinema as counter-cinema. In C. Johnston (ed.), *Notes on women's cinema* (pp. 24–31). London: SEFT.

Johnston, C. (Ed.). (1975). *The works of Dorothy Arzner: Towards a feminist cinema*. London: British Film Institute.

Kaplan, E. A. (1983). *Women and film: Both sides of the camera*. London: Routledge.

Khoo, G. C., Barker, T., and Ainslie, M. J. (eds). (2020). *Southeast Asia on screen: From independence to financial crisis (1945–1998)*. Amsterdam: Amsterdam University Press.

Lee, S. (2020). *Cinema and the cultural Cold War: US diplomacy and the origins of the Asian Cinema Network*. New York: Cornell University Press.

Lim, D. C. L., and Yamamoto, H. (2012). *Film in contemporary Southeast Asia: Cultural interpretation and social intervention*. London: Routledge.

Magnan-Park, A. H. J., Marchetti, G., and Tan, S. K. (eds). (2018). *The Palgrave Handbook of Asian cinema*. London: Palgrave Macmillan.

Marchetti, G. (2021). Women as cross-cultural intermediaries within the Chinese diaspora: The search for Esther Eng in S. Louisa Wei's *Golden Gate Girls* (2013). In E. Ben-ari and H.-W. Wong (eds), *Cultural intermediaries in East Asian film studies*. London: Routledge.

Mulvey, L. (1975). Visual pleasure and narrative cinema. *Screen*, 16(3), 6–18.

Rawnsley, M.-Y. T. (2013). The distribution and exhibition of Chinese and Asian cinema in the UK: A Chinese Film Forum UK symposium, Cornerhouse, Manchester, 28–29 March 2012. *Screen (London)*, 54(4), 534–39.

Riley, D. (1987). Does sex have a history? 'Women' and feminism. *New Formations*, *1*, 35–45.

Rosen, M. (1973). *Popcorn Venus: Women, movies and the American dream*. New York: Avon.

Wang, L. (2011). *Chinese women's cinema: Transnational contexts*. New York: Columbia University Press.

Wei, S. L. (2014). 'She wears slacks': Pioneer women directors Esther Eng and Dorothy Arzner. In W. Fu and E. C. Chan (eds), *Transcending space and time: Early cinematic experience of Hong Kong: Book III. Re-discovering pioneering females in early Chinese cinema and Grandview's cross-border productions* (pp. 110–44). Hong Kong: Hong Kong Film Archive.

White, P. (2015). *Women's cinema, world cinema: Projecting contemporary feminisms*. Durham: Duke University Press.

Women Film Pioneers Project, WFPP. (n. d.). *About the project*. Retrieved from https://wfpp.columbia.edu/about/

Yau, S. T. K. (2009). The early development of East Asian cinema in a regional context. *Asian Studies Review*, *33*(2), 161–73.

# PART I

# GENDER REPRESENTATIONS

Chapter 1

# A Cinema of Pleasure: He Xiaopei's Home Video Aesthetics and Queer Feminist Politics

Hongwei Bao

> I have two girlfriends. They also have their own partners apart from me. Many people ask me about my relationship. For them, polyamory seems unbelievable like these flying starlings. So I made this film. My name is Xiaopei. This is my girlfriend Jaya, my girlfriend Sue and Sue's boyfriend Orvil. I was born in Beijing. I grew up and live in Beijing . . .

With these words narrated in the director's voice-over, Chinese queer and feminist filmmaker He Xiaopei's (何小培) 2010 film, a twenty-six-minute documentary titled *Polyamorous Family* (多性恋家庭), begins.[1] The opening sequence of the film shows the Brighton Pier at dawn, images of family members as their names are mentioned in the film, as well as black-and-white photographs from an old album.[2] These voice-overs and images are accompanied by a mixed style of background music incorporating electronic sounds and traditional Indian string instrumentation. All the images and music have meanings for He Xiaopei, as they are all related to different phases of her life. For example, the Brighton Pier is shown because her partner Sue lives in Brighton, and the pier is one of their favourite places to visit. An Indian-style music was used in the film because He Xiaopei's other partner Jaya lives in India. The film has a small filming and production crew that consists primarily of He Xiaopei's family and friends. The interviews with different individuals, which comprise the core part of the film, were conducted by Sue's sister. The film editor Yuan Yuan is He Xiaopei's friend and work partner. In other words, the whole film is about He Xiaopei's life and family; it was made by, for and about her family and friends. Such a film resembles a home video – videos about one's family life and made for domestic consumption – and this seems a consistent feature of He Xiaopei's films.

*Polyamorous Family* was He Xiaopei's debut film. It was deliberately under-publicised and therefore little known to the public, in part because

Figure 1.1 'Woman with a movie camera' (courtesy of He Xiaopei)

of the intimate nature of the film's subject-matter. However, this film set the tone for many of her later films. Over the next decade, He Xiaopei made around ten films. They share many things in common: all of them are documentaries, although many have strong narrative strands; some are as short as three minutes, while others are feature-length; most of them are made transnationally across continents, involving different languages and cultures and constituting a good example of what Felicia Chan (2017) calls 'cosmopolitan cinema'; most feature He Xiaopei's own life, family and friends; most are extremely candid about love, sex and intimacy and articulate a strong queer feminist political stance; many were made with a digital video camera on a shoestring budget, and they often manifest a 'home video'-style and aesthetics. How do we understand the close relationship between the filmmaker's life and the autobiographical narratives of these films? How do we make sense of the close alignment between He Xiaopei's home video aesthetics and queer feminist politics?

This chapter examines He Xiaopei's films and filmmaking career to discern how they help her articulate a queer feminist politics. He Xiaopei (Figure 1.1) is one of the best-known queer and feminist filmmakers and activists in contemporary China. She has made ten films so far, including *The Lucky One* (宠儿 2012), *Our Marriages: When Lesbians Marry Gay Men* (dir. He Xiaopei and Yuan Yuan, 奇缘一生 2013), *Yvo and Chrissy* (如此生活 2017), *Playmates* (玩伴 2019) and *The Bad Women of China* (中华坏女人 2021). Referred to as a 'pink crusader' (Zhang, 2013),

He Xiaopei was a pioneering queer activist in 1990s Beijing and played a crucial role in China's Lesbian, Gay, Bisexual and Transgender (LGBT) movement (He, 2001). Since the 2000s, she has been known as one of the most articulate advocates of queer feminist politics in China. Her politics is consistently manifested in her films and in her social and political activism. This chapter situates He Xiaopei in the global women's cinema tradition, highlighting He Xiaopei's queer feminist intervention in the feminist debate about the use of pleasure in feminist cultural politics. It also examines the close relationship and dynamic interaction between her personal biography and the narrative, style, content, aesthetics and politics of her films. I suggest that He Xiaopei's films can be best described as a 'cinema of pleasure', films celebrating women's sexual pleasure and sexual agency, and that their 'home video' format and aesthetics effectively facilitate the expression of a queer feminist politics.

## Women's Cinema and the Politics of Pleasure

The question of pleasure has been an important issue in feminist film scholarship since the 1970s. While some scholars and filmmakers embrace the use of entertainment and visual pleasure in women's cinema, others advocate the complete destruction of visual pleasure in order to articulate a feminist alternative to mainstream aesthetics and politics. Claire Johnston, a pioneer of feminist film criticism, critiques Hollywood as a patriarchal 'dream factory' and suggests that 'a strategy should be developed which embraces both the notion of films as a political tool and film as entertainment' (1973, p. 31). This strategy, for Johnston, is to develop women's cinema as a form of 'counter cinema', although Johnston does not rule out the political potential of entertainment cinema made by women filmmakers:

> [W]omen's cinema must embody the working through of desire: such an objective demands the use of entertainment films. Ideas derived from entertainment films, then, should inform the political film, and political ideas should inform the entertainment cinema: a two-way process. (Johnston, 1973, p. 31)

In contrast, feminist film scholar Laura Mulvey (1975) advocates the use of experimental film language and avant-garde aesthetics to destroy the visual pleasure derived from mainstream narrative cinema. Entertainment cinema, according to Mulvey, reproduces patriarchal ideologies, and the audience's visual pleasure is usually derived from the objectification of women. A feminist politics of cinema can only be achieved through the destruction of visual pleasure by means of innovative and avant-garde cinematic form, language and aesthetics, in order to facilitate a detached, critical film-viewing experience:

> The first blow against the monolithic accumulation of traditional film conventions (already undertaken by radical film-makers) is to free the look of the camera from its materiality in time and space and the look of the audience into dialectics, passionate detachment. There is no doubt that this destroys the satisfaction, pleasure and privilege of the 'invisible guest', and highlights how film has depended on voyeuristic active/passive mechanisms. (Mulvey, 1975, p. 816)

Following Johnston's and Mulvey's trailblazing writing, feminist film scholars have explored women's filmmaking in different contexts and articulated various ways in which women's cinema can articulate feminist politics. Alison Butler (2003) argues that women's cinema should be seen as a minor cinema which exists inside other cinematic traditions, inflecting and contesting the codes from within. In other words, it can rework, but does not have to appear radically different from mainstream film forms and aesthetics. Patricia White (2015), Sophie Mayer (2016)[3] and Olivia Khoo, Anna Grgić and Eva Jørholt (2021) look beyond the Western film canon and at diverse histories, traditions, forms and aesthetics of women's cinema in different parts of the world. Lingzhen Wang (2021) examines well-known mainstream women filmmakers in China's Mao and post-Mao eras to discern the crucial role that women filmmakers play in articulating socialist politics and proletarian culture; their films belong neither to commercial cinema nor elite culture; rather, these filmmakers strategically draw on and critically make use of popular culture and entertainment forms to articulate a socialist feminist politics. Gina Marchetti (2021) focuses on women filmmakers in Hong Kong to argue for the transnational nature and global impact of their filmmaking. Jinyan Zeng (2022) examines the use of documentary by women filmmakers in feminist activism in mainland China. Behind the proliferating feminist filmmakers and scholarship, the issue of pleasure seems to be a persistent theme. Filmmakers and scholars have answered the following question in different ways: how does women's cinema engage with the issue of visual pleasure? Does the articulation of a feminist politics necessitate the complete erasure of visual pleasure? If not, what would a feminist cinema of pleasure look like? Does it matter if the filmmaker is a queer woman? What role does sexuality play in women's cinema and feminist politics? This chapter uses He Xiaopei's films and filmmaking career as a case-study to examine how pleasure can be used to articulate a queer feminist politics.

## Becoming a Queer Feminist in Post-Mao China

> The hills trained me to be a professional shepherd and the Himalayas turned me into a full-time mountaineer. A government job made me an economist while the women's movement and gender studies converted me into a feminist. Participating in LBGTQ organisations in China helped me to realise there are many people, especially people with disabilities, HIV-positive women, bisexual women, sex workers, who are also oppressed due to their gender and sexualities. This is why I set up the Pink Space Sexuality Research Centre and promote sexual rights and sexual pleasure among people who are oppressed. (He Xiaopei, cited in CCC 2012)

The above statement, written by He Xiaopei for a film screening event, nicely sums up her personal biography. It also explains how and why she became a queer feminist, filmmaker and director of a women's rights NGO – the Pink Space Sexuality Research Centre (Pink Space, for short). As contemporary China's leading queer feminist filmmaker, He Xiaopei's life-story is deeply connected to the transformation of feminism and the LGBT movement in post-Mao China; it also reveals the hopes and frustrations of gender- and sexuality-related social movements in an authoritarian, neoliberalist state.

He Xiaopei was born in Beijing to an intellectual family before the Cultural Revolution. Her mother was a foreign language teacher, and her father, a Malaysian Chinese, was an economist. Like many peers in her youth, she was influenced by the Maoist ideology claiming that 'women and men are all the same' (*nannü douyiyang* 男女都一样) and endorsed China's state and socialist feminism (Balian, 2021). Her choice to study economics at university and her decisions to become a civil servant and later a mountaineer were informed by her interest and personality, without being hindered by gender stereotypes. Because of her active training in sports, she developed a masculine build and is often seen as a tomboy (or T) in the Chinese lesbian community. Although she experienced sexism and gender-based discrimination in her youth and at work, gender and sexuality were not seen as an important part of her identity at the time, largely because of the heteronormative and patriarchal environment in which she grew up and because of the state's feminist values that she internalised.

The 1990s witnessed the emergence of China's grassroots feminism and LGBT movements (Engebretsen, 2014; Kam, 2013); it also marked the formative years of He Xiaopei's gender and sexual politics. Around the 1995 UNWCW (United Nations World Conference on Women), many grassroots women and LGBT NGOs were set up in Beijing. Living in Beijing and being fluent in English, He Xiaopei found herself in the middle of all these exciting developments. She attended the UNWCW NGO Forum and met many international lesbian activists in the 'lesbian tent'. She socialised with international queer activists, including Susie Jolly (also known as Sue), who was based in Beijing at the time and later became He Xiaopei's girlfriend. Together, a group of queer activists in Beijing organised house parties, nights-out in bars and clubs, cultural salons, as well as a pager hotline which provided free psychological counselling over the telephone for LGBT people in China. The height of this was a celebration of the Stonewall Uprising, disguised as a 'birthday party' at the Half and Half bar in 1996 (He, 2001). It was in these years that He Xiaopei started to identify herself as a lesbian and an activist. Although working for the State Council, the Chinese government's official think-tank, and designing China's healthcare reform at the time, her real interest was in NGO work, and she saw grassroots organising as a way to make social change out of a rigid state bureaucratic system.

In the late 1990s, He Xiaopei went to the UK to pursue further education and to find the best way to contribute to China's social change. She first completed an MA in Gender and Development at the Institute of Development Studies (IDS) in Brighton, where she was introduced to feminist and queer approaches to development studies. At IDS, a group of scholars had been dissatisfied with the long-standing negligence of and conventional sex-negative approach to women and LGBT issues in development studies; they were committed to changing the situation. Traditional approaches often see sex in negative and heteronormative ways, as either a disease or a moral panic, or restricting it to the realm of heterosexuality; the group sought to highlight the importance of gender and sexuality, and they encouraged policymakers to treat sex positively, recognising the pleasurable and transformative aspect of sex in human relations and social change (Cornwall et al., 2008). Studying at IDS spoke to He Xiaopei's life experiences and had a positive impact on her very open and liberal attitudes towards sex. She then completed another MA in Sexual Dissidence at the University of Sussex, where she studied queer theory and met many gender- and sexual-nonconforming people – including Chrissy, whose life He Xiaopei would later document in the film *Yvo and Chrissy*. He Xiaopei's Master's study at IDS and Sussex played an important role in shaping her feminist and queer politics. In 2003, she was offered a PhD scholarship in Gender Studies at the University of Westminster to study with the renowned gender studies scholar Harriet Evans. Her PhD thesis was titled *I am AIDS: Living with the epidemic in China*.

Conducting fieldwork in China in the 2000s for her PhD research turned out to be a transformative experience for He Xiaopei. At the time, China was in the middle of an AIDS crisis. Gender and sexuality, although at the heart of the epidemic intervention, had long been neglected by the Chinese government, due to its reluctance to recognise LGBT people's existence and their rights. As soon as the link between LGBT and AIDS was officially established in 2004, AIDS also stigmatised LGBT people in significant ways. A homonormative gay identity politics began to emerge in China's LGBT communities in response to the stigmatisation of gay identity. In other words, AIDS was a double-edged sword in mainland China: its policy and intervention not only contributed to the public recognition and stigmatisation of gay identity, but it also led to the domination of gay men's groups in the LGBT communities and the rise of gay identity politics in mainland China (Bao, 2018).

After meeting and talking to many people living with HIV, He Xiaopei realised that the mainstream discourses about AIDS in China had prioritised men's over women's experiences. Besides, they were largely negative and even misleading, constructing people living with HIV as passive, medicalised subjects instead of active subjects and real human beings with their own agency. She also felt that people living with HIV were even more marginalised than lesbian and gay men. However, there existed very few groups and support networks for them at the time. She wondered if there was a way to recognise the sexual agency of people living with HIV in AIDS intervention. As soon as He Xiaopei completed her PhD thesis in 2006, she returned to China. In 2007, she founded Pink Space, an NGO dedicated to exploring women's sexuality. Pink Space was set up to promote 'sexual rights and sexual pleasure among people who are oppressed' (CCC, 2012), including women living with HIV, heterosexual women who are married to gay men and people living with disability. All these marginalised gender, sexual and desiring subjects constitute the main subjects of He Xiaopei's films. Pink Space experimented with innovative ways to engage with minority subjects, including organising meet-up and support groups, curating photo exhibitions and compiling a newsletter. At a Pink Space meeting, He Xiaopei met a woman living with HIV in the last days of her life, who agreed to record an audio diary and also be filmed by He Xiaopei. After the woman had passed away, together with Yuan Yuan, He Xiaopei completed the film *The Lucky One* (Bao, 2020). When the film reached 100,000 hits on a Chinese video-streaming website and was invited to international film festivals, He Xiaopei started to realise the wide public reach and positive social impact of films.[4] In her own words, '[f]rom that moment, I said I'm only making films now'

(He Xiaopei, cited in Balian, 2021). Since then, He Xiaopei has focused on making documentary films. Most of her films are about her own life and the lives of people with whom she is familiar. They are made low-budget and with a portable digital video camera. Over time, she has developed a highly autobiographical, subjective and intimate way of filmmaking – a cinematic strategy for many women filmmakers (Yu, 2019). Although He Xiaopei's films are primarily about marginalised subjects, they differ significantly from mainstream representations. Her films portray the everyday life of these marginalised people, showing them in three dimensions. If mainstream representations about minority subjects are often full of tears, He Xiaopei's films mostly reveal their happiness, joy and optimism. Gender, sexuality and intimacy are important components of this affective engagement. Indeed, most of He Xiaopei's films are pleasurable to watch and even laced with a sense of humour and fun. Many of the films are sex-positive, showcasing a strong feminist and queer political stance. He Xiaopei's films are a good exemplar of what I call 'a cinema of pleasure', an aesthetics that celebrates gender, sexuality, intimacy and life.

## A Cinema of Pleasure

Leading an NGO, He Xiaopei sees many blind spots in existing global development policies and China's domestic social policies, including their continuous neglect of issues regarding sex and sexuality, associating these issues with disease (such as AIDS) or moral degradation, or seeing them as hazards from which people should stay away. He Xiaopei advocates a sex-positive approach instead:

> We do not focus only on discrimination and violence faced by those who break sexuality norms or negotiate the power dynamics of relationships. We also take a positive approach to sexuality, and create opportunities for sharing experiences of pleasure, to enable people to find affirmation in their sexual feelings and interactions. (He, 2019, p. 107)

He Xiaopei explains the work of Pink Space in the following way: 'Pink Space believes that sexual rights are for everyone, whether you are poor, gay or living with disabilities. Much of our work is with marginalised people who are oppressed due to their gender and sexuality' (2016, p. 561). He Xiaopei's positive approach to sexuality has been inspired by the work undertaken at IDS, which adopts a 'pleasure-based development' approach: 'One lens through which development can be re-envisioned is that of a focus on pleasure, rather than on misery and harm [. . .]

it seems obvious that pleasure should be at the heart of making sex safer' (Cornwall and Jolly, 2009, p. 9).

He Xiaopei's 'pleasure principle' in NGO work is reflected in her films, which I call 'a cinema of pleasure' that celebrates gender equality, sexual diversity and embodied agency. For her, everyone has the ability and right to enjoy pleasure, regardless of their gender, sexuality, class, race, nationality, or other intersectional differences. Pleasure should be understood in a capacious way to encompass a wide range of bodily, emotional and sensorial affects, and sex is only one of them. Pleasure, therefore, becomes a radical and egalitarian social force that can be used to empower individuals and social groups – especially those who are marginalised – and that connects people with one another for mutual understanding and radical care. These ideas have found a clear expression in most of He Xiaopei's films.

He Xiaopei's first open-access and widely circulated film, *The Lucky One*, serves as a useful example (Figure 1.2). The film features the last days of Zhang Xi, a working-class Chinese woman living with HIV. Instead of depicting the agony and despair of a dying person, He Xiaopei chose to portray Zhang's joy, happiness and dreams instead. Through Zhang's own narration and He Xiaopei's interview, Zhang is represented on screen as a positive, optimistic and determined person who loves life and the world against all odds. Even her memory of a son lost at birth a long time ago is narrated in a vivid and dramatic way, as if he were still living and around her. Through Zhang's storytelling, it transpires that she enjoyed having sex and had many sexual partners. Zhang described herself as 'the lucky one' (*chong'er*) – which also informs the title of the

Figure 1.2 *The Lucky One* (screenshot)

film – and He Xiaopei's film captures her charisma and optimism. More importantly, the filmmaking process was informed by participatory film- and videomaking methods, which allowed the filmed subjects to speak on their own terms (Bao, 2020). Indeed, by learning to use a camera and voice recorder to document her life, Zhang exercised the power to tell her stories and to do so in her own way, even though she did it by making up stories and by conflating fantasy with reality. In the long history of the cinematic representation of people living with HIV, *The Lucky One* strikes as a good example of portraying filmed subjects not as poor and powerless victims, but as active agents who are able to tell their own stories and control how these stories should be told.

*Love You Too* is a sixteen-minute documentary made by He Xiaopei in 2017.[5] The film documents an art workshop in which He Xiaopei, collaborating with Spanish artist Jose Abad Lorente, worked with children living with mental disabilities in a care home. These children were usually seen as having low intelligence and insufficient social skills and, therefore, are difficult to communicate with. The support offered to them by the institution and by society was limited to a physical, material and survival level without attending to – or even recognition of – their emotional needs. Working with art and food, the children were encouraged to express their feelings, emotions and desires. In doing so, they learned to use language – verbal and nonverbal – to express their likes and dislikes, pleasure in tasting food and emotional attraction to aesthetic beauty. In the film, the children are seen to be freer to express their feelings and more courageous to talk about sex than adults. This challenges not only the social prejudice against these children, but also the myth that they do not have sexualities. More importantly, these children's joy and happiness draws attention to the role of social and medical institutions such as care homes and mental health hospitals in disciplining people's minds and desires.

Another 2017 film, *Yvo and Chrissy*, shifts the filming location from China to Brighton, a small town located in the south of England where He Xiaopei had studied and lived. This sixty-minute documentary centres around the lives of two people: Yvo, whom He Xiaopei met in a diving club; and Chrissy, who studied together with He Xiaopei at the University of Sussex. Yvo and Chrissy share an open attitude towards gender, sexuality and identity: while Yvo was particularly open about her sex and sexuality, the male-born Chrissy identified with the female gender but refused to conform to conventional notions of femininity. Neither person wants to be confined by rigid identity categories, and the openness of their gender, sexuality and desire becomes the best explanation for what queer can mean. Yvo and Chrissy also have in common a critical attitude towards money, capitalism and the middle-class lifestyle. Yvo voluntarily gave up a large inheritance from her family and leads a bohemian life as a poet and performing artist. Chrissy left his hypocritical middle-class foster home and also gave up the male privilege with which he was born. Both lead a free, anarchist and nomadic lifestyle. Both consider that the true liberation of desire must be accompanied by a trenchant critique of neoliberal capitalism which disciplines desires through the consumer lifestyle and identity categories.

In her writing about the above films, He Xiaopei (2019) reflects on the intertwined relationship between gender, sexuality, desire and other intersectional identities. She notes that structural issues and socio-economic conditions have marginalised many individuals and groups, denying them access to bodily and affective pleasures. These people's lives are no less – and perhaps even more – colourful than their mainstream and middle-class peers. Their affective worlds deserve to be acknowledged and respected. Her films endeavour to document their lives, presenting their rich desires to the audience and making people think critically about the social structures and ideologies that marginalise these experiences. She writes:

> Poor and marginalised individuals are not short of feelings, emotions, or experiences, and in many cases are rich in desires. These films therefore apprehend the desires of the poor and marginalised people, how they articulate and fulfil their desires, and why it is important to recognize desires at these margins. (He, 2019, p. 66)

A 'cinema of pleasure' is therefore not merely a celebration of diverse genders, sexualities and desires. It also calls for the recognition and critique of oppressive social structures – including capitalism, patriarchy and heteronormativity – in disciplining and controlling desires. It seeks to liberate desires not through the inscription of identity categories and the endorsement of existing social structures, but through unleashing desire in its multiplicity and polymorphousness and situating them in decentralised, egalitarian and life-affirming social relations.

## Queering the 'Home Video' Genre

In an interview, He Xiaopei talked about the subject-matter of her films:

> I always film people around me: friends and the family. They are very close to each other and trust each other. They can be very relaxed when filming and appear very natural in a film. The family video has the power to touch people. If a story can touch the family, it can touch other audiences too. (He Xiaopei, cited in Balian, 2021)

Familiarity with filmed subjects makes it easier to film them; it also gives the filmmaker some authority over the subject-matter. This inevitably raises the issue of the objectivity and subjectivity of documentary filmmakers. Inspired by feminist and queer epistemologies, such as Audre Lorde (1984)'s writing on the uses of the erotic and Donna Haraway's (1998) writing on situated knowledges, He Xiaopei does not shy away from talking about her own feelings, experiences and intimate relations in front of the camera, seeing this as a powerful tool to challenge heteropatriarchy. This political stance is rare among independent Chinese filmmakers, most of whom have followed a 'camera on the wall'-type of direct cinema tradition (Robinson, 2013). Being a 'woman with a movie camera' not only entails centring on women's lives and experiences in terms of subject-matter, but also necessitates exploring alternative perspectives, aesthetics and politics. Foregrounding female filmmakers' gender, sexual and political subjectivity through authorial inscription has been a very important method for women's filmmaking in contemporary China (Wang, 2011).

He Xiaopei's words also point to the importance of the 'home video' genre. The 'home video' has a long history in global screen culture, although most home videos are not seen as proper films because of the intimate nature of the subject-matter, limited circulation and exhibition, as well as the long-established hierarchy in professional and amateur production. With the open release, wide circulation and increasing professionalisation of home videos, one can ask: what if home videos are not merely private? What if they are shown online, on the big screen and at film festivals? How can the aesthetics and politics of home video be strategically used to empower marginalised communities who have traditionally been denied access to the 'big screen'? Home videos are often characterised by their 'lightness' (Voci, 2010) – lightness not only in terms of media and technology (for example, a portable digital video camera), but also in terms of subject-matter and style. Paola Voci identifies some strategies of the 'small screen', which include 'preferences for genre blending, emphasis on brevity, playfulness, and open-ended and fragmented formats' (p. xx). These strategies embody important aesthetic and political potentials:

> [T]hese moves participate in the making of a light vision of cinematic avant-garde, while at the same time creating new spaces where collectivity and individuality are negotiated and where boundaries between elite and popular culture are affectively blurred and dissolved. At a broader and deeper level, *lightness* fulfils the need for unsanctioned, unregulated, and intensely private realities both within and without the borders of legitimate cultures. (Voci, 2010, p. xxi, emphasis in original)

Indeed, the small screen of the 'home video' genre can help open up spaces for what is considered marginal, unspeakable, intimate and radical, bringing it to human consciousness and the public sphere. Sex, sexuality and intimacy seems a fitting topic for this genre, and through this format queer feminist politics also finds an appropriate medium for its expression.

Many of He Xiaopei's films can be seen as falling into – or at least being informed by – the 'home video' genre. They include her first film *Polyamorous Family*; *Gay Cats*, a three-minute short about her cats; *Playmates*, a film about children playing together; and *The Bad Women of China*, a 2021 film about her mother and family history.[6] All these films are about private family lives, but they also have a public dimension; that is, they address important social issues and political questions. They were made to share with a bigger audience and to trigger public debates about the issues concerned. For example, *Polyamorous Family* was made to introduce the concept of polyamory to the LGBT communities, against a homonormative gay identity politics which prioritises the agenda of same-sex marriage. *Playmates* documents two children of different skin colours growing up together, through which the possibility of intercultural communication is explored. *The Bad Women of China*, a documentation of her family history, is He Xiaopei's tribute to her mother who passed away in 2019. The film challenges dominant and stereotypical narratives about Chinese women – often dubbed as 'the good women of China' (Xinran, 2003) – as passive and silent subjects of racism and heteropatriarchy. All these films subvert social norms and celebrate gender and sexual nonconformity with humour, pleasure and even laughter. They have a very intimate feeling for the viewing audience, as if the audience were incorporated into He Xiaopei's life circle and became part of her extended family.

He Xiaopei's films also go beyond her immediate family and document alternative formations of family and kinship. For example, her 2013 film co-directed with Yuan Yuan, *Our Marriages: When Lesbians Marry Gay Men* – together with its 2019 sequel *Happily Ever After* – followed the lives of a few 'cooperative marriage' couples; that is, a marriage of convenience voluntarily formed by lesbians and gay men to cope with the pressure from their parents and society to enter heterosexual marriage (Figure 1.3). This type of 'cooperative marriage' is usually condemned by mainstream society, which sees it as a form of 'fake' or 'sham' marriage. It is criticised by LGBT activists, as it 'betrays' the 'authenticity' of being gay. In making the film, He Xiaopei engages with the public debate on 'cooperative marriage', critiquing both heteronormative and

Figure 1.3 *Our Marriages: When Lesbians Marry Gay Men* (DVD cover; courtesy of He Xiaopei)

homonormative values in family, marriage and kinship, as well as opening them to nonconventional – and indeed very queer – forms. While her films have queered the concept of *jia* (home/family), they have also queered the home video genre often deemed private and apolitical.

## Conclusion

This chapter has introduced Chinese queer feminist filmmaker He Xiaopei's films. By making strategic use of the home video genre to create a 'cinema of pleasure', He Xiaopei's films have contributed to the development of queer feminism in China and globally. They have also showcased what women filmmakers in East Asia have done to foreground women's sexual pleasure, highlight their sexual agency and push the boundaries of world cinema. If, for Mulvey, a feminist politics of cinema can only be achieved through the destruction of visual pleasure,

He Xiaopei's films demonstrate otherwise: a queer feminist film can also be pleasurable to watch and is no less politically engaged.

## References

Balian, H. (2021). Episode 08: filmmaker He Xiaopei. *The Beijing sessions* (1 March). Retrieved from https://thebeijingsessions.com/episodes/episode-08-xiaopei
Bao, H. (2018). *Queer comrades: Gay identity and tongzhi activism in postsocialist China*. Copenhagen: NIAS Press.
Bao, H. (2020). Queering development: Participation, power and pleasure in the participatory video *The Lucky One*. *Feminist Media Studies*, 20(4), 530–47.
Butler, A. (2003). *Women's cinema: The contested screen*. New York: Wallflower Press.
CCC. (2012). Documentary screening event and discussion: *The Lucky One*. Contemporary China Centre, University of Westminster (5 June).
Chan, F. (2017). *Cosmopolitan cinema: Cross-cultural encounters in East Asian film*. London: I. B. Tauris.
Cornwall, A., Correa, C., and Jolly S. (eds) (2008). *Development with a body: Sexuality, human rights and development*. London: Zed Books.
Cornwall, A., and Jolly, S. (2009). Sexuality and development theory. *Development*, 52(1), 5–12.
Engebretsen, E. L. (2014). *Queer women in China: An ethnography*. London: Routledge.
Haraway, D. (1988). Situated knowledges: The science question in feminism and the privilege of partial perspective. *Feminist Studies*, 14(3), 575–99.
He, X. (2001). Chinese queer (*tongzhi*) women organising in the 1990s. In P.-C. Hsiung, M. Jaschok, and C. N. Milwertz, with R. Chan (eds), *Chinese women organising: Cadres, feminists, Muslims, queers* (pp. 41–59). Oxford: Berg Publishers.
He, X. (2016). Pink Space and the pleasure approach to sexuality and the development industry in China. In W. Harcourt (ed.), *The Palgrave Handbook of gender and development* (pp. 561–71). New York: Springer.
He, X. (2019). Rich in desire: Sexualities and fantasies deriving from poverty, stigmatisation and oppression. In J. D. Luther and J. U. Loh (eds), *'Queer' Asia: Decolonising and reimagining sexuality and gender* (pp. 65–84). London: Zed Books.
Johnston, C. (1973). Women's cinema as counter-cinema. In C. Johnston (ed.), *Notes on women's cinema* (pp. 24–31). London: Society for Education in Film and Television.
Kam, L. Y. L. (2013). *Shanghai lalas: Female tongzhi communities and politics in urban China*. Hong Kong: Hong Kong University Press.
Khoo, O., Grgić, A., and Jørholt, E. (2021). Introduction to special issue: Women's world cinema. *Studies in World Cinema*, 1(2), 115–20.
Lorde, A. (1984). *Sister outsider: Essays and speeches by Audre Lorde*. Berkeley: Crossing Press.
Marchetti, G. (2021). Where in the world are Chinese women filmmakers? Transnational China and world cinema in the twenty-first century. *Studies in World Cinema*, 1(2), 121–44.
Mayer, S. (2016). *Political animals: The new feminist cinema*. London and New York: I. B. Tauris.
Mulvey, L. (1975). Visual pleasure and narrative cinema. *Screen*, 16(3), 6–18.
Robinson, L. (2013). *Independent Chinese documentary: From the studio to the street*. Basingstoke: Palgrave Macmillan.

Voci, P. (2010). *China on video: Smaller-screen realities.* London: Routledge.
Wang, L. (2011). *Chinese women's cinema: Transnational contexts.* New York: Columbia University Press.
Wang, L. (2021). *Revisiting women's cinema: Feminism, socialism and mainstream culture in modern China.* Durham: Duke University Press.
White, P. (2015). *Women's cinema, world cinema: Projecting contemporary feminisms.* Durham: Duke University Press.
Xinran. (2003). *The good women of China: Hidden voices.* New York: Vintage.
Yu, K. T. (2018). *'My' self on camera: First person documentary practice in 21st century China.* Edinburgh: Edinburgh University Press.
Zeng, J. (2022). Desiring feminism in Chinese documentary. *Chinese Independent Cinema Observer, 3,* 142–78.
Zhang, Y. (2013, July 28). Pink crusader. *Global Times.* Retrieved from https://www.globaltimes.cn/content/799610.shtml

## Notes

1. He Xiaopei's 2010 film *Polyamorous Family* is available on YouTube: https://www.youtube.com/watch?v=VlRClrQmbGg&t=46s
2. To avoid the confusion between He Xiaopei's surname (He) and the third person singular in English (he), I spell out the filmmaker's name in full and use her preferred personal pronoun 'she/her/hers' to refer to the filmmaker.
3. Editors' note: Sophie Mayer now publishes as So Mayer.
4. He Xiaopei's 2012 film *The Lucky One* is is available on YouTube: https://www.youtube.com/watch?v=talIgb09mfk&t=49s
5. He Xiaopei's 2017 film *Love You Too* is available on YouTube: https://www.youtube.com/watch?v=_rH-tZvEZNA
6. He Xiaopei's 2010 film *Gay Cats* is available on YouTube: https://www.youtube.com/watch?v=3b8ikYX3PNY. Part of her 2021 film *The Bad Women of China* can be viewed at: https://www.youtube.com/watch?v=mg1PINnB3k0

Chapter 2

# Work Ethic(s) of Being a Woman: Images of Female Labour in Hong Kong Cinema (1950s–60s)

*Fiona Y. W. Law*

Different from today's general impression that the masculine images of action heroes and kungfu masters have dominated Hong Kong cinema and attracted its global and local audiences, it was women's films and their female audiences that defined the city's popular cinema before the 1970s. Before the opening of TVB (Television Broadcasts Limited) in November 1967, when housewives and young women could stay at home enjoying free entertainment, cinemagoing was a major activity – especially for women who were economically productive and in control of their leisure expenditure. The vibrant film scene was underpinned by the blossoming film exhibition business; according to Chung Po-yin (2004), there were approximately seventy-three film theatres scattered across the tiny city by the early 1960s, during which post-war urbanisation began. In light of this prosperous cinemagoing scene, film critics such as Sek Kei (1996) identified female spectatorship as contributing to a major proportion of mainstream audiences of the time, before the era of action heroes arrived. As Sek Kei (1996) notes, the growing number of young female stars cast in film at that time was to 'cater to the fantasies and aspirations of housewives in this audience, particularly those women who worked part time in certain home industries to increase their family income' (p. 30). The mainstream female spectatorship is also reflected in the film production from the 1950s to 1960s, when melodrama, Cantonese operatic drama, family drama, romantic comedy and related female-oriented genres comprise the major body of films produced.

According to Annette Kuhn (1987), one of the defining generic features of the woman's film as a textual system is its construction of narratives motivated by female desire and processes of spectator identification governed by a female point-of-view. In Mary Ann Doane (1987)'s study of a particular corpus of Hollywood films from the 1940s to the early 1960s, a 'woman's film' is defined as a genre that deals with the female protagonist through her narrative point of view and unfolding problems that are defined as 'female' – for example, problems that revolve around domestic life, family, children, self-sacrifice, the relationship between women and production versus women's relationship with reproduction. Usually combined with other popular genres – such as melodrama, horror, film noir and the musical – the woman's film is directed towards a female audience as well. Although Doane's classification and discussion stem from the emergence of woman's socio-economic-cultural power as a post-war social phenomenon in the US, this analytical framework is also applicable to Hong Kong's situation during the same period, especially regarding the connection between the rising female spectatorship and the development of popular genres. Instead of following the discussion of conventional feminist film theories through the critical discourse of psychoanalysis, this chapter addresses and identifies the importance of female spectatorship as social subjects or social audiences, with the understanding that these female spectators are actual members of cinema audiences whose economic power affords them the power of consumers able to make meaning and partake in pleasures that in turn formulate and define the mainstream woman's films. In addition to examining how the film company's calculation of its potential female audience demographic is reflected in generic development, narrative construction, star production and even fandom, this chapter aims to investigate the characteristics of the woman's film as a crucial part of popular cinema in Hong Kong during the 1950s and 1960s, by exploring the archetypal figures of womanhood as cinematic representation and how these figures structure the narrative features of Hong Kong Cantonese cinema at that time.

With female spectatorship as a target and feeding the audiences' desire to make sense of their social roles as modern women, Cantonese cinema during this period stressed the portrayals of women's stories regardless of genre and aesthetics. Although filmmaking was not yet a job that women at that time could generally consider, cinema offered them diverse imaginations that being a woman itself was a job, and these films became archetypal groundwork in both representing the advent of industrial capitalism and addressing the female workforce within and beyond the domestic sphere. Ranging from selfish landladies to devoted domestic servants, from day-dreaming factory girls to hard-working nightclub girls, from innocent mistresses to jealous housewives, Cantonese cinema outlines and highlights not only the clash between traditional and modern values, but also the work ethic(s) of being a woman as their society progressed toward economic restructuring. Selected films will be introduced as illustrations of these character archetypes. Through this survey of these least examined cinematic images in Hong Kong cinema, this study also aims to explore an alternative historical perspective in understanding how shifting spectatorship, stardom and generic development are preceded by these herstories.

## Female Figures Before the 'Strong Career Woman' (*nü qianren*) and the 'Kong Girl' (*gang nü*)

There are several factors leading to the growth of female spectatorship in Hong Kong, such as the improved education levels of women, a growing economic power of women whose participation in the labour market ranges from blue collar to white collar, the emergence of 'full-time' middle-class housewives, the emergence of feminism as a Western cultural import, and a new generation of young female baby boomers who are more exposed to both local and imported popular culture. These social factors, together with the overall urbanisation of modernising society, structure a multi-layered formation of womanhood that illustrates the co-existence of the old and new values in the city's imaginary gender discourse. This is a period when sexual conservatism, social hierarchy, gender stratification, the feminist liberation of women and Confucian values struggled against each other among younger and older women. The idea of a patriarchal family and the moral responsibilities as daughters, mothers and wives also seem to contradict and comply with women's growing economic independence and self-awareness as social agents. Women's films in Cantonese cinema of the 1950s and 1960s therefore can tell us something about how these conflicting values create distinctive local elements that contribute to a unique gender discourse of Hong Kong from within and beyond screen culture. Among the enormous corpus of Cantonese film productions from the period, there has been a large variety of female character archetypes from urban settings: landladies, maidservants, domestic workers, rich heiresses, filial daughters, nightclub girls, office ladies, family teachers, middle-class housewives and factory girls. Their character traits are often repetitive, blended and similar across different films, likely because most of these popular films were quick productions and their familiarity to audiences could effectively generate resonance, which in turn constructs and consolidates a communal spectatorship. As Cheng (1985) also observes, the Cantonese cinema in the 1950s and 1960s created 'intelligent, independent, and firm woman characters' (p. 44) who were pioneers for contemporary female images.

While there has been no comprehensive scholarly research on such female representations in this period, the changing image of the modern woman in contemporary Hong Kong is generally defined through the wide use of two popular slang terms in the local context: the image of the 'iron lady' or the 'strong career woman' (*nü qianren*) since the late 1970s, and the image of the 'Kong Girl' (*gang nü*) since the 2000s. Both labelling descriptions of young women in Hong Kong emerged from popular cultural representations. The 'iron lady' or 'strong career woman' generally denotes powerful middle-class women who are usually seen as threatening competitors to men in the workplace. On the surface, her desire to excel at economic productivity overrides and compromises her sexual desire and reproductive desire for intimate affectivity. This character trope comes from singer-actress Liza Wong's successful performance as the strong-willed, self-conscious female protagonist in the local TV drama series *A House Is Not a Home* (1977), in which Wong plays the role of Lok Lam, a diligent but ignored daughter born of a rich man's mistress in a traditional big Chinese family. Lok Lam not only establishes her own business running a fashion magazine, but also struggles to save her family business, a major construction company in the city, from bankruptcy. The enormously successful reception of this TV drama series, especially among housewives and young women at the time, led to the emergence, popularisation and advocacy of this role-model image of the strong, heroic woman who manages to create her own career and stays defiant against traditional family values, without destroying them. The pragmatism and ideology of social progress celebrated by the fast-growing economic prosperity of Hong Kong society in the late 1970s defined this middle-class career woman as a mainstream social product whose formation of agency seems to disrupt her mother's generation, in which women were generally considered to be obedient, diligent, quiet and reluctant to resist against unfairness.

Transformed from the 'strong career woman' image of the late 1970s, young women in Hong Kong have been coined as 'Kong Girls' or 'Hong Kong Girls' since around the 2000s, and the slang term is still being used among the public today. Young women in Hong Kong nowadays are generally labelled, if not stereotyped, as 'Kong Girls', meaning that they are a combination of worshippers of materialism, addicts of consumer culture and self-centred manipulators of their boyfriends and husbands. These features were, as Donna Chu (2014) analyses, generally gathered from numerous local online forum discussions over the course of the early 2000s and were popularly circulated as common characters of young females, who may also self-identify as such. But in addition to such seemingly derogatory categorisation, 'Kong Girls' also embody positive attributes, such as a sense of righteousness, emotional authenticity, a strong calibre and a sense of resilience in the workplace. 'Kong Girls' therefore take an ambivalent and sometimes opportunistic stance in feminism, and their images also become unique representations in Hong Kong cinema from the 2000s, especially through the performances by local actress-singers such as Sammi Cheng, Miriam Yeung and Stephy Tang. Romantic comedies by Johnnie To and Wai Kar-fai – such as *Needing You* (2000), *Love on a Diet* (2001), *Fat Choi Spirit* (2002), Edmund Pang's *Love in a Puff* trilogy (2010, 2012, 2017) and Patrick Kong's urban romance films such as *Marriage with a Fool* (2006) and *Love is Not All Around* (2007) – all show female protagonists with these features of 'Kong Girls' who are both independent and dependent by different degrees at the same time.

Derived from both the 'strong career woman' and the 'Kong Girl', the cultural configuration of womanhood in Hong Kong has been tending towards a general sense of toughness and a mixture of paradoxical features, which could be illustrating hybridised ideologies of conservatism and orthodoxy (as in Confucian family values and binary gender roles), as well as progressive resistance and a liberalist outlook (as in their performance as feminist fighters for patriarchal values embedded in social practices). This interesting combination of hybridised ideological embodiments, as I will illustrate, may be rooted in their mothers' generation who were young female labourers and film audiences in the 1950s and 1960s, watching women's films as their source of imaginary identification and social empowerment. The conceptualisation of femininity and the assumption of traditionally passive womanhood in the context of Hong Kong are therefore called into question, as the character traits of 'strong career woman' and 'Kong Girls' can be found in popular woman's films from earlier decades.

In light of the need to trace the early development, if not genealogy, of how the modern Hong Kong woman is cinematically visualised, narrated and formulated in relation to the development of women's film and related popular genres, this chapter focuses on the image of woman labourers and women as labourers in Hong Kong Cantonese cinema in the 1950s and 1960s. This is a period which is rarely researched, while current scholarly works mainly pay attention to the historical framework of Hong Kong's colonial, post-colonial, national and translocal trajectories with its cinematic neighbours, such as mainland China, Taiwan and Southeast Asia, as contextualised by the Cold War (Chang, 2019; Chu, 2003; Fu, 2000; Mak, 2018, 2019; Ng, 2021). Although these works comprehensively outline the socio-political context for understanding the formation of Hong Kong cinema by tracking the transnational mobility of film personnel and industrial networking, offering a background knowledge to foreshadowing the later success of Hong Kong popular cinema, more work needs to be done to examine the narrative patterns, generic development, stylistic articulations, cultural configurations and other textual elements of the films produced in this period. To further contextualise this period through the women's stories, it is found that women on screen are often attributed social values, moral duties and contrasting expectations from tradition and modern culture, all of which illustrate the ideological clashes, cultural dynamics and moral dilemmas that their female audience could either identify with or internalise in their own formation of womanhood as social subjects. In these popular films, being a woman is not only being a woman, but also working to become a woman, working as a woman and being a woman in the workplace. The images of woman labourers are also double-layered illustrations of women as labourers in the developing society. Beyond the screen, these female images offer references and idealised projections for spectatorial identification and consumption. Thus, womanhood and femininity are not only culturally defined, but also socially practised through these cinematic representations of female archetypes, the narrativisation of these characters and their consumption among female audiences as popular cultural products.

## Work Ethic(s) of Being a Woman: On-Screen Representations and Beyond

The 1950s and 1960s were a transformative period for Hong Kong, when the mobility of personnel, inflow of capital and common people's desire for a stable life worked concurrently to engineer the development of the city. The rapid changes that took place spatially, ideologically, culturally and economically could also be understood through Zygmunt Bauman's (2000) concept of liquid modernity, when society is moving from modernity to late modernity, when private consumption is celebrated over work, and when social inequality is most distinctively illustrated through different practices of consumption. Cinemagoing could be one of these emerging forms of consumerist activity. In this regard, the actual female audiences, who themselves were active consumers of popular entertainment, were also the flawed consumers who were not entirely resourceful. This means that their freedom to choose and pick a film for leisure entertainment with their own money did not coincide with their freedom as an individual member of society, which defined them as part of an anonymous labour force. The limitation of class and gender stratifications is thus in need of an escapist emancipation through cultural consumptions that would not be economically threatening. Therefore, the relationship between on-screen female images and off-screen female spectators should not be simply understood as an imaginary construction of female subjectivity or identification; the act of cinemagoing itself as an economic activity could also be an emancipatory social performance of women's limited, or perhaps growing, freedom as collective consumers.

By examining these cinematic images of female labourers, this chapter attempts to open the discussion with the following questions: first, how are women of different ages and social classes in the 1950s and 1960s represented in a way that offers an alternative perspective for understanding Hong Kong's gendered localism and urban modernity, at a time when it, as a post-war society, was undergoing modernisation, industrialisation and cinematisation? This sociological viewpoint is to be seen through the transformation of women's social positioning in the transitional post-war society. Some women participated in the growing market economy as factory workers, office workers, entertainers, nightclub girls, or waitresses; others would literally 'work' in domestic spaces as maidservants and landladies (rent collectors who live in the same place as the tenants). In most cases, women's social roles as mothers, daughters and wives are their primary 'work', and women as such need to get other jobs in order to fulfil their duties as mothers, daughters and wives. Economic contribution has always been at stake, and this practical necessity among different types of working women is also a major driving force in the narrativisation of many woman's films. Based on the assumption that cinematic representations create desirable figures or objects of fantasy for their spectator, these female labourers on screen complicate such functionality of identification. Their references to the real-life situations of their female audiences and the highly formulated and sometimes clichéd narratives both create a desire for consumption and disrupt the cinematic fantasy at the same time.

Second, how are these women's everyday stories narrated, textualised, dramatised, fantasised and archived on the silver screen, and how might these cinematic stories in turn formulate Hong Kong women's ways of living? In this regard, working women or female labourers on screen are seen as major signifiers for female audiences to identify with. Through the cinematised images of their own social roles, female audiences see themselves as both ordinary and extraordinary members of a modern society which was also in the process of changing. Post-war Hong Kong society was undergoing a major transformation or economic restructuring when manufacturing industries, consumer culture, urbanisation, imported popular cultures and exported products defined the ideology of progress much celebrated by the official discourse, which encouraged one to believe in the work ethic of embracing a can-do attitude. How does such a positive and practical outlook further offer imaginary elements in defining womanhood in Hong Kong?

The practicality of being a woman is most effectively shown in various cinematic images of the female labourer, ranging from the woman whose work is located in the domestic space that does not belong to her, such as the landlady or rent collector, the home teacher, and the domestic worker or maidservant; over the woman who needs to leave her domestic milieu for work to support her family, such as the factory girl and the nightclub girl; to the woman whose 'career' is synonymous with her domestic life, such as the full-time housewife in a middle-class family. Oftentimes the narratives about these female labourers also represent the clash between the leftist critique of urban capitalism and its celebration through conflicting ideologies, such as feminism and consumerism. Against this interwoven and sometimes disruptive social discourse of change and continuity, women are both empowered and disenchanted by these changing opportunities and crises at the same time. Femininity in this regard is an identity project of both becoming and resisting the modern, and women's individual sense of duties is under an enormous burden. They need to sustain the status quo and embrace transformation when their workplace is often entangled with the domestic space. In an attempt to stimulate discussions concerning the questions raised above, three sets of character archetypes of female labourers will be introduced and analysed in the following sections, in order to illustrate the different work ethics of being a woman in Hong Kong Cantonese cinema. While the attribution of these character archetypes and formulated generic traits is often associated with their different social class backgrounds, age-groups, work natures, positions in the domestic sphere and family, as well as the mutative cultural dynamics of the times, the following discussion attempts to explore and prepare for an alternative inquiry into gender representations, the cinematic narrativisation of women's agency and the trending of popular genres through these woman's films of the 1950s and 1960s.

## 1. The Landlady and the Housemaid as Images of Social Critique

The Cantonese cinema of Hong Kong in the 1950s, according to P. K. Leung (2000), commonly showcased the binary opposition between the urban and the rural, with the former being connotative of colonial Hong Kong and the latter of mainland China. Other than the ideological differences represented through such binary settings, especially through the narrative closure when the protagonists need to make the decision of whether to stay in the city or move to the countryside, the crowded living environment in the city also produced several character archetypes, defining Hong Kong cinema as urban cinema since the post-war period. Among the various types of characters whose traits connect to both the growth of the city and clashes of ideologies, some are formulated as working-class women whose social class and gender role illustrate the emerging cultural clashes. For example, the landlady, or female rent collector, in social realist melodramas of leftist productions, such as *In the Face of Demolition* (1953, dir. Lee Tit), embodies and triggers social critique. Interestingly, although she never plays the role of protagonist, the image of the female rent collector in these films tends to be portrayed as a fierce-looking middle-aged housewife whose husband is economically unproductive, usually jobless or addicted to gambling and alcoholism, and as such it is the landlady who brings in the family income. Although she is addressed as 'the landlady', she is not necessarily the owner of the property. In most of these films, she often is a hired person who shares the flat with other tenants, from whom she collects the rent every month. Given this special position in the household, the landlady is often portrayed as exploitative, practical and lacking sympathy for the other tenants who may struggle to earn money for their rent payments. In many cases, the pressures and threats imposed by the landlady become a major driving force within the narrative.

While the actual property owner is seldom represented or shown in the narrative (Kei, 1985), this 'managerial' and seemingly powerful female figure has also gradually become a cinematic stereotype for ordinary middle-aged women who are themselves portrayed as being stuck in a state of in-between-ness. Although she may act and speak in an authoritative manner, the landlady is also burdened by her work requirements. When the tenants are not able to pay their rent, she either has to drive them out or compensate for the rent herself. During *In the Face of Demolition*, the landlady and her husband are also heavily in debt, and in order to secure her job, she becomes even tougher in pressurising the penniless tenants. In this narrative structure, the landlady often represents the selfishness that is associated with urban decadence and capitalism; as the stereotype becomes more commonly found in Cantonese films in the 1960s, the stingy, mean-looking landlady is also occasionally transformed from a derogative figure in social realist melodrama into a clownish comic character in urban comedy. Although the figure of the landlady remains a supporting character, she is a popular archetype that recurs in popular films, regardless of their ideological stance. Although this particular social class or work type has gradually disappeared as result of Hong Kong's transformation into a neoliberal, international financial centre, which has altered public housing provision as social benefit for those who are economically underprivileged, the figure of the landlady occasionally re-appears in films as a nostalgic reminder of previous decades. For example, in Stephen Chow's *Kungfu Hustle* (2004), the apathetic, cynical landlady is reminiscent of the figure from *The House of 72 Tenants* (dir. Chor Yuen, 1973), which is based on another film by the same title, from 1963 (dir. Wong Wai-yat). Through their shared character traits, all these landladies defy the notion of the traditional Chinese housewife who is obedient to the husband, as in these films the husbands are now subordinate to the landladies.

Other than the landlady who works in the household, the maidservant (commonly known as *amah*) constitutes another type of working woman in a domestic setting that is not hers. Historically, in a social practice that dates back to the early twentieth century, *amahs* are unmarried young women from Southern Chinese regions, who are life-contracted to upper-middle-class families and spend their lifetime serving the same family across generations. Thanks to the long years with the same host family, many of them develop strong emotional attachments to the host families, while also forming an intimate sisterhood among themselves. The title of the film *Sworn Sisters* (dir. Ng Wui, 1954) refers to the cultural practice in which these women become affectively tied by mutual vows to develop their communal life as sisters. This is also a very interesting matriarchal social structure that resists and re-envisions motherhood, as many of these maidservants become surrogate mothers to the children of their host families. Long before Ann Hui's *A Simple Life* (2011), which tells the story of a maidservant who gets old and needs her surrogate child to take care of her in return, *Sworn Sisters* explored the different destinies and tragic experiences of four maidservants who have different outlooks onto the future: Ah Choi wishes to get married and have her own family, but is found to have cheated with a married man; Ah Ho, the aged maidservant, sacrifices her life savings to help the failing business of her host family who immediately fire her after having taken her money; Ah Juen's superstition leads to the death of her niece who is her only relative; and Ah Sam wishes to spend her retired life in a Buddhist nunnery but is swindled out of almost all her money.

Produced by the leftist company Union Film, this social realist melodrama makes a stern critique of the social hierarchy created by this maidservant tradition, as well as exposing the impossibility for women to sustain this work ethic when their personal lives are compromised. In the opening sequence, documentary footage and an off-screen narrative voice introduce this group of women in Hong Kong society. By showing the images of maidservants in real life, as they are busy with preparing meals and taking care of children, the opening footage contextualises the narrative of the film and frames its critical position. Similar to the landlady, the local life-contracted maidservant has largely disappeared in domestic and economic life in Hong Kong, particularly since the mass importation of domestic workers from the Philippines since the 1980s. The traditional *amah* maidservant's resilient work ethic, internalised exploitation and inferiority complex, lacking the sense of a secure future, are all combined in these films to reflect on Hong Kong society in the immediate post-war period, where hard work does not necessarily pay off. As a character archetype, the maidservant is often set as a supporting role in film narratives, representing the suppressed agency of these figures, or sometimes also functioning as the helper of the hero in family melodramas. Apart from films such as *Sworn Sisters* and *A Simple Life* where the maidservant is featured as the protagonist, stories of local maidservants are relatively under-represented, despite the fact that this group of working women were part of the mainstream workforce in post-war Hong Kong society.

## 2. The Factory Girl Fantasia

While the landlady and maidservant are associated with social realist melodramas as supporting characters, other types of working women are represented through different popular genres. The best-known and most popularly represented female labourer in the 1960s is the enormous population of factory girls in Hong Kong. While Hong Kong was becoming a leading industrial city in the region, the many nameless female workers who produced these products and contributed to this narrative of economic success are often overlooked. Recent films such as *McDull Prince de la Bun* (dir. Toe Yuen, 2004) and *The Way We Are* (dir. Ann Hui, 2008) pay brief tributes to these hardworking factory girls from decades ago, and a number of romantic comedies in the 1960s addresses this social position of young women. Different from the critical, social realist articulations of the landlady and the maidservant as mature adults or middle-aged adults, factory girls are often represented as teens or young adults – this is also related to the fact that female factory workers at that time were mainly born in the post-war period. Through fantasised narratives in the genre of romantic comedies, popular films about factory girls were further glamourised by young female stars who had just emerged at that time. The frenzied, competitive fandoms of Connie Chan and Josephine Siao, for example, defined the emerging local popular culture among baby boomers in the mid-1960s.

These filmic representations address the lives of docile, diligent and filial daughters working in factories (both outside and within the home), who produced a variety of consumer products for the world market (Siu, 2010). On the one hand, popular representations of these young local working-class women on screen outline the productivity of Hong Kong as part of the world economy; on the other hand, the narrative portrayals from these women's perspectives suggest the evolving nature of women's social position. When working women were more often represented in supporting roles in the 1950s and their necessity to offer economic support to their families was introduced as the cause of narrative events with tragic results, working women gradually became cinematic protagonists in the 1960s. The changing generic trend from social realist melodrama to romantic urban comedy also signalled an evolving representation of women's agency. Discussing the cinematic stories of factory girls and teddy girls, Chang (2019) suggests that these filmic texts become a 'milieu of negotiation' (p. 151) where female agency can exist within the patriarchal systems of the family economy and industrial modernity, by reconciling gender conflicts among the social classes of 1960s' Hong Kong. This 'milieu of negotiation' is also unsettled, contested and made ambivalent when issues of gender and social class intersect with differences in ideological values between generations, against the backdrop of an increasingly urbanised society. Summarising the characteristics of Cantonese cinema in the 1960s, Fu (2000) points out that the generational conflicts between the baby boomers and their parental generation resulted in a tendency to foreclose ideological contradictions through cinematic works. When women's economic power and education advanced among young female adults, the woman's film was also incorporated and blended into the overall emergence of youth films.

One of the earliest films focusing on the factory girl is *Blooming Under a Cool Moon* (dir. Fung Fung, 1960). It features Law Yim Hing as the female protagonist, Chik Hon Mui (literally translated as 'cool plum blossom'), who yearns for freedom and economic advancement by leaving the countryside and working as a factory worker in the city. However, her dream of freedom does not come true when she is entangled in a love triangle with her cousin (played by Law Kim Long) and the factory manager (played by Lam Kar Sing) and at times is harassed by the villainous factory owner. The romantic tragedy is set up with the expectation that the factory girl's freedom of romantic love will be compromised. In the film, Hon Mui's pre-marital pregnancy has to be concealed, because her real love, the factory manager, is allegedly killed in a train accident. In order to survive in a conservative society where pre-marital pregnancy is perceived as shameful, she has to accept marriage to her cousin. She then has to leave home to earn money as a singer when her husband loses his job. The melodrama snowballs into a series of tragic events and complications of romantic relations, underpinned by the burden of Confucian values. The film's didactic tone and emphasis on morality are not unique at the time, but the emerging character archetype of the factory girl also illustrates the increasingly challenging lives of young women when the irreversible progress of the society compels them to and simultaneously forbids them from pursuing a life of their own volition.

The tragic melodrama of failing female agency in *Blooming Under a Cool Moon* is expanded with more detailed inquiry into the factory girl's social situation and her growing agency in *The Blossoming Rose* (dir. Chiang Wai Kwong, 1968). With similar plot elements – such as pre-marital pregnancy, the myth of upward social mobility and the factory girl's transformation into a nightclub singer – Connie Chan's articulation of the factory girl Ho Siu Ping is narrated through a romantic tragedy rather than a failed family melodrama. Unlike *Blooming Under a Cool Moon*, in which family values and parental roles play a burgeoning part in hindering the female protagonist's decisions, there is almost an absence of parental voice and family pressure over the course of *The Blossoming Rose*. Instead, there is a detailed portrayal of the everyday life of factory girls at that time, showcasing their daily routines between the workplace and leisure time. In addition to the hectic schedule as a factory worker, Siu Ping also attends night school where she can acquire knowledge beyond the industrial world of manufacturing. This yearning for knowledge and a hidden note of a growing agency to shape her outlook also contextualises her romance with the part-time night schoolteacher Lee Hon Chung (played by Woo Fung), a Prince-Charming-like university student whose overseas study is later financially supported by his rich girlfriend. The night school is here represented as an intersecting milieu of romantic fantasy and social mobility, where young adults can live in an alternative world and create a different interpersonal network at night-time, a time when everyone is a part-timer who sacrifices leisure activities for self-improvement. Romantic affairs also grow among these diligent students and teachers. In contrast to Hon Chun's capitalistic, aristocratic girlfriend who seems to be detached from social reality, Siu Ping fulfils the role of a hard-working housewife who takes care of Hon Chung's mother and of a devoted mother who raises their child by working as a nightclub singer while he is away for study. As in most romantic tragedies at the time, there is a series of misunderstandings from Hon Chung, making Siu Ping's sacrifice more dramatic and inducing sympathy.

Despite the narrative twists and tragic events, *The Blossoming Rose* closes with a happy ending when the lovers reunite after having resolved all their misunderstandings. The tear-inducing end of this Cinderella tale not only validates the film as a typical 'weepie' – a genre that commonly characterises the popular understanding of a woman's film – but it also presents a combination of realist resonances and fantasised desires for its factory girl audiences. Interestingly, this aggrandisation of female fantasy is highlighted through the promotional advertisement of this film in newspapers. As shown in the newspaper advertisement of the film (Figure 2.1), bonus footage about a local beauty pageant competition was shown at the screenings of *The Blossoming Rose*. According to the description on the advertisement, the footage showcased the crowning ceremony of the local beauty queen, led by the most popular female stars from both Mandarin and Cantonese cinemas at that time, such as Ling Bo, Le Di, Connie Chan and Josephine Siao. This beauty competition was co-organised by the film company and a cigarette brand, and it highlighted the glamourous, celebratory moment of victory, of being crowned the new modern beauty of the city. Such an encouragement to make dreams come true is further reinforced by an advertisement in the same newspaper, recruiting dancers for the film company. Beyond the textual configuration of a fairy tale about the factory girl within the film, these two extratextual events create a multi-layered production of female fantasy for actual female audiences at that time: it offered the promise that, in addition to being a spectator who could easily identify with the female protagonist, factory girls in real life could also join the pageant or train as a dancer – and potentially become a movie star.

Although the aftermath of the 1967 leftist riots led to a growing social awareness and local concern among the public, and although the global counterculture and youth cultures prompted local young adults to be more socio-politically engaged, popular films such as *The Blossoming*

Work Ethic(s) of Being a Woman    43

Figure 2.1 Newspaper advertisement of *The Blossoming Rose*, Wah Kiu Yat Po, 2 February 1968

*Rose* continued to draw in audiences, offering an escapist outlook from the uncertain reality where young adults found themselves voiceless and lacking control. The pragmatism of social upward mobility, the petty enjoyment of consumerist culture and the fantasy generated by popular culture were mainstream concerns among working-class women, whose growing sense of agency was also defined by their rising economic autonomy. Throughout the 1960s, the factory girl was a popular character archetype and served as the female protagonist in urban romantic comedies, such as *Three Love Affairs* (dir. Mok Hong-si, 1963), *Movie Fans* (dir. Wong Yiu, 1966) and *Three Flowers of the Factory* (dir. Sung Ming, 1967). In these urban comedies, the everyday life of the factory girl is portrayed in a light-hearted way. Diverting from the industrialising, entrepreneurial working environment in modern society, the factory in these films was often represented like a high school, where the young women, bonded by friendship, are both disciplined by the institutionalisation of economic production and tactically resistant to male managers who impose exploitative power over them. In many of these films, the factory girls have already left their parents and live together as roommates in shared housing, and they sometimes go on group dates in their leisure time. Replacing the school, the factory becomes the educational locale where the young women learn survival skills, acquire economic power, develop friendships and affective relationships, and reimagine their female agency through everyday practices as independent individuals. These mass-produced, cinematic fantasies of the factory girls are, in a sense, locating a utopic imaginative world where female desire is encouraged to blossom. The self-reflexive, intertextual elements of fan culture and moviegoing within and beyond these urban narratives build up a multi-layered realm of fantasy with which female audiences could directly engage.

### 3. The Pedagogic Comedy of the Middle-Class Housewife

Unlike the landlady, the maidservant and the factory girl, the role of middle-class housewife is not work that is defined through economic exchange for human labour with a contracted relationship between employers and employees. However, within the narrative logics of the films discussed, it is commonly understood that the social position of a middle-class housewife is the ideal status or 'work' position to which a working-class woman would generally aspire. Being a middle-class housewife who does not need to do household chores might be the most fancied goal for most young single women in these films. Being loved by her husband, who is usually the director or manager of a business company, this fashionable, modern and spoilt housewife was a very popular image in Cantonese cinema during the 1960s. Quantitatively, films related to middle-class housewives have outnumbered that of the character archetypes introduced in the previous sections. This might be because cinematic representations of the middle-class housewife were not especially new to Chinese popular cinema at the time. Sang Hu's Mandarin film *Long Live the Missus!* (1947)[1] is probably the most renowned urban screwball comedy from an earlier period, focusing on the figure of a middle-class housewife who experiences multiple challenges in her marriage, from financial issues to a cheating husband. Written by Eileen Chang, this Mandarin film follows her recurring motif of the dysfunctional marriage. In fact, Chang coined the term 'female marriage officer' (*nü jiehunyuan*) in her short-story 'Flower Withered' (*huadiao*, 1944) to describe how marriage was the only 'job' that young middle-class women could pursue for a successful life, because they had no capacity to work as office ladies or shopkeepers. In Chang's description, the differences between marriage and work are almost indiscernible for middle-class women; but for working-class women, getting married to a manager and forming a middle-class family of their own functioned as an aspirational 'dream job' of achieving upward mobility.

Different from the satirical tone of Chang's Mandarin comedy, the portrayal of housewives in Cantonese cinema is, from the female audience's perspectives, more idealised and shaped by growing feminist sensibilities. Different from working-class housewives who needed to handle all the housework themselves, middle-class housewives rely on the maidservants to take care of the heavy chores, while they would take on the managerial role in assigning duties to the employed domestic labour. With increasing leisure time, the middle-class housewife can engage in different social activities. In her discussion of the development of feminism in modern Japan, Vera Mackie (2003) uses the term 'housewife feminism' (p. 132) to describe the rising power of women in post-war Japan, where the increased economic growth, industrialisation and nuclearisation of families led to rising intellectual debates on the social roles of women through the publication of feminist magazines. The social identity of housewives and domestic labour became the core of this debate within Japanese feminist circles, and it was argued that being a housewife should also be recognised as a profession. Although there is yet to be a thorough study on the growth of feminist movements in Hong Kong within the same period, popular cinema offers a brief glimpse into how feminist ideas have been incorporated in popular discourse through representations of middle-class housewives. However, instead of advocating a progressive outlook, feminist ideas and women's communal activities represented in these films have been implied as being destructive to the normative everyday life of modern women, and these films function as pedagogical comedies from which female audiences could learn a lesson about how to be an amiable middle-class housewife.

For example, unmarried office lady Kit Fong (Ting Ying) in *Three Females* (dir. Mok Hong Si, 1960) is perceived as an irresponsible employee by her employer (who is also her brother-in-law). He immediately fires her, upon discovering that she took leave from work to attend a feminist meeting. The chair of the feminist club Mui Lai Ling (Carrie Ku Mei) is represented as an addicted Mahjong player who spends all day and night either playing the game or taking part in feminist activities and who completely ignores her children and husband. As these activities disturb their daily domestic routines, both female characters have lessons to learn over the course of the plot's development. Being laid off and having to leave home, Kit Fong encounters difficulties in renting a room and finding a new job – she is stuck in the practical dilemma of whether to get married to her fiancé because, on the one hand, the landlady only takes in married couples as tenants and, on the other hand, the prospective employer does not hire married women. In the case of Lai Ling, her neglecting her family leads to an accident with a fire that almost ruins everything. The film, while being an urban comedy, is also a pedagogic text that educates its audiences about the social roles of wives and husbands. The third female figure in this film, Kit Yu (Law Yim Hing) is Kit Fong's elder sister who is constantly suppressed by her domineering husband. In contrast to Kit Fong and Lai Ling, Kit Yu is a traditional woman who obeys her husband; her husband, as a clichéd patriarchal figure, keeps a mistress. Although Kit Yu does not need to do housework and although she can lead a luxurious lifestyle, she remains voiceless in the family because she is economically unproductive, and because her maternal family needs her husband's financial support. In Kit Yu's case, marriage is not too different from an employment relationship in which the husband plays the role of a controlling boss with his economic power. However, the narrative twist of the film lies in the husband's epiphany when Kit Yu has a miscarriage. The reconciliation and revelation experienced by the three couples draw on a pedagogic closure of the film, by stressing a 'balanced' marriage in which both husband and wife need to take responsibility for producing a functional family.

The pedagogic tone of urban comedies about middle-class housewives or young couples is rather common in the period. As a preparation for the moral lesson at the narrative closures, stereotypical or binary character traits are employed for educational effect. For example, the character traits of middle-class housewives are often portrayed as unproductive, spoilt, materialistic, selfish and even matriarchal. Mahjong playing is the major activity in which they engage to pass time, and they seldom show maternal affection to their children. The husbands, however, are usually quiet, patient, pragmatic and uninterested in household matters. Sometimes the husbands submit their power and express fear of their fierce-looking wives who are suspicious of them having extramarital affairs. In *Two City Girls* (dir. Mok Hong Si, 1963), Fan Kam Ping (Lam Fung) is the wife of the businessman Chui Sek Wah (Cheung Ying Choi), who openly spoils her by letting her do whatever she likes in the household, such as playing Mahjong overnight and setting up various house rules for her own convenience. In contrast to Kam Ping, their family teacher Tang Sau Man (Ting Ying) is the well-mannered, hardworking and conscientious young woman who not only teaches Kam Ping's daughter but also handles all personal matters and even prepares breakfast for her – according to the house mistress's special requests. Such binary contrasts of a selfish middle-class housewife and a reliable working-class, but well-educated young woman set up an interpretative framework for film audiences to critique the commonly aspirational social position of the middle-class housewife. The narrative development also follows the formulated expectation that Kam Ping will experience a revelation and learn her lesson after some critical events. The character archetype of the middle-class housewife, as a crucial generic element in woman's film, structures and consolidates the didactic formalism for Cantonese cinema in a period when popular cinema was a major cultural text for the audience to shape and reflect on their own social agency.

## Concluding Remarks

From today's perspective, the variety of female labourers in Hong Kong's popular cinema from the 1950s and 1960s has now become among the most important archival representations of gender roles. Against the colony's economic development during these two decades, these various images of female labourers had been the dominant representations, as they directly responded to the lived experiences of young women who were stuck between traditional roles and societal modernisation. The dynamics, contradictions and negotiations between the residual and emergent social and ideological values illustrate the pre-emergence of a modern female agency. Among all these romantic comedies, there are shared narrative traits of using pretension or performance as survival skill – both for the narratological purpose of plot development and as an indication of class fantasy. For example, factory girls and ordinary workers pretend to be rich people in courtship, a factory owner's son pretends to be poor, many housewives pretend to be single in order to get an office job, several single women pretend to be married for other reasons, and so on. All these female characters play with a mode of performance or masquerading in constructing, fantasising about and transgressing the fixed, binary views of modern marriage against Chinese traditions.

This chapter mainly serves as a survey of selected images of female labourers in Hong Kong's Cantonese cinema in the 1950s to 1960s. While the discussion above offers an overview of selected character archetypes in examining the growing female workforce on screen, further research into the popular cinema of this period is needed. By introducing these prominent female images, I hope to explore the extent to which these various archetypal screened heroines and their female spectatorship could explain the uniqueness of Cantonese cinema, as compared to other regional and national cinemas of the same period. The urban and modernising settings in Hong Kong Cantonese films of the 1950s and 1960s are effective reminders, if not comparative cinematic representations, of a variety of films during the same period – for example, the inter-war Japanese woman's films produced by Shochiku Studio through popular genres, such as *Shomin Eiga* or *Shoshimin Eiga* (film narratives about the salaryman or salarywoman) and Classical Hollywood romantic comedies or woman's films in the 1940s. Looking back from today's viewpoint, these stories of everyday lives and women's multi-layered struggles and delights in Cantonese cinema are texts worthy of study for rethinking Hong Kong's cinematic history, especially in connection with the conceptualisation of women's labour, or women as labourers, as they are shown through the different waves of global feminism, as well as in the discussion of world cinema.

## References

Bauman, Z. (2000). *Liquid modernity*. Cambridge: Polity Press.
Chang, J. J. (2019). *Screening communities: Negotiating narratives of empire, nation, and the Cold War in Hong Kong cinema*. Hong Kong: Hong Kong University Press.
Cheng, Y. (1985). The world according to Everyman. In *The traditions of Hong Kong comedy* (pp. 41–45). Hong Kong: The Urban Council of Hong Kong.
Chu, D. (2014). Kong Girls and Lang Mo: Teen perceptions of emergent gender stereotypes in Hong Kong. *Journal of Youth Studies*, 17(1), 130–47.
Chu, Y. (2003). *Hong Kong cinema: Coloniser, motherland and self*. London and New York: Routledge.
Chung, P. (2004). *Xianggang ying shi ye bai nian* [香港影視業百年]. Hong Kong: Joint Publishing.
Doane, M. A. (1987). *The desire to desire: The woman's film of the 1940s*. Bloomington and Indianapolis: Indiana University Press.
Fu, P. (2000). The 1960s: Modernity, youth culture, and Hong Kong Cantonese cinema. In P. Fu and D. Desser (eds), *The cinema of Hong Kong: History, arts, identity* (pp. 71–89). Cambridge: Cambridge University Press.
Kei, S. (1985). The city and the village. In *The traditions of Hong Kong comedy* (pp. 32–35). Hong Kong: The Urban Council of Hong Kong.
Kei, S. (1996). The war between the Cantonese and Mandarin cinemas in the sixties, or how the beautiful women lost to the action men. In *The restless breed: Cantonese stars of the sixties* (pp. 30–33). Hong Kong: The Urban Council of Hong Kong.

Kuhn, A. (1987). Women's genres: Melodrama, soap opera and theory. In C. Gledhill (ed.), *Home is where the heart is: Studies in melodrama and the woman's film* (pp. 339–49). London: British Film Institute.

Leung, P. K. (2000). Urban cinema and the cultural identity of Hong Kong. In P. Fu and D. Desser (eds), *The cinema of Hong Kong: History, arts, identity* (pp. 227–51). Cambridge: Cambridge University Press.

Mackie, V. (2003). *Feminism in modern Japan citizenship, embodiment and sexuality*. Cambridge: Cambridge University Press.

Mak, G. (2018). *Xianggang dian ying yu Xinjiapo: Leng zhan shi dai Xing Gang wen hua lian xi, 1950–1965* [香港電影與新加坡：冷戰時代星港文化連繫, 1950–1965]. Hong Kong: Hong Kong University Press.

Mak, G. (2019). *Leng zhan shi qi Xianggang dian mao ying pian de 'ling lei gai bian' yu chong pai* [冷戰時期香港電懋影片的'另類改編'與重拍]. Beijing: Zhonghua shu ju.

Ng, K. K. K. (2021). *Zuo tian jin tian ming tian: nei di yu Xianggang dian ying de zheng zhi, yi shu yu chuan tong* [昨天今天明天：內地與香港電影的政治、藝術與傳統]. Hong Kong: Chung Wa Book Publisher.

Siu, H. (2010). Women of influence: Gendered charisma. In H. Siu (ed.), *Merchants' daughters: Women, commerce, and regional culture in South China* (pp. 169–96). Hong Kong: Hong Kong University Press.

# Notes

1. There have been several films titled *tai tai wan sui* (literally translated as 'long live the wife') in Mandarin and Cantonese cinemas since the 1940s. Other than San Hu's 1947 film, Wong Tin Lam's Mandarin comedy *Darling Stays at Home* (1967) also uses the same Chinese title. Bi Hu's Cantonese comedy *Long Live the Wife*, or *Three Cheers for My Wife* (1948) also takes this Chinese title. While the three films have different narratives, Bi Hu's Cantonese film portrays a domineering, capable housewife whom her timid husband nicknames the 'empress'; this showcases an early tendency to strong housewife representation.

Chapter 3

# 'Functioning on the Fringes': Interrogating New South Korean Womanhood and Millennial Trauma in *Microhabitat* (2017)

## Dave McCaig

*Microhabitat* (*Sogongnyeo*, dir. Jeon Go-Woon, 2017) is a film that has gained global critical attention and praise for its poignant portrayals of millennial womanhood in South Korea. Formally sparse in style, *Microhabitat* follows the emotionally charged personal lives of a group of thirty-something city-dwelling friends struggling through the challenges of contemporary urban life as middle age beckons. Throughout the film particular focus is placed on the collective emotional trauma that millennial women face within a patriarchal society. The lead character, Mi-so (Esom) goes through a period of her thirties in which her life seems to edge further into a spiralling dissociation from the expectations of a stable, comfortable middle-class existence as the narrative progresses. We first encounter university graduate Mi-so on a stark winter evening, shivering with cold and carefully counting what little money she has in her sparsely furnished, barely habitable apartment. Her friends seem to have gained some identifiable markers of middle-class stability, such as tastefully decorated apartments and marriage. But as we follow Mi-so's interactions with them, it becomes ever apparent that all is not so well beneath these superficial surfaces and that their life is also plagued by trauma. As 'elder' millennials they, too, are shakily navigating through previously established markers of womanhood, such as marriage, fulfilling careers, stable relationships and home ownership.

Released during a volatile period in local generational and gender politics in which both millennials and women are demonised, *Microhabitat* will be assessed in this chapter as a valuable reflection of the modern public environment in South Korea, where the nation has seen a dramatic increase in collective feminist voices against the upswing of widespread misogynistic groups. *Microhabitat* will also be appraised as a significant cultural document in relation to recent changes in South Korea, changes that have ensured a collective political strengthening of women's narratives through artistic and wider civic life.

The nonconformist Mi-so drifts from one almost uninhabitable living space to another, whilst making some money doing casual work, cleaning houses so that she can exist on the fringes of contemporary Seoul. She struggles to make the rent, warm her home and feed herself with the money from her irregular employment. Mi-so's life on the fringes is obviously extreme, but in general *Microhabitat* depicts post-university life for the circle of friends as one of confined mobility. As many commentators have noted, high student loan repayments, unstable employment and unaffordable housing keep this demographic in a state of socioeconomic precariousness (Cho and Stark, 2017, p. 120). University education became one of the most desired markers of middle-class status in South Korea from the 1990s onwards (Lett, 1998, p. 159) as a contrast to the present day, photographs of the friend's university days are used by the director as a quiet yet stark flashback device to suggest that their life in higher education was a rather hedonistic and carefree period filled with hope, glee and camaraderie. Of course, a relatively happy-go-lucky state of mind and decadent lifestyle is regularly enjoyed by the young and the higher end of the middle classes. These inclusions bring forward an early suggestion of the importance of class as a motif running through *Microhabitat*. Mi-so and her friends may not be unfamiliar with the mores of a comfortable middle-class life growing up; it is just now more out of reach for the group in adulthood. This short flashback device through still images works well as an intermittent and stark mechanism that acts as an antithesis to the temperance of their contemporary existence where some of them still come off as lonely and unfulfilled despite having, or having previously gained, some markers of material wealth and life-partners. For instance, in a lengthy scene, one of the group, Dae-yong (Lee sung-wook), breaks down in tears in front of Mi-so as he laments his sad post-divorce life with an unfulfilling dead-end white-collar job.

Recent displays of feminist political unity in South Korea have highlighted the tension within contemporary gender politics and, in order to unpack *Microhabitat* as a significant reflection of this ongoing period of volatility, a brief overview of recent nationwide events will be necessary. Significant movements include the ongoing *Molka* (hidden camera) rallies, the determination of the candlelight protests and, most constantly, the ongoing earnest work of Megalia's digital and physical activism against the increase in displays of online and material misogyny. The emergence of Megalia sits alongside other progressive South Korean digital-centred feminist collectives, such as B-wave Korea and DSO. These can be highlighted as being characteristic of some of the seismic shifts and articulations of action from South Korean gender activists. Ignited by and united against the tolls of national patriarchy and misogyny, these collectives are attempting to repurpose life narratives for women across generational and class categories. The roots of these advocations of solidarity have grown rapidly as the millennial generation has come of age. As Jeong and Lee (2018) imply, the inter-merging of digital and physical feminist-activism is a development from earlier forms of collective cyber-feminist resistance: most significantly, the response to the advancement of restrictive and misogynistic homosocial cyberspaces in the 1990s. The 'masculine expectation' of female behaviour and 'womanhood' online within male-dominated network communities of the period necessitated female led collectives that 'socialised the female users as proto-feminist subjects' (p. 707).

Despite these dramatic developments, some Western critics seemed to depoliticise the film and contexts through their readings of *Microhabitat* and focus attention on the more wistful elements of Jeon's feature that '*celebrate* the simplest aspects of life wrapped up in bittersweet melancholy' (Haag and Rieser, 2018). Others brought forward an awareness of contemporary South Korean life and produced more complex and politicised appraisals. These indicated that the film contained critiques 'not just of modernity, but of a neoliberal, patriarchal capitalism' (Sheu, 2022). As women's participation in and around the South Korean film industry increases and public debate concerning the role of millennials in South Korean life continues, this chapter further argues that *Microhabitat* can be positioned as a rather complex thesis on and around these local upheavals, as public narratives of gender divide, discrimination and conflict continue to advance with the recent election of the 'anti-feminist' Yun Suk-yeol to office as president of South Korea in 2022 (Rashid, 2022).

As a term denoting a period of adulthood for a female person, 'womanhood' is increasingly fluid and politically charged within global public discourse. In the context of South Korea, it carries significant weight historically, as the patriarchal and misogynistic underpinnings of Confucianism stubbornly remain. As Howson and Yecies (2015) observe, women's studies cannot be separated from these legacies when critiquing women-led South Korean cinema. And indeed, daily life in South Korea stays trapped within the corrupt foundations of a historic hegemonic masculinity that grants supremacy to men and assigns subservience to women in an ongoing period of neo-Confucianism. Despite political democratisation in the 1980s and the collective radical actions of cyber-feminist groups against male-led online and physical hostility, harassment, assault and cyber-bullying from the early 1990s onwards, these divisions are becoming more radical. More recently, the term gained further political significance and a compelling symbolic charge, as 2015 saw a throng of #iamafeminist tweets posted in an attempt by South Korean feminists to collectively 'reboot' their cause. This indicates that forms of South Korean womanhood and female resistance to misogyny are now 'collectively reclaiming feminist identity in the face of prevalent anti-feminist sentiment in Korea' (Kim, 2021, p. 76).

Within South Korea the '*sampo*' generation, meaning 'three giving up' generation, is now widely used as a disparaging term to describe those born between the early 1980s and the mid- to late 1990s. Seemingly surrounded by the temptations and transitory pleasures of modern, cosmopolitan city-living that they can ill afford, Mi-so and her peers are visualised as ghostly presences set aside from the mainstay of a middle-class that enjoys the pleasures of metropolitan society. Her generation is portrayed as stuck in time, unable to linearly progress and reach the markers of adulthood. In such a state, they embody a 'precarious, intermittent, (affective) and "just-in-time" subjectivity' (Shaviro, 2010, p. 60), where the trauma of continually reforming their identity to suit differing conditions and situations continuously overshadows their life. Since a South Korean newspaper initiated the term in 2011, '*sampo*' has progressively been modified as a derogatory term for millennials. As the millennial generation staggers into their forties, various unflattering denominations have garnered a wide cultural currency. '*Opo sedae*' or 'five giving up generation', for instance, describes those who have, additionally, given up on employment and home ownership. Today, the term '*wanpo sedae*' or 'total giving up generation' is extensively used by South Korean media as a distraught byword for the national moral panic to describe those millennials who have discarded hope in interpersonal relationships, physical and mental health, and appearance. These terms have become common parlance as a generational stereotype and are widely used nationally to describe the hopelessness that seemingly engulfs many in this demographic (Moon, 2020).

In *Microhabitat*, millennial characters are more complicated than this. Many ways of urban millennial living are represented, for both male and female characters. All are discordant with a healthy and settled adult life. Post-university life for Mi-so's friends is illustrated as a myriad of frustrated, compromised and downbeat existences that reflect the uncertainty of modern life for this now 'not so young' generation. Characters who do get married (a more traditional pathway) are unhappy with their life. Jeong-mi's husband is very dictatorial and, as she confides to Mi-so, a 'domestic' existence of raising children is not fulfilling and bleakly contrasts with her once-youthful ambitions. Another marriage, Dae-yong's, ends in divorce after his wife finds out about loan repayments that they need to make after renting a new apartment, while one of Mi-so's university friends is demonstrably distressed at the cramped living situation in her husband's home and restaurant, psychologically suffocated by having to care for her elderly mother and father-in-law.

As *Microhabitat* reaches its final act, Mi-so is single, destitute and becomes ever more physically and emotionally dissociated from her group of friends who have families and some semblance of a career to fill their days. As her life spirals ever downwards, living conditions worsen to homelessness, and even casual cleaning jobs become scarce, Esom plays Mi-so as an increasingly ethereal presence who, despite the harsh tribulations of her day-to-day life on the fringes of urban society, is not given to the excesses of overwrought emotional responses to the trauma that surrounds her. The film offers no immediate solutions to her current situation, and our time spent with her may only be a liminal stage in her life, but for the duration of the film she appears to forgo much ambition and has 'given up' on some facets of her life, such as steady and fulfilling employment. However, it would be inaccurate to say that Mi-so is completely emblematic of the dominant representation of the '*wanpo sedae*'. Reflecting the perceived individualistic, materialistic and pleasure-driven nature of the millennial generation (not just in South Korea), Mi-so is depicted as finding happiness and solace in her consumption of whisky in swanky bars and smoking pricey cigarettes as a form of '*shibal biyong*'. This can be loosely translated as a '*fuck it expense*' that gives the individual temporary pleasure and release from the stress of an uncertain future and a present beset by social and economic problems (Kim, 2019). Such indulgences are demonstrative of fashionable trends among South Korean millennials partaking in expensive treats as a psychological surviving tool under bleak and uncertain conditions. The photos of her university days have already heavily hinted that Mi-so may have enjoyed a middle-class upbringing before the uncertainty of her current existence, and the obvious pleasures of these conspicuous markers of status re-enforce this. Furthermore, Mi-so appears to thrive on her relationship with her long-term boyfriend from her days as a student, Han-sol (Ahn Jae-hong), and seeks to re-form connections with her contemporaries from university as a form of comfort and momentary escape against her prevailing poverty-stricken nomadic existence. Bittersweet solace in the past and an idealised bohemian life in her university band provide Mi-so with temporary escape from the harsh realities of life on the fringes of modern urban society.

This need for some overblown materialistic satisfaction as an anchor against the trauma and uncertainty of life for millennials can be aligned with Mi-so and her indulgence in costly whisky and cigarettes. Grant McCracken (1990) claims that a reliance on high-end consumer goods for temporary gratification heightens during periods of both national and personal destabilisation. The consumption of these luxury goods acts as a temporary anchor in unstable times – they are markers of 'an ideal life lived' (p. 85). McCracken also asserts that this ideological calibration can be both future- and past-oriented, so his theorisations can also be applied to the camaraderie, joy and hope contained within the university photos that Mi-so often ambles through. This time spent in trendy bars sipping expensive whisky and reminiscing over an idealised past are clearly only transitory respites from the harsh realities of Mi-so's descent from the comforts of the bourgeois, as the downward trajectory of home and work life continues.

As Moon (2020) implies, Korean Confucian-based patriarchy assigns men to public spaces and women to private spaces. This naturalises the confinement of Korean women to the domestic sphere. Thereby, women are defined not as individuals, but as social subjects whose worth is measured by service to men (husbands, fathers and brothers) and family. We see numerous depictions of this confinement within *Microhabitat*. We are first introduced to Mi-so as she completes one of her casual cleaning jobs in a gentrified upscale apartment. Positioned as a series of long takes, these drawn-out performances of (paid and unpaid) domestic labour within the private space of an idealised middle-class 'home' are placed throughout the narrative. As she goes through the monotony of her cleaning duties, she is consciously framed with what seems a deliberate reference to the numerous film adaptations of *The Housemaid* (*Hanyeo*, dir. Kim ki-young, 1960). In particular, the director of *Microhabitat* utilises some of the by now iconic imagery of women and domestic service from the 2010 adaptation (by Im Sang-soo). In *Microhabitat*, a distanced and static shot of Mi-so, functionally attired, in her client's minimalist and pristine bathroom cleaning the bathtub, uncannily recalls the similar setting and hunched housemaid's pose used in the promotional materials upon release of the 2010 adaptation – an adaptation that presents the story as a graphically horrific melodrama set among the lustful and morally corrupt higher echelons of South Korean society. The account centres on a female domestic help shattering the set-up of a well-to-do family through calculated sexual manipulation and presenting female sexuality and material wealth as sites of corruption and trauma. *The Housemaid* has been adapted through various cultural interpretations, to critique the time of production and always with bourgeois objects of desire foregrounded in the frame so as to hammer home the dangers of a life based on 'sinful' materialist and corrupt pleasures. From the omnipresent television set and piano in the lounge of the 1960 version to the sleek, blindingly white bathrooms, polished floors and minimalist layout typical of Mi-so's client's city dwellings, examples of 'good taste' and domestic status markers blatantly illustrate the material desires of the established and aspiring middle classes. In *Microhabitat*, Jeon positions our heroine, Mi-so, less as a threat to the projected and idealised harmony of middle-class family life and corruptive sexuality and more as a phantasmal presence on the edge of the lives of those for whom she cleans and of her university friends. By not conforming to strict, patriarchal norms, Mi-so can never fully manifest as a being in South Korean society. As such, she remains fluid and ethereal. By the end of the film, Mi-so has become so spectral that she no longer 'sofa surfs' in her friends' homes; instead, she lives on the periphery of the metropolis, on a patch of wasteland in a small tent. Fleeting shots of Mi-so as she returns to her tent from her favourite whisky bar reinforce this spectrality.

While accepting displays that fit the roles of mother/wife/daughter in public, Confucian-based patriarchy seeks to render invisible depictions of women who are not part of a normative heterosexual family system. Illustrative of this are the gendered reactions to the Doenjang women who make themselves visible and radically conspicuous through luxury beauty, fashion and consumption. Local cyber-led anti-feminist groups such as 'New Men in Solidarity' have demonised these young women and constructed narratives of outrage, sinfulness and selfishness around them (Grouard, 2021), positioning them as vain females who scrimp, save and sacrifice to gain temporary pleasure and status from the relative performance of affluence gained by consuming these products. Representations of her female peers further complicate our understanding of this generation through *Microhabitat*'s vision of a modern urban-based millennial existence and South Korean womanhood. The rigid gendered demarcations of the post-war dictatorship that conceived of women's roles as largely domestic and subordinate to male breadwinners and family members have been eroded through and beyond the democratisation period of the 1980s, a period which ensured the increasing participation of women in higher education and a rise in the publicly vocal efforts of feminist activists. However, a degree of despondency remains through the staggered progress towards gender equality in the face of a largely conservative society such as South Korea; put simply, '[m]en are not catching up with women's demands' (Anon, 2020, p. 8).

This is an era where working women are deemed the new poor of the neoliberal economy in South Korea. Disproportionately, women within *Microhabitat* are depicted as struggling to pay for housing, heating and other necessities. Mi-so herself moves from a small, sparsely furnished flat, which she cannot heat, to increasingly derelict accommodation. Provided with the opportunities for more highly paid employment, as her boyfriend is, Mi-so may not, at the end of the film, have been reduced to living in a tent on the outskirts of Seoul. Similarly, one of her friends from university must share a small, cramped home with her husband and his elderly parents. This is a living situation with which she becomes increasingly frustrated. Even some female characters who, on the surface, seem to be living more affluent lifestyles are depicted as being in very precarious, impermanent situations or forms of work. One of Mi-so's cleaning clients, who lives in an expensive apartment, supports her luxurious lifestyle by sleeping with rich men for money and goods. Upon learning that she has fallen pregnant, Mi-so's client breaks down in tears, realising that soon she will no longer be able to carry on in this line of work and maintain such a lifestyle.

Within *Microhabitat* the difficulties of finding stable, long-term employment are played out by Mi-so's experience, as the film follows her struggle to find a suitable place to live. Her feelings of hopelessness, loneliness and depression are also experienced by several of her male and female friends. As film scholars such as Choi (2010) have noted, these portrayals are familiar throughout South Korean cinema during tempestuous periods within national history. The female-centred melodrama of the golden period, such as *Madame Freedom* (*Jayu Buin*, 1956) and *The Housemaid* (*Hanyeo*, 1960), were distinctly emphatic in the way in which they illustrated national trauma through individual experience. During this era, the temptations brought on by the perverse pleasures to be found within accelerated modernity and the perils of conspicuous consumption were projected through representations of unhinged womanhood and out-of-control female sexuality. Ultimately moralising in their approach to the genre, these excessive actions by female and male characters typically led to violent encounters and the break-up of the traditional family unit.

Women in *Microhabitat* are still centralised as leading troubled existences. Throughout the film, women are positioned as inanimate and secondary to the patriarchal wishes and ideals that define them against male counterparts and partners as new global citizens. Mi-so's boyfriend is given the opportunity to work abroad, become the traditional, masculine provider, to earn enough money over two years to be able to return to South Korea and provide a home for him and Mi-so. Similarly, her bandmate and friend, Jeong-mi, is tied into a seemingly loveless marriage with a man who, conveniently for her, works away from home much of the time. Jeong-mi, however, appears to be bored with her life, trapped and confined to the home where she must take care of her baby son. Mi-so also has traditionally female domestic facets to her character as she cooks and cleans in her role as a housekeeper, and her former bandmate, Rok-yi, attempts to entrap her in a marriage for a more strictly feminine role. However, Mi-so wants to be free to do what she wants. She has the freedom to enjoy traditional and nontraditional, nonconforming facets of femininity. In a period of millennial and feminist critical curtailment, Mi-so, because of her peculiar outlook, emerges as a strong feminist archetype with her choice to live life through her unique personal desires and wants.

It is constructive to set the film within wider cultural trends and locate *Microhabitat* as part of a global wave of recent 'herstory' film narratives. The term 'herstory' can be traced back to the early 1970s, via Robin Morgan in the underground *Rat* newspaper, and unites anthologies such as *Sisterhood is Powerful* (Morgan, 1970). The use of 'herstory' flows and seeps out beyond these continuing volumes as a symbolic charge for feminists worldwide and has recently found revised vigour and usage when analysing women-authored films. As such, Jeon's film accompanies a list of contemporary global cinema constructed by female authors from South Korea, such as Kim So-Jung's *A Blue Mouthed Face* (2018), Boo Ji-young's *Cart* (*Ka-teu*, 2014) and Hong Sung-eun's *Aloners* (*Honja saneun saramdeul*, 2021). These confidently sit alongside female-authored Western output, such as *Burn, Burn, Burn* (Chanya Button, 2015) and *Jeune Femme* (Léonor Serraille, 2017). All of these 'herstory' films need to be widely celebrated as a collective reframing of cine-feminism. Their nuanced and complex portrayals of millennial womanhood – or, more aptly, millennial life in pieces – focus on characters' tropes of traumas while they attempt to function on the fringes of modern metropolitan life. The magnitude of this recent female-focused movement alongside the global growth of anti-misogyny movements, such as #metoo and the gender-oriented themes that they display, recalls recent theoretical assertions for the amendment of the previously established physical geographies of the transnational in film studies. As Lim argues, a decentralisation and a rethinking in terms of 'non-nation based new waves' (2019, p. 5) alongside national conditions is now required by feminist activists and scholars.

Confucianist-based male privilege continues to exert suffocating restrictions on South Korean women's civic and cultural lives. This necessitates a growing need for popular culture films such as *Microhabitat* to function as a means to critique gender and generational politics and prompt public political discussion. As Kim (2021) implies, gender-based activism since the tremors enabled by the feminist 'reboot' of 2015 (p. 81) has been so persuasive in contemporary public life that 'it has become nearly impossible to discuss any aspect of any sector, from politics and religion to culture and the economy, without raising gender issues' (p. 77). In turn, *Microhabitat* proposes to contribute to ongoing debates on the amplified waves of dissent within South Korean platforms. A new generation of South Korean female creatives is appearing on the global stage as prominent feminist subjects with profound voices to represent, reflect on and shape local culture. Many of these have formed collectives. These include networks such as the Women in Film Korea organisation founded in 2000 and Jeon's own progressive Gwanghwamoon filmmaking organisation.

Hieu Chau (2020) proclaims that, as Korean cinema comes into its second century, women filmmakers, both independent and commercial, are now bringing forward important and profound feature-length content that exposes gender-based local morals and policies. Many women South Korean filmmakers have, for instance, begun to critique the sexual violence prevalent within patriarchal, Confucian societies. Films such as *Gull* (2020) and *An Old Lady* address the 'untold stories' (Goh, 2020) of sexual violence and discrimination within Korean society. Park (2020, p. 91) theorises that the recent revival in South Korean cine-feminism can be heralded as 'a new method for critically reshaping Korean film historiography and media ecosystems from a feminist perspective'. But we need to be slightly cautious in fully embracing this assertion while women are still under-represented in production and screen roles. As Montpelier (2018) highlights, in the year of the cinema release of *Microhabitat*, only 25.8 per cent of local commercial films featured a female lead, while only 8.4 per cent were directed by a woman. The South Korean film industry remains male-led and -focused, while female directors are still side-lined for funding in the mainstream industry and discouraged from going into creative production roles such as cinematography. Women directors are still being herded into specific mainstream 'female' genres such as romantic comedies. As Darcy Paquet (2017) highlights, a 'walled garden' persists for many talented women in the industry.

Within the much-celebrated South Korean golden age of melodrama (1955–72), the 'women's film' (Ablemann and McHugh, 2005, p. 9) developed a consistent but fluid genre that is 'somewhat distinct in the alignment or proximity between traumatic historical circumstances and melodramatic narrative' (p. 3). Jeon's debut feature continues this local predilection for personalising the political within melodramatic forms. *Microhabitat* forwards a clear realignment on the struggles of contemporary millennial womanhood that consciously deviates from the globally popular male-centric blockbuster cinema of the immediate post-IMF period. This was a stylistically innovative and thematically intense period of auteur-marketed cinema, led by globally celebrated male directors such as Park Chan-Wook (*Oldboy*, 2003) and Lee Chang Dong (*Peppermint Candy / Bakha Satang*, 1999). These films attempted to make sense of the national fiscal and political disaster through a male-led personalisation of national trauma. As Kim (2004) highlights, this was a highly visible period of projected remasculinisation for South Korea and reflected in mainstream national cinema as the shockwaves of the post-IMF period continued to displace the nation and violently disrupt modernity and previously rigid patriarchal structures within employment and domestic life.

*Microhabitat* sharply observes the male characters within the group of post-university friends and their individual tribulations. But these are invariably shaped and influenced by the female perspective of Mi-so as a central character who is physically present in the majority of the scenes and acts as a confidante for their outbursts of trauma. The struggle of male friends becomes intertwined with her experiences as generational differences and concerns are highlighted. In one scene, we witness the emotional turmoil of her friend, Kim Rok-yi (Choi Deok-moon), who is unable to leave his parental home and who cannot form a relationship with a woman, even though he desperately wants to get married. However, rather than understand this issue from the perspective of the male, as another victim of the female imperative to put work and career before marriage and children, we perceive it from the perspective of Mi-so, as Rok-yi's parents attempt to initiate an intimate relationship between the two platonic friends. In one scene, Mi-so is staying at her bandmate Rok-yi's home which he shares with his parents. Keen for their son to marry, Rok-yi's parents lock Mi-so in the house as their prisoner, leaving her a carton of cigarettes so she has no reason to leave. In response, Mi-so is seen desperately trying to escape the overbearing would-be in-laws and the physical confines of the house, as well as the expected role that patriarchal society has laid out for her.

Representations of South Korean millennial women and their struggle against frequent overbearing and patriarchal expectations, such as Mi-so's awkward encounter with Rok-yi's parents, need to be viewed as an ongoing and profound component of these interconnecting spheres of contemporary culture, collective activism and political positioning. The societal tremors created by Cho Nam-joo's controversial feminist novel in 2015 and later film adaptation, directed by Kim Do-young, titled *Kim Ji-young: Born 1982 (82 Nyeonsaeng Gim Jiyeong,* 2019), are clearly a significant part of this equation. Widely hailed as one of the most important modern feminist novels in the socially conservative nation, it relays the life of the ordinary Korean woman of the title in her thirties, as she encounters gender discrimination, exclusion and violence in her work and family. As such, the novel and film adaptation join *Microhabitat* as part of a recent proclivity within South Korean culture to critique, rather than just present, the complex relationships involved in women's modern millennial life.

The roots of this proclivity come from a burgeoning national feminist movement in the 1990s that was, in part, emboldened by the translation of Western-led academic works on body politics, the male gaze and the monstrous-feminine, filtered through various initiatives such as the Seoul International Women's Film Festival (Park, 2020, p. 93). In connection, *Microhabitat* can be evaluated as part of, but also apart from these contemporary female-driven practices alternative to the dominant, local, mainstream cultural modes – most predominantly, the success of the action heroine cycle. This cycle includes films such as *The Villainess* (2017) and *The Witch* (2018) which 'marginalise(s) Korea's own diverse creativity, experimentalism and alternative voices and discourages or leaves little room for alternative cultural practices in film, television and other media forms' (Kim et al., 2017, p. 316). As the current wave of feminist activism continues within popular media forms, politically charged, independent female filmmakers such as Jeon have tended to take a different direction to 'reflect on and critique the dynamics of interpersonal relationships in Korean society – and, more specifically, the impact of traditional Confucian ideals on contemporary gender relations' (Yecies and Shim, 2016, p. 11). Rather than representing revolutionary, systematic change, however, these films have, as some critics argue, 'moments of reformism' (Howson and Yecies, 2015). That is not to say, however, that such moments of reformism could not develop into a wider, more impactful movement.

Ideals of a spiritual and physical 'home' and the pressure of societal expectations prevail throughout *Microhabitat*. As the likelihood of home ownership has become increasingly eroded with continual house price spikes, not just in South Korea but throughout densely populated areas worldwide, and the cost of living in developed cities continues to rise, many millennials' lives are increasingly characterised by temporary and liminal spaces. The context of 'aspirational' living has dramatically shifted, and a lack of permanence dominates generational living. As Arnett (2000) shows us, a new life period has emerged for young people in industrialised countries whereby 'emerging adulthood' proposes a not so clear transition between adolescence and adulthood. Previous markers of progressive adulthood are now erased, and the responsibilities of mature life are not as easily reached by millennials. Youths are 'getting stuck in time without the means to become adults' (Allison, 2009, p. 90) according to previously established norms. Despite Mi-so and her friends clearly being in their thirties, much of their individual financial and emotive insecurities would not look out of place in a post-college movie centred on young adults in their early twenties. This is frequently demonstrated through Mi-so and her friend's displays of confessional emotional vulnerability in their scenes together. Traumatic private and public breakdowns, as well as impermanence on the fringes of urban society amongst Mi-so and her peers, run through the film. Aspirations for the women of the 'new poor' are simply reduced to a comfortable and safe dwelling. Mi-so and her friends attempt to navigate the novel life narratives that local millennials are experiencing as compromise and sacrifice dominate employment and domestic life.

Jeon confirms this emanation of hardship and sacrifice within modern urban life as a constant for Mi-so and her circle of millennial friends. As concerns about the rising cost of city-living and shelter for young people continue to accompany gender equality as a political priority for many millennials in South Korea (Guina, 2022), Jeon's portraits of troubled lives and shared crises are further legitimised. As she discusses, 'I approached it in a way where I wanted to sort of convey the idea that to have your own place in Seoul, every one of us has to give up on something in their living' (Vélez, 2018). In addition, Mi-so's scenes with her disenchanted friends extend the themes and complexity of individual and generational despondency and emotional destitution. As Jeon construes, '[i]n the case of the first friend, she has to give up rest; there's no rest for her. The second one, she's lost her dream. The third one, he's in debt. The fourth one is still living with his parents; he's not able to become independent. I think that's what I wanted to convey' (Vélez, 2018). In the case of Mi-so, she has no permanent home of her own. She eventually sofa-surfs so that she can afford her '*shibal biyong*' treats and earns what she can through domestic cleaning. This type of casual and impermanent work is widespread among women in South Korea, particularly among those without university education. A lack of meaningful employment opportunities characterise life for this demographic; those christened as *peaksu* or 'good for nothings' in the national mainstream media. This generational gap regarding wealth and opportunities is one which will resonate with millennials globally. There is a commonality here between many developed societies' reactionary, popular media channels, who label youths as work-shy and demonstrating a complacency that is wrecking national and international economies.

Ultimately, *Microhabitat* needs to be considered in relation to surrounding socio-political, economic and production contexts and should be viewed as part of ever-developing local and international spheres of feminist-led culture. As this chapter has argued throughout, it is a filmic interrogation with essayistic qualities, on the pressures of modern post-university millennial life in South Korea. Jeon reveals no immediate solutions to the troubled existence of the group of friends. Instead, she offers a glimpse into their continuing emotional and financial hardships, as the ruptures in social and political life continue to traumatise the nation. The text and contexts need to be consumed and engaged as part of an ongoing period in South Korea in which the spectator and the art form function on a correspondent and progressive level. These should be considered as parallel components of an era within which people increasingly perform as enlightened actors in personal and national civic life and operate as active participants in transmedial conversations around the injustices of urban and generational poverty and misogyny. Jeon Go-Woon's portrait of millennials functioning on the fringes suggest that the dramatic changes in identity, lifestyle and culture within South Korean society bring forward a charge of generational dissent that accompanies, but does not eclipse, a resilient model of South Korean womanhood.

## References

Ablemann, N., and McHugh, K. (2005). Introduction: Gender, genre and nation. In N. Ablemann and K. McHugh (eds), *South Korean golden age melodrama: Gender, genre and national cinema* (pp. 1–15). Detroit: Wayne State University Press.

Allison, A. (2009). The cool brand, affective activism and Japanese youth. *Theory, Culture and Society*, 26(2–3), 89–111.

Anon. (2020). South Korean women are fighting to be heard. *The Economist*, 45, 9189.

Arnett, J. (2000). Emerging adulthood: A theory of development from the late teens through the twenties. *American Psychologist*, 55(5), 469–80.

Chau, H. (2020, October 26). Video essay: The women directors leading South Korean cinema into its next century. *Filmed in Ether*. Retrieved from https://www.filmedinether.com/video-essays/the-women-directors-leading-south-korean-cinema-into-its-next-century/

Cho, H., and Stark, J. (2017). South Korean youth across three decades. In Y. Kim (ed.), *The Routledge handbook of Korean culture and society* (pp. 119–33). London and New York: Routledge.

Choi, J. (2010). *The South Korean film renaissance*. Middletown: Wesleyan University Press.

Goh, K. (2020, November 10). A new wave of Korean filmmakers are tackling sexual violence through cinema. *Vice*. Retrieved from https://i-d.vice.com/en_uk/article/akdg4p/london-korean-film-festival-new-wave-of-female-directors-tackling-sexual-violence

Grouard, A. (2021, November 30). South Korean women fight back as disillusioned young men seek to cancel feminism. *This Week in Asia*. Retrieved from https://www.scmp.com/week-asia/people/article/3155871/south-korean-women-fight-back-disillusioned-young-men-seek-cancel?module=perpetual_scroll_0&pgtype=article&campaign=3155871

Guina, A. (2022, March 10). How South Korea's Yoon Suk-yeol capitalized on anti-feminist backlash to win the presidency. *Time*. Retrieved from https://time.com/6156537/south-korea-president-yoon-suk-yeol-sexism/

Haag, M., and Rieser, A. (2018, November 30). Review: *Microhabitat* and *The poet and the boy* at LKFF. *The Glasgow Guardian*. Retrieved from: https://glasgowguardian.co.uk/2018/11/30/review-microhabitat-and-the-poet-and-the-boy-at-lkff/

Howson, R., and Yecies, B. M. (2015). Korean cinema's female writers-directors and the 'hegemony of men'. *Gender, Equal Opportunities, Research*, 16(1), 14–22.

Jeong, E., and Lee, J. (2018). We take the red pill, we confront the DickTrix: Online feminist activism and the augmentation of gendered realities in South Korea. *Feminist Media Studies*, 18(4): 715–17.

Kim, H. K. (2004). *The remasculinization of Korean cinema*. Durham: Duke University Press.

Kim, J. (2019, July 4). Why young Koreans love to splurge. *Foreign Policy*. Retrieved from https://foreignpolicy.com/2019/07/04/why-young-koreans-love-to-splurge-shibal-biyong-millennial-fuck-it-expense/

Kim, J. (2021). The resurgence and popularization of feminism in South Korea: Key issues and challenges for contemporary feminist activism. *Korea Journal*, 61(4), 75–101.

Kim, J., Unger, M. A., and Wagner, K. B. (2017). The significance of beyond *hallyu* film and television content in South Korea's mediasphere. *Quarterly Review of Film and Video*, 34(4), 315–20.

Lett, D. P. (1998). *In pursuit of status. The making of South Korea's 'new' urban middle classes*. Cambridge: Harvard University Press.

Lim, S. H. (2019). Concepts of transnational cinema revisited. *Transnational Screens*, 10(1), 1–12.

McCracken, G. (1990). *Culture and consumption: New approaches to the symbolic character of consumer goods and activities*. Bloomington: Indiana University Press.

Montpelier, R. (2018, February 14). Study: Women are under-represented onscreen and off in Korean film. *Women and Hollywood*. Retrieved from https://womenandhollywood.com/study-women-are-underrepresented-onscreen-and-off-in-korean-film-b180dc7d2edc/

Moon, G. (2020, January 9). The young Koreans pushing back on a culture of endurance. *BBC Worklife*. Retrieved from https://www.bbc.com/worklife/article/20200108-the-young-koreans-pushing-back-on-a-culture-of-endurance
Morgan, R. (1970) *Sisterhood is powerful*. New York: Vintage Books.
Paquet, D. (2017, August 3). The (few) women breaking through in Korean cinema. *Sight and Sound*. Retrieved from https://www2.bfi.org.uk/news-opinion/sight-sound-magazine/features/women-korean-cinema
Park, S. H. (2020). South Korean cine-feminism on the move. *Journal of Japanese and Korean Cinema*, 12(2), 91–97.
Rashid, R. (2022, March 11). 'Devastated': Gender equality hopes on hold as 'anti-feminist' voted South Korea's president. *The Guardian*. Retrieved from https://www.theguardian.com/world/2022/mar/11/south-korea-gender-equality-anti-feminist-president-yoon-suk-yeol
Shaviro, S. (2010). *Post cinematic affect*. Ropley: Zero Books.
Sheu, C. J. (2022, March 28). *Microhabitat* is an Ozu adaptation in both story and heart. *The News Lens: Arts and Culture*. Retrieved from https://international.thenewslens.com/article/164710
Vélez, D. (2018, July 25). New York Asian 2018 interview: Director Jeon Go-woon and actor Ahn Jae-hong talk love and poverty in MICROHABITAT. *Screen Anarchy*. Retrieved from https://screenanarchy.com/2018/07/pending-nyaff-2018-interview-director-jeon-go-woon-and-actor-ahn-jae-hong-talk-love-and-poverty-in-m.html
Yecies, B., and Shim, A. (2016). *The changing face of Korean cinema: 1960 to 2015*. London: Routledge.

Chapter 4

# The Female Gaze in Xu Jinglei's *Letter from an Unknown Woman* (2004)

Bérénice M. Reynaud[1]

One night, a man receives a letter from a woman. She claims that they have met several times in the past, have been lovers and even conceived a child, now dead, but that he never knew who she was. Before dying, she sends this letter confessing her life-long passion for him while remaining unidentifiable. This is the plot of Xu Jinglei's second directing work, *Letter from an Unknown Woman* (2004), adapted from Stefan Zweig's 1922 novel. Set in mainland China in the 1930s and 1940s, the film received several foreign and domestic film festival prizes and confirmed Xu as a notable filmmaker. Besides directing, Xu Jinglei also produced, adapted, edited and starred in the film. Ann Kaplan (2011) and Guo Shaohua (2018) comment on the prevalent gaze of the heroine; however, they both describe the character's gaze as a reversal of the male gaze. I argue that the female gaze displayed is actually of a different sort.

The concept of the female gaze is almost as old as that of the male gaze. However, it does not have a set definition. It is generally admitted as an alternative gaze for cinema; some see it as a gender inversion of the male gaze like Guo and Kaplan, some insist on the female director's perspective (Dirse, 2013, French, 2021), others on the female character's perspective and the way she is presented in film (Brey, 2020). In China, the female gaze is more frequently associated with the she-economy that has been steadily developing over the past decade. In this context, the female gaze is understood as a reversal of the male gaze. The issue is that the inherent power dynamics are therefore not really questioned and consumption remains the main goal. As Li Xiaomeng astutely puts it, 'although women can exert their "reversed gaze" to observe male celebrities' sexualized bodies and actions, they are still constrained in an idealized, power-laden heterosexual relationship that eventually serves the corporate agenda and reinforces the patriarchy' (Li, 2020, p. 66). When it comes to cinema, the study of the female gaze, whether of its definition or usage, has been sparse and only quite recently entered the discourse in Chinese academia and abroad.

This chapter draws from recent works by French scholar Iris Brey (2020) and Australian scholar Lisa French (2021), which have shed a new light on how to approach film with this tool of analysis. In her book on women's documentary, Lisa French defines the female gaze as the female director's subjectivity that is situated and personal, but still influenced by her 'experience of living as female' (French, 2021, p. 1). Brey uses a feminist phenomenological reading that considers the audience of a film as lived bodies watching other bodies, perceiving and feeling their actions and sensations. She says: 'If we were to define female gaze, it would be a look that gives subjectivity to the female character, allowing the viewer to *feel the experience* of the heroine but without identifying with her' (Brey, 2020, p. 36; emphasis added). She adds: '[I]t is not only a question of having a central female character, but to be at her side. We don't simply watch her do things, we do them with her' (Brey, 2020, p. 37). The female gaze applies to both the story and the *mise en scène* of the film. Brey lists a few criteria in each aspect:

> Narratively speaking: (1) the main character must identify herself as a woman, (2) the story is told from her perspective, (3) her story challenges the patriarchal order. From a formal point of view, (1) the audience has to feel the female experience thanks to the *mise en scène*, (2) if the bodies are eroticized, the gesture must be conscious (Laura Mulvey demonstrated that the male gaze results from the patriarchal unconscious), (3) the visual pleasure of the audience does not result from a scopophilic impulse (to take pleasure by looking at a person by objectifying them, like a voyeur). (Brey, 2020, p. 69)

Thus, the audience experiences a specifically female perspective that is also inscribed in a particular socio-cultural context. It is not the only way to produce feminist films, but it certainly is, as Brey further argues, a 'crucial and urgent approach since the female characters whose existence will be felt and who will come out of the status of object have been so far absent, erased, minimized and above all discriminated from our screens and our culture. The female gaze can help us to see and look outside the dominant model' (Brey, 2020, p. 45). Brey's theory, of course, has its limits; she mostly discusses white female directors and the phenomenological aspect is far from being systematic for the audience and does not work for every film. Nonetheless, Brey's approach helps us unpack Xu Jinglei's *mise en scène*, while French's perspective is useful to situate the director in her practice. The analysis will be divided in two parts. The first will focus on how the director conveys the heroine's perspective, while the second will discuss how the film subverts male-dominated narratives and China's patriarchal order. Max Ophüls's 1948 Hollywood adaptation of the same novel will serve as an important point of comparison.

## 1. Voice-Over and Image-Maker

The film inserts itself in a certain continuity in women's filmmaking in China since 1949, where the female voice-over is a recurring feature that conveys women's perspective. It is often an adaptation of a literary work, most of the time a woman's autobiography, where the character's story is told in a flashback, with the voice-over commenting on it. Films of the 1980s have been commented on and connected to the surge of women's autobiographies in the same decade, which aimed to explore the authors' experiences and subjectivities (Wang, 2019, p. 9). This enhancement of the female experience inspired women filmmakers such as Zhang Nuanxin with *The Drive to Win* (*Sha'ou* 沙鸥, 1981), *Sacrificed Youth* (*Qingchun ji* 青春祭, 1986) or Hu Mei's *Army Nurse* (*Nü'er lou* 女儿楼, 1984). However, recent work by Wang Lingzhen (2011) reveals that the voice-over was also previously used in the 1960s, as in Dong Kena's *Small Grass on the Kunlun Mountain* (*Kunkun shan shang yike cao* 昆仑山上一棵草, 1962). In each of these works, the voice-over helps to convey the heroine's subjectivity and to complexify her. Thus, the films strive 'to assert a woman's voice against the dominant discourse of communist ideology' of the time (Cui, 2003, p. xvi). In this perspective, the voice-over helps the female character to develop her self-consciousness and individuality, while having limited leverage. *Letter from an Unknown Woman* actually goes a step further, because its female gaze not only determines the film's *mise en scène* but also enables more agency to its heroine.

The film's story is told through a first-person voice-over narration, taken directly from the letter written by the unknown woman. Except for the opening and ending scenes, most of the film is a flashback of the heroine's memories as she recounts them. Since she is the only narrator, she orients our perception of the story as she selects which event she retells, dismisses or lingers on, depending on its importance in her eyes. The voice-over helps to connect the three parts of the unknown woman's story (as a teenager, then as a student and later working as a courtesan under the name of Miss Jiang and raising her son), separated by two major ellipses lasting a few years each time. Each ellipsis is indicated by a sequence of abstract or descriptive images, while the voice-over narrates what happened to the heroine during that time. The voice-over also comments on the events as they take place, highlighting what she is feeling at that moment, which is often emphasised by a slowed-down image on screen, on the one hand, and the film's soundtrack, on the other hand. Finally, the voice-over tells us the heroine's thoughts, which enhances our perception of the story from her point of view.

Writing on voice-over narration in film, Sarah Kozloff (1988) talks about the 'image-maker' or the formal narrator of the film. They are the one who arranges sounds and images to create the film, orchestrating the whole ensemble for the audience. In comparison to the voice-over that is often subjective, the image-maker can be seen as a more objective, neutral and omniscient figure. Therefore, the audience can turn to them if the voice-over narrator is unreliable. But what happens most of the time is that . . .

> . . . the voice-over narrator is so inscribed in the film as to seem as if [they have] generated not only what [they are] saying but also what we are seeing. In other words, films often create the sense of character-narration so strongly that one accepts the voice-over narrator as if [they] were the mouthpiece of the image-maker either for the whole film or for the duration of [their] embedded story. We put our faith in the voice not as created but as creator. (Kozloff, 1988, p. 45)

In other words, the audience may think that the voice-over narrator's perspective is aligned with the image-maker's, especially if the character talking to us is also present on screen. Cui Shuqin has commented in the same way about Fei Mu's *Spring in a Small Town* (小城之春, 1948), arguing that, when '[p]ositioned as narrator and character, the female voice and figure are designed to control both the diegesis and nondiegesis' (Cui, 2003, p. 28). In *Letter from an Unknown Woman*, the illusion is almost perfect. It is very easy to believe that what we see on screen is a projection of the heroine's mind, not only because of the voice-over but also because of the prominence of her senses.

## 2. Gazing and Feeling(s)

The director of *Letter from an Unknown Woman* made the interesting choice to shoot in a *siheyuan*, a traditional courtyard house. This setting favours proximity between the characters, as in this kind of housing privacy is virtually non-existent: noises and smells travel easily from one house to another, and an open door dividing the courtyard areas allows the neighbours to peek inside. The heroine, especially as a teenager, takes advantage of this situation to spy on Mr Xu. When she returns a few years later, she rents a room with a window overlooking the house's entrance to catch a glimpse of him when he goes out. The prominence of her gaze is also emphasised by the fact that we have to wait twelve minutes into the film to finally see Mr Xu's face; when it finally happens, it is through her eyes. Until then, the actor was always positioned far from the camera or turning his back to it so that his face was concealed from the audience. By doing so, the character entirely mediates our perception of him. However, it is worth noting that, even if the heroine mostly watches Mr Xu unbeknownst to him, she does it with longing. Her gaze is never voyeuristic in the sense that the man is not sexualised or even shown naked in the scenes of their sexual encounter, which differs from how the male gaze usually works.

While less prominent, her other senses are also involved. Hearing, smelling, and even touching is highlighted in the voice-over narration. The heroine recalls the effect that the man's voice had on her, making her unable to resist him. She mentions the perfume filling his room, and she is shown caressing the objects decorating his place in a few close-ups, the sensorial tour serving as a form of foreplay before she has sexual intercourse with him. All these elements thus add a sensual tone to her story and contribute to making the audience share her experience and her perspective.

Another instance of this 'sensual narration' is a striking scene taking place in a theatre where the heroine completely takes over the role of the image-maker. The audience then only perceives reality through her eyes and her senses. In this scene, Xu Jinglei depicts the swirling of emotions that surge through the character when she sees the man she loves. Although it does not really advance the narrative, it is charged with dramatic tension. This is what the experimental filmmaker Maya Deren (Deren et al., 2000) calls a moment of 'vertical narration', or a 'poetic' scene. These moments are meant to create an emotion, a feeling, while the 'horizontal narration' entails actions that advance the narrative. Deren talks about a pyramidal figure, a build-up that leads to an illumination of this moment in the story, which is precisely what happens in this scene. As I will demonstrate, we may even talk of an intensification of the moment. The scene takes place in the third part of the story, when the heroine is working as a courtesan under the name of Miss Jiang. It begins with an establishing shot that travels across a theatre. The camera moves across a curtain to reveal the theatre space, allowing us to catch a glimpse of what is happening on the stage – a duel between a male and a female warrior – and pans to the box where Miss Jiang is seated with her companions, including the army captain she is seeing, currently sulking. The editing is next divided between the box and the theatre stage, as the frame gradually narrows on Miss Jiang while she suddenly notices Mr Xu with a woman in another box.

This scene displays a rare moment in the narrative: the heroine losing her composure. In the beginning, she is confident, almost cold, when she comments on the captain's mood. In the previous scene, he tried to bring up marriage, but she resolutely turned him down. In the present scene, she explains to her friend that, like many others before him, he thought that she would eventually fall in love with him. Her patronising tone and loud words are meant as a rebuke to the captain and a reminder about the nature of their relationship: he is only a client who pays for her time. The contrast in her attitude is perceptible when she notices Mr Xu, as she is unable to resist her attraction to him. Even if she tries to ignore him and his current flirtation, she unconsciously turns her body towards him and can no longer focus on the play. As if hypnotised, she is unable to take her eyes off the movements of his fingers following the rhythm of the show's drums, revealed in a close-up of his hand. Then the editing accelerates, mirroring the speeding-up of the drumming, the camera now alternating between the actors fighting on stage, Miss Jiang and the writer's fingers. Miss Jiang then appears dizzier and dizzier. Her state is emphasised on screen by the constant whirling of the actors, and one of the flags adorning their costumes. This visual and auditory acceleration makes the audience feel the vertigo that overtakes the heroine, experiencing the same sensory saturation as she does. She suddenly seems to break from this daze and asks her companions to leave, claiming that she has a headache. As soon as she stands up, the music stops, signifying that the fight is over. Nonetheless, the camera never returns to the stage, and consequently we do not know who won the fight. The next scene is thankfully silent, allowing the character as well as the audience to recover from the previous one. As Miss Jiang smokes a cigarette in her bathroom, the tension that has risen in the previous scene finally subsides. The horizontal narration can start again.

This scene constitutes a moment of vertical narration, where emotions are building up and intensified by the *mise en scène*, and where the audience experiences what the heroine is feeling. As Miss Jiang watches the fight on stage, she sees herself trying to resist her attraction to Mr Xu while witnessing his endless string of love affairs. For tonight, she prefers to withdraw and takes a break before reclaiming the narration. Besides making the audience share the character's experience and see things from her perspective, Xu Jinglei's directing also 'challenges the patriarchal order' (Brey, 2020, p. 69), first by refusing sexual voyeurism in the film's *mise en scène* and then by making a feminist figure out of her heroine.

## 3. The Female Gaze and Visual Pleasure

In her conception of the female gaze, Brey rightfully does not dismiss visual pleasure but opposes any form of voyeurism and objectification of characters, regardless of their gender. Voyeurism means receiving sexual pleasure by secretly watching other people's nudity or people in their intimacy, which often shapes the perspective of a film's audience during sex scenes. On the contrary, with the female gaze, the audience participates and shares in the experience of the characters: '[T]hey are aware of being an active body participating in the experience of watching a film or a play' (Brey, 2020, p. 155). This is reflected in Xu Jinglei's intentions for the sex scenes. When asked about it, she said that she was not worried about censorship by the Chinese authorities, because she used an approach 'not too vague but not too straightforward either' (Xie and Wu, 2004). According to her, the point was to 'make the audience feel the sexual desire between the two characters' (Xie and Wu, 2004), and she managed to do so with a careful *mise en scène* that successfully avoids any voyeurism.

In the film, during the first night that the couple spend together, the young woman is inexperienced and lacks confidence at first. Placing her face at the centre of the frame and leaving the writer with his back to the camera makes us focus on the expressions on her face as she experiences her first tremors of pleasure. The proximity with her body as he places his hands on her encourages the audience to vicariously share her feelings – we, too, can almost feel his fingers on our skin. In a last shot, the writer takes her top off as she turns her back to the camera and she lays down, going off screen. The next shot shows them after sex, the writer asleep while she watches him, satisfied. During their second night, she is more proactive and propositions him to go back to his place. There, she is very passionate and places herself on top of him, which is a rare sight in film overall. Once again, her face is in the centre of the frame as they kiss on the bed, but this time, the next shot shows the bed through the gap between two panels of a screen that separates it from the rest of the room. The lovers, however, are not visible; only some vague movement can be detected on the side through the cross-ribbed glass panels. The play of light and shadow behind the glass signals that the lovemaking is still happening, but the absence of visuals thwarts the scopophilic impulse. The camera does not linger but moves backwards, making the initial gap disappear, and keeps going until a bouquet of white roses appears on the left, carefully arranged in a vase. These roses are the ones that the heroine sends anonymously to the writer every year for his birthday. The camera movement thus focuses our attention on

Miss Jiang's devotion and reminds us of the significance of this moment for her: she is reunited with the man she loves. The emotion is emphasised also by the increasing intensity of the film's soundtrack as the bouquet appears in the frame. Thus, each night, the *mise en scène* makes the passion visible but neutralises the voyeuristic gaze by refocusing our attention on what the heroine is feeling at that moment, or accentuates the emotional dimension of the scene for her.

## 4. A Feminist Character?

Scholars have noted that there is an initial imbalance between the man and the woman, but that they gradually reach a certain equity (Guo, 2018; Zhang, 2011). The writer is older, more educated and wealthier than the young girl when they first meet. However, Miss Jiang steadily closes that gap. She studies at a university in Beiping, which was not the case for many women at that time in China, and later on her job as a courtesan provides her with a modern and westernised lifestyle, just like he had enjoyed until then. In the same way, her love for him evolves over time. She nearly worships him as a child, but over time she becomes more lucid about his personality and behaviour.

The evolution of their relationship can actually be observed visually. In the first part of the film, the young girl bumps into the man by accident and has to raise her eyes to look at his face. The man apologises in English, which asserts his cultural superiority over her, while she does not dare to speak. The voice-over next reports that she fell in love with him then. In the second part, they meet again in a demonstration. Hiding from the chasing police, they take shelter in the stairwell of a building. The heroine is positioned two stairs below him, but this time she smiles at him, holds his gaze and initiates physical contact. Finally, in the third phase, the characters meet at a ball, through mutual friends. There is no longer any physical hierarchy, as they are seated side by side. She has no trouble looking him in the eyes and teasing him. In this milestone scene, Mr Xu becomes a partner of seduction rather than an object of adoration.

In a few interviews, Xu Jinglei openly declared her preference for the heroine over the writer and makes an analogy between her interpretation of the story and her personal maturity:

> This work has seen me mature. [ . . . ] When I read it for the first time, [. . .] I read it as a Qiong Yao novel, with this man so bad and this infatuated and pathetic woman. It was completely different ten years later: this time I thought that the man was pathetic while the woman was very strong.

> She didn't give him a child; she actually made a child for herself. (Yang and Wei, 2009, p. 264)[2]

In Zweig's novel, the narrative unfolds as a tragic one-sided love story. In the film, Xu argues that the woman certainly would not have had a long-lasting relationship with that man; in her opinion, the woman had a very satisfying life, living according to her principles (Xie and Wu, 2004). The result is a radically emancipated heroine on screen, which is why I agree with Cai Shenshen (2017) that this qualifies her as 'a female figure ahead of her time, an emancipated woman in terms of thought, behavior, and values' (p. 73). Indeed, Miss Jiang is educated, which was not common for women back then. She refuses to marry and, with her work as a courtesan, she earns enough money to sustain her son and herself, as well as to secure the best education there is for her child – therefore opposing women's gender roles and expectations then and now, as well as patriarchal control over her sexuality. Regarding prostitution, the filmmaker has purposely set the action before 1949 in order to avoid censorship. She could have changed the plot, as did Max Ophüls in his Hollywood version by marrying the heroine to another man, but she kept it that way. As she says:

> [T]he heroine later becomes a prostitute, which would be impossible to shoot if the story was set nowadays. I wanted to film a simple love story without adding too much historical context that could have raised moral judgement. In the end we changed it to about the same epoch as the novel and it worked very well. (Xie and Wu, 2004)

Indeed, there is no moral judgement about the heroine's actions and decisions. Contrary to the original work, there is no self-criticism in the film's narration. When she mentions her job, she simply says, 'I go with other people, people who can provide such an existence for me, regardless of their age'. The filmmaker's portrayal of the protagonist's work is a glamorous one, however: the captain she is seeing is a dashing young man, and she seems to enjoy a lavish lifestyle with him and her friends. At the same time, she is also shown being a real professional, adamant about her work boundaries, as we have seen in the theatre scene. While Xu says that she wanted to avoid censorship to focus on a love story, it is tempting to see it as a convenient way to cover up more controversial details, such as prostitution, sex outside marriage, one-night stands and illegitimate children. Under the pretence of telling a love story, the film thus addresses sensitive issues regarding women, which are still relevant today in China.

Xu's perspective on the story may also be influenced by her celebrity status. Before becoming a director, she was already a famous actress. She is one of the 'four *dan* 四旦', a title awarded to popular Chinese actresses in the 2000s. On the one hand, her celebrity is an advantage to promote her work; on the other hand, being a public figure leads people to establish parallels between her films and her personal life (which can be useful in terms of promotion as well). For example, Guo Shaohua compares the waiting heroine of the novel to the actress waiting for a good script (Guo, 2018). Xu has explained before that she was immediately successful when she started acting in *Cherish Our Love Forever* (*Jiang aiqing jinxing daodi* 将爱情进行到底, 1998), but that the next offers were always based on the same model (Yu, 2016, p. 247). This could explain why she gave so much agency to the character of Miss Jiang, who is played by Xu herself. Becoming a director after acting, especially if she acts in her own films, can be seen as reclaiming control over her career by monitoring both her image and the narratives in which she takes part. Next, like her heroine, Xu Jinglei dates but is not married (and still is not to this date). Cai sees this detail as a reflection of the director's personal life: this 'avant-garde female character in the established Chinese social and moral contexts mirrors her own proclivity and beliefs [in her films] as she is a self-determining woman who disregards old-fashioned ethical constraints and governs her own life course' (Cai, 2017, p. 73). Moreover, Xu can use her single status to fuel the fans' imagination who project her being with her also single male co-stars (Cai, 2017).

## 5. An Empowering Death

Another aspect that emphasises the heroine's independence and agency is in how she dies. The first sentences of the letter clearly state that Mr Xu is reading the words of a dead woman, but the circumstances of her death are never detailed. Two scholars have advanced the view that the woman commits suicide after writing this letter, but they do not provide any argument to support this statement (Guo, 2018; Li, 2007). Nonetheless, the circumstances of the character's death remain ambiguous in Xu's film, in comparison to Zweig's work or even Ophüls's adaptation. In the original story, the woman says that she may have the same illness that just took her son:

Perhaps I shall not be able to speak to you entirely clearly, perhaps you will not understand me – my mind is dulled, my temples throb and hammer, my limbs hurt so much. I think I am feverish myself, perhaps I too have the influenza that is spreading fast in this part of town, and I would be glad of it, because then I could go with my child without having to do myself any violence. Sometimes everything turns dark before my eyes; perhaps I shall not even be able to finish writing this letter – but I am summoning up all my strength to speak to you once. (Zweig, 2013)

And she finishes with the following:

I cannot write any more. My head is so heavy; my limbs ache; I am feverish. I must lie down. Perhaps all will soon be over. Perhaps, this once, fate will be kind to me, and I shall not have to see them take away my boy . . . I cannot write anymore. (Zweig, 2013)

In Ophüls's film, the voice-over also insists on the fever that the character endures and stops abruptly when the woman character on screen collapses on her desk. The image then becomes blurred, signifying the woman's vision as she loses consciousness. In contrast, the voice-over of Xu Jinglei's film does not describe any symptoms of illness or weakness; she just ends her letter by saying that she cannot write anymore.

During her last appearance on screen, Miss Jiang is shown standing and looking out of her window in her apartment. The camera then pans down to her desk in the foreground, where a frame with a picture of her late son is prominently placed, and keeps panning over the letter resting on it, before the image fades to black. During that scene, the women does not look weak or ill. Her posture seems more contemplative. Nothing confirms nor denies the possibility of a suicide, but a death by illness appears unlikely. The director did not comment on the heroine's death, except that her son's passing took away her will to live without further elaboration (Xie and Wu, 2004). It is then open to interpretation. Zweig's heroine does not exclude suicide when she writes 'then I could go with my child without having to do myself any violence' (Zweig, 2013). In her eyes, her approaching death, once she is relieved of her confession, is a blessing.

Taking her own life would actually be more in character for the heroine in Xu's film. Now that her son – her reason to live after going through war, losing her family and friends in the process – is dead and since she was repeatedly disappointed by Mr Xu, with whom she may never have had a lasting relationship, she could choose an end on her own terms. Doing so would add to the agency that the filmmaker has given her. Miss Jiang was shown as remarkably independent for her time – and even for today – sustaining herself and her son without complying with patriarchal rituals such as marriage and legitimate offspring. If she had let herself die of illness, it would have made her a tragic and sacrificial figure. Suicide actually asserts her autonomy. By sending the letter after her death, she prevents Mr Xu from finding her and responding to her, which could be seen as a punishment beyond death. But, more importantly, she stays in control of her narrative until the end. From this perspective, the suicide hypothesis better matches the heroine's character and supports once again her agency.

In conclusion, Xu Jinglei transformed her heroine into a more independent figure and addressed many controversial issues in Chinese society, without condemning them. She is a good example of how women filmmakers negotiate their position on the film market. She amasses enough of a following and recognition as an auteur, and her movies are shown in domestic theatres. Her strength of character and her ability to navigate the market requirements are, according to Cai, the keys to the successful career she has had so far. At the same time, the female gaze displayed in *Letter from an Unknown Woman* not only highlights a female perspective and agency, but also contributes to the disruption of dominant (masculine) narratives and ways of filming. The female gaze, in its different manifestations, provides then a new frame to discuss Chinese cinema, provided that the filmmaker's perspective is situated and historicised.

## References

Brey, I. (2020). *Le regard féminin: Une révolution à l'écran* [The female gaze, a revolution on screen]. Paris: L'Olivier.
Cai, S. (2017). *Contemporary Chinese films and celebrity directors.* Basingstoke: Palgrave Macmillan.
Cui, S. (2003). *Women through the lens: Gender and nation in a century of Chinese cinema.* Honolulu: University of Hawai'i Press.
Deren, M., Miller, A., Thomas, D., Tyler, P., and Maas, W. (2000). Intervention at the Poetry and the Film: A Symposium (1953). Transcribed by A. Sitney (ed.), *Film culture reader* (pp. 171–86). New York: Cooper Square Press.
Dirse, Z. (2013). Gender in Cinematography: Female Gaze (Eye) Behind the Camera. *Journal of Research in Gender Studies*, 3(1), 15–29.
French, L. (2021). *The female gaze in documentary film: An international perspective.* Cham: Palgrave Macmillan.
Guo, S. (2018). Wenyi, Wenqing and pure love: The European imaginary in Xu Jinglei's films. *Journal of Chinese Cinemas*, 12(1), 41–58.
Kaplan, E. A. (2011). Affect, memory, and trauma past tense: Hu Mei's *Army nurse* (1985) and Xu Jinglei's *Letter from an unknown woman* (2004). In L. Wang (ed.), *Chinese women's cinema: Transnational contexts* (pp. 154–70). New York: Columbia University Press.
Kozloff, S. (1988). *Invisible storytellers: Voice-over narration in American fiction film*, Berkeley-Los Angeles-London: University of California Press.

Li, J. (2007). Chinese feminisms and adaptation-as-translation readings of *Letter from an unknown woman*. *Comparative Literature and Culture*, 9(4). Retrieved from http://docs.lib.purdue.edu/clcweb/vol9/iss4/4

Li, X. (2020). How powerful is the female gaze? The implication of using male celebrities for promoting female cosmetics in China. *Global Media and China*, 5(1), 55–68.

Wang, L. (2011). Socialist cinema and female authorship: Overdetermination and subjective revisions in Dong Kena's *Small grass grows on the Kunkun mountain* (1962). In L. Wang (ed.), *Chinese women's cinema: Transnational contexts* (pp. 47–65). New York: Columbia University Press.

Wang, L. (2019). Zhang Nuanxin and Social Commitment in 1980s Chinese Women's Experimental Cinema. *Camera Obscura*, 34(3), 1–29.

Xie, X. 谢晓, and Wu, J. 伍洁敏 (2004, April 7). *Xu Jinglei shouci jiemi laixin: Zhebu yingpian huiling guanzhong gandong* 徐静蕾首次解密'来信': 这部影片会令观众感动 [Xu Jinglei decodes *Letter* for the first time: This movie will be touching]. *Nanfang dushi bao* 南方都市报 [Southern Metropolis Daily]. Retrieved from http://ent.sina.com.cn/m/c/2004-04-07/1514358136.html

Yang, Y., and Wei, S. L. (2009). *Nüxing de dianying: Duihua zhongri nüdaoyan* 女性的电影: 对话中日女导演 [*Women's cinema: Dialogues with Chinese and Japanese female directors*]. Shanghai: Huadong shifan daxue chubanshe.

Yu, W. 宇文翮 (2016). *Shaozhuangpai daoyan baogao* 少壮派导演报告 [Young and vigorous directors in China: Interviews with the new wave of filmmakers]. Jinan: Shandong huabao chubanshe.

Zhang, J. (2011). To become an auteur: The cinematic maneuverings of Xu Jinglei. In L. Wang (ed.), *Chinese women's cinema: Transnational contexts* (pp. 293–310). New York: Columbia University Press.

Zweig, S. (2013). *Letter from an unknown woman and other stories* (A. Bell, trans.). London: Pushkin Press.

## Notes

1. All citations in French and Chinese are translated into English by the author.
2. Editors' note: Qiong Yao novels are discussed in Xuelin Zhou's chapter in this volume.

Chapter 5

# *Ichi* (2008): Female Stars and Gender Representations in the *Zatoichi* Franchise

Jonathan Wroot

The majority of the *Zatoichi* films made in Japan reflect gender biases that are systemic of the contexts in which they were made, as well as the perception of female stars, in terms of their popularity and commercial viability within certain roles. The *Zatoichi* films and TV series have typically been interpreted through their leading Japanese men – from Shintaro Katsu,[1] to later iterations by Takeshi Kitano in 2003, and Shingo Katori in 2010. Katsu originally played the blind masseur who wandered eighteenth-century Japan, with a sword hidden in his cane, in twenty-six films from 1962 to 1989, as well as in 100 TV episodes (broadcast from 1974 to 1979). There was also the gender-flipped reboot released in 2008, *Ichi*, directed by Fumihiko Sori, where Haruka Ayase played the sword-wielding protagonist. This was a potential turning point for the franchise, as well as for *chanbara* (sword action) films in twenty-first-century Japanese cinema. Following earlier examples, such as *Azumi* (2003) and *Azumi 2* (2005), here was another film that could show how one of Japan's most popular genres can be led by Japanese female stars as much as by male ones. However, since the relative critical and commercial disappointment of *Ichi*, the most successful domestic and international *chanbara* films continue to be male-dominated – from *13 Assassins* (2010) to *Blade of the Immortal* (2017) and the *Rurouni Kenshin* franchise (2012–21). Nonetheless, the production context of the 2008 film demonstrated how the film's studio and producers were aiming for commercial success, as can be seen from the cast and crew involved in the project.

Despite these aims, the poor reception of *Ichi*, in addition to its aesthetics and narrative content, illustrates particular trends related to Japanese cinema. First, notwithstanding the efforts of the film to make its female protagonist as heroic as Katsu's original incarnations, *Ichi* still falls into tendencies to which other *Zatoichi* titles and *chanbara* features frequently adhere. The Ichi character is shaped by her femininity, particularly through her sexuality, looks and place in society, and this ultimately affects how the narrative is resolved. Ichi instead could have potentially asserted her sword-fighting skills and independence from other (predominantly male) characters, as Katsu's original protagonist often did. The filmmakers intended to incorporate the tropes of popular romantic films in Japan at the time, in order to capitalise on the previous successes of female stars. However, these efforts were not recognised by Western critics, nor did this equate to commercial success in Japan. What the film ultimately illustrates is the way in which female characters have constantly been used in the *Zatoichi* franchise, from the 1960s onwards, as well in other popular Japanese action films. When on-screen, such characters tend to be romantic interests or damsels-in-distress, with villainous or heroic turns being few and far between. As is perhaps expected, especially with a film series that originated in the 1960s, male stars within the franchise do not have this problem, especially when they play the protagonist.

This chapter will situate the case-study of *Ichi* within established findings concerning franchise media, studio production contexts, popular culture and star personas. The *Zatoichi* films and TV episodes are subject to these trends within their Japanese production history that stretches across five decades. Unfortunately, as these trends are so entrenched, and since the *Zatoichi* franchise is so recognisable due to its popular male protagonist, it means that these factors also affect the performance of the female cast on-screen – whether or not they are portraying the protagonist.

Although this chapter is limited to the case-study of *Ichi* and the *Zatoichi* franchise, these findings do have wider implications for popular *chanbara* films, the production of action cinema within Japan and gender representation on-screen. Derek Johnson states that 'franchising – and the study of it – should remain of significant value to those who want to understand how and why the culture industries reproduce shared culture' (Johnson, 2013, p. 26). Richard Dyer offers a similar argument in his influential study *Stars* (1979) – specifically, that such personas have a significant cultural impact due to their multiple facets:

> star-as-person : star-as-image
> star-as-image : star-as-character
> star-as-auteur : star-as-text
> star-as-self : star-as-role
> and . . . star-as-essence : star-as-subject
> (Dyer, 1998, p. 161)

Dolores Martinez (2009) has concluded, by way of investigating Japanese cinema, that by studying films as anthropological artifacts, popular culture is found not to be static, especially when it has a global impact. In a contrast to this notion, however, the history of female characters, stars and gender representation within popular franchises, such as the *Zatoichi* series, shows that some aspects of popular culture and film production can remain static over many decades.

## *Ichi* within the *Zatoichi* Franchise: Illustrating New and Constant Directions

The success of Takeshi Kitano's 2003 remake, *Zatoichi*, opened the door to many new and possible interpretations of the famous blind swordsman. Kitano famously said that he wanted to make his portrayal of Zatoichi as far removed from Shintaro Katsu as possible. Apart from cutting his hair short and dressing in unremarkable period garments, such as brown or grey cloaks and sandals, Katsu did little to change his appearance. However, Kitano would decide to dress in blue and black cloaks, while carrying a red cane concealing his sword and dyeing his hair blond. Five years later, Haruka Ayase would not go to such extremes with her costume in *Ichi*. Her naturally brown hair is kept loose, and her cane sword is concealed in a plain bamboo scabbard, as was the case with Katsu's swordsman. Her kimono is ragged and multi-coloured, which is distinctive visually and also apt, as the character cannot see the clothes in which she dresses. The biggest contrast from previous feature films is that the protagonist is female. But despite this unique hook, in terms of plot and characterisation, *Ichi* would not stray far from the *Zatoichi* formula.

At first, this seems like a strength for the film, as Ayase's protagonist can finally prove that a female swordsman is as capable as the legendary male character. Instead of being a travelling masseur, Ichi is a travelling musician and singer who carries her *shamisen* (three-stringed lute) as well as her cane sword. After being dismissed from one house, she cuts the fingers off a groping male servant after trying to find shelter from the snow. In the next scene, she kills two *yakuza* who are trying to get away from a blind prostitute without paying for her services. Shortly afterwards, Ichi meets Toma (Takao Osawa), a trained samurai who cannot draw his sword, due to a past tragedy – which leads to several moments where he relies on her sword skills (as well as her ability to hear the way in which the dice land in a *yakuza* gambling den). Although coincidence leads to Toma being mistaken for a master swordsman and the pair being embroiled in a local gang feud, the film's scenes and narrative structure do not shy away from presenting Ayase's character as a formidable warrior. However, this changes after her first encounter with the film's chief villain, the flamboyant, one-eyed and constantly cackling Banki (Shido Nakamura).

Banki is not just a clichéd villain because of his outlandish garb, his loud and brawling *yakuza* gang, and the fact that he resides in a shadowy cave. He is also a fan of the monologue. He takes pleasure in first defeating Ichi by countering her back-handed draw of her cane sword. Then Banki explains that he fought the legendary blind swordsman Zatoichi several years earlier, and that he was determined to triumph over his sword-fighting style. Ichi has also been searching for Zatoichi, who may be her father, but Banki simply says that he died of a disease. Ichi is then imprisoned in Banki's cave, where she experiences a flashback to Zatoichi leaving her with a blind musician troupe as a child, but also visiting every now and again to train her in sword fighting. Instead of herself escaping, as the original Zatoichi often did (from many a prison), Ichi instead has to be rescued by Toma. Ichi now seems depressed and despondent, although by the end of the film she does not entirely trust Banki's story and implies that she may still look for the man who raised her. However, before she does emerge from her stupor and kill Banki, she and Toma give in to their feelings and spend the night together. This seems to have two consequences – first, Toma can now draw his sword when Banki attacks the local town; and second, Ichi is 're-energised' so that she can face Banki again, but only after Toma has died before she reaches the battle.

Structurally speaking, *Ichi* follows the formula of previous *Zatoichi* films and many others within the broader category of *chanbara*. Ichi's journey brings her into contact with other travellers and, eventually, a town where a rivalry between *yakuza* gangs is brewing. Through certain coincidences and plot developments (such as killing two of Banki's *yakuza* early on, and Toma being mistaken for a master swordsman), Ichi is forced to face and kill many of the antagonists, including Banki. But the film's rigidity, in terms of plotting and structure, ultimately extends to gender roles within the narrative, which in turn continues long-standing trends within the franchise (and *chanbara* films) from the 1960s. While this can be evidenced from the film's narrative and production context, another figure within the 2008 film also helps to emphasise this point. In the flashbacks to Ichi's earlier life, Zatoichi is portrayed by Tetta Sugimoto, who wears a costume and haircut similar to Katsu's original portrayal. As will be explained, factors relating to Japanese film production in the 2000s will be noted as influencing the film's inception, casting and production. However, the film is also determined to honour previous portrayals of the blind swordsman and to continue long-standing trends and tendencies within the franchise.

Before further highlighting the shortcomings of *Ichi* in terms of gender representation, by linking it to other portrayals of women within the *Zatoichi* franchise, it is necessary to outline the production context of the film. This helps to explain why the plot of *Ichi* and its character motivations play out in certain ways on-screen. Even though these aspects can be heavily critiqued in terms of the history of gender stereotypes within the *Zatoichi* films and other *chanbara* titles, they also situate the film within wider trends found in Japanese popular films and media at the time. Fumihiko Sori directed the script, written by female writer Taeko Asano. These credits, as well as the portrayal of Ichi by popular actress, singer and model Haruka Ayase, were a likely formula for commercial success, especially considering Sori's previous successful film releases (*Ping Pong*, 2002; *Vexille*, 2007). Ayase's multimedia idol status also fit well into the star-persona-mould shaped by Katsu and Kitano. However, *Ichi* grossed just over $4 million dollars at the Japanese box office and ranked 84 out of 100 in terms of domestic and international releases for 2008 in Japanese cinemas. This ultimately disappointed Kodansha, Warner Bros and the TV network Tokyo Broadcasting System (TBS), who had put up most of the funds for production. Multiple theories can be put forward now for the film's lacklustre performance (as will be suggested later). But the focus on a female protagonist and the introduction of a doomed romance between Ichi and Toma was very much part of the zeitgeist in the 2000s, in terms of popular Japanese media narratives.

Japanese audiences love romantic stories, whether in book, film, *anime* or *manga* form (Kono, 2010; MacWilliams, 2014, pp. 137–54; McDonald, 2015, pp. 3–84). The possibility that *Ichi* was trying to capitalise on this success in Japan, rather than simply continue a tried and tested formula, is indicated by the film's acting and script credits. Both Haruka Ayase and Takao Osawa were no strangers to action films before *Ichi*, but a more significant link between the two is that they appeared in television (Ayase) and film (Osawa) versions of the same romantic novel, *Crying Out Love, in the Center of the World*. Both the feature film and series were released in Japan in 2004. The novel, originally titled *Socrates in Love* (by Kyoichi Katayama and published in 2001), concerns an engaged young man who suddenly comes across audio tapes reminding him of a romance that he had as a teenager with a young girl who died of leukemia. Despite such a melancholic premise, the novel and its many adaptations have captured the imaginations of audiences in Japan and other East Asian countries (Lai, 2013). Furthermore, the scriptwriter for *Ichi*, Asano, had worked mostly on romantic films and TV series before (and since) her reimagining of Zatoichi – such as *Love 2000* (2000) and *A Symphony of Us* (2006).

Such plotting, however, came across as strange to Western fans of *chanbara*. Following the international success of Kitano's 2003 *Zatoichi* film, a gender-flipped reboot of the character may have also been positively received. As romantic dramas such as *Crying Out Love, in the Center of the World* were not being widely exported from Japan, the critical reception of *Ichi* outside of Japan expressed discontent and confusion about some of the characterisation and plotting. For instance, Calum Waddell, writing for *NEO*, a monthly magazine published in the UK focusing on Asian popular culture, stresses that the film is one of two halves, where the second part is a major contrast from the first. In this respect, he believes that it departs too much from the original *Zatoichi* series and becomes too focused on its romance subplot, summing up his views by stating 'Less talk, more action please' (Waddell, 2009). Similar comments are put forward by other critics, such as the *London Evening Standard* stating that 'the fight scenes are better than the dialogue' (Malcolm, 2009); *Sight and Sound* said that 'Ayase brings little to the character apart from a doe-eyed demeanour' (Clarke, 2009); *Time Out London* saw it as a 'limp femme take on Japan's popular *Zatoichi* franchise' (Jenkins, 2009); and *The Times* thought that it was an 'uninspired reimagining of the *Zatoichi* legend' (Maher, 2009). Yes, these are male critics, from predominantly British publications, but at the time of writing this chapter no critical reception from Japan was accessible. However, the lacklustre domestic box-office performance of the film, at just over $4 million, is an indicator of the Japanese audience reaction to the film. Four years earlier, the film adaptation of *Crying Out Love, in the Center of the World* grossed almost $73 million. And yet both films were based on popular stories and characters, concerning romantic stories, with popular stars in their casts. Other than the partial view of the critical reception that is currently available, the latter aspect mentioned here – star personas – combined with the long-running popularity of the *Zatoichi* character and franchise, may offer some answers as to why there was such a contrast with the critical and commercial success of *Ichi*.

## In the Land of the Blind Swordsman, Star Power and Gender Stereotypes Are King

Star power and franchise formulas are significant factors within the study of popular culture and cinema history, as shown in much published research. Certain views of stars given by the *Zatoichi* franchise and its production context align with concepts established by Richard Dyer in *Stars* (1979) – particularly the notions of 'star-as-image' and 'star-as-character'. This is also found within star studies that have continued since Dyer's work, especially within the East Asian film and media industries, where stars are frequently interpreted as a constellation of images and popular characters. In 2009, Deborah Shamoon investigated the evolution of Misora Hibari's star image from sexualised child actor to a righteous and virginal young girl. Mats Karlsson is one of several scholars to examine the star persona of Setsuko Hara. His 2015 book chapter situates Hara's identity within the rigid Japanese studio system, of which Shintaro Katsu was also a product. While such case-studies are historical, parallels are found between stars of the past and present across many national borders, as demonstrated in the chapters of *East Asian Film Stars* (Leung and Willis, 2014). Here, carefully constructed star images are examined in relation to the careers of Kyo Machiko, Brigitte Lin, Donnie Yen, Chow Yun Fat and Zhang Ziyi, among others, although changes are often necessitated by shifts between East Asian and Hollywood studios. Differing star images have also been found within the study of different genre categories. In 2001, Aaron D. Anderson argued that analyses of martial arts films often reduced female heroines to either sexualised objects, or mobile, athletic and feminine; and although David Brown only writes about male martial arts actors' bodies in 2008, his categories of 'martial-artist-as-actor', 'actor-as-martial-artist' and 'the enhanced martial-artist-as-actor' can easily be adapted to the successful martial arts actresses now found in East Asian countries. This could have been attempted in the analysis of *Ichi* (2008). However, the characterisation of the protagonist and the performance of Ayase do not emphasise her martial arts skills, as much as they do particular gender stereotypes.

When looking back on the history of the *Zatoichi* films and TV series, depictions of gender are very strongly linked to stardom. Judith Butler's views on gender still underscore much writing and research in this area, especially points such as 'what we take to be an internal essence of gender is manufactured through a sustained set of acts, posited through the gendered stylization of the body' (1990, p. xv). This is particularly seen in the consistent performances of Katsu and other actors as Zatoichi, in addition to his female co-stars. Across the whole franchise, Ichi is often found to be kind, selfless, amiable, as well as morally justified in his bloody actions (he is only reluctant to draw his sword throughout the films made in the 1960s). Portrayals of women support this view of the character and, in turn, the star identity of Katsu. Female co-stars often require saving through Ichi's actions, either through violence or words of wisdom. This can lead to changes of heart in women who are at first villainous, or victims of injustice may fall in love with him – leading Ichi to stress that he is 'no good' as a blind man, a killer and a gambler, so he never settles with any woman. As a result, a changing roster of female stars (both emerging and established) were brought into the films and episodes through these supporting roles. This is perhaps understandable for a long-running franchise about a particular male character, but there was often a limited variety to the supporting roles offered to female co-stars.

This partially explains why later portrayals of the Zatoichi character seem to struggle to move away from gender stereotypes, especially in relation to women. This long history and rigid formula will now be explained in this section before the film *Ichi* is re-situated within it. The *Zatoichi* film series began in 1962, with *The Tale of Zatoichi* (dir. Kenji Misumi). The adaptation of a short story by Kan Shimozawa (first published in 1948), the film was a surprise success for the studio Daiei. It helped to cement Shintaro Katsu's status as one of their top stars, following the growing success of the *Akumyo (Tough Guy) yakuza* films which started in 1961. A sequel was quickly produced in the same year, which included many more fight scenes and villains for Katsu's blind warrior to vanquish. Simply named Ichi, meaning 'one', the 'zato' suffix means 'blind'. The character wanders innocently into nineteenth-century Japanese towns, looking to offer his services as a masseur and take part in some gambling when the chance arises. In every single film and TV episode, this inevitably leads Ichi into violent trouble with the local *yakuza*, requiring him to unsheathe his sword hidden in his walking stick and to use it with deadly force. Zatoichi was not just another popular *jidai-geki* (period drama) character, but also a hero of the *chanbara* (sword action) genre, as well as the *matabimono* (drifter stories) genre. In many interviews, Katsu claimed to have had a blind servant in his family as a child; alongside his regular training with a sword, this helped him to fulfil what would become his signature role. It would also allow him to incorporate his other famous talents, such as playing musical instruments, singing, dancing, as well as defending and wooing the female characters. Twenty-five films were made from 1962 to 1973, then 100 TV episodes until 1979, followed ten years later by Katsu directing his final on-screen performance as Ichi. Even after his death in 1997, the role continued to be associated with Katsu, through anniversary celebrations, re-releases, stage performances, as well as official and unofficial lookalike actors.

For better or worse, both star and actor became inseparable. As Donald Richie noted about Katsu in 1978, there was an 'absence of anything and anyone when Zatoichi is not there' (Richie, 2005, p. 164).

A recurring trait throughout the *Zatoichi* franchise is the changing roster of female cast members in every instalment, whether a film or TV show. This was varied in the later remakes from 2003 onwards, as the lead actors also changed, but it was also an established part of the formula within the Shintaro Katsu films from the 1960s and 1970s, as well as the later TV series. Female co-stars would often try to use the franchise to establish or continue their own success on-screen. If this did not happen, their appearances in *Zatoichi* instalments may become what was most remembered about them. There were sometimes exceptions to these trends, but in most cases star power was drawn into the *Zatoichi* franchise to help promote Katsu's own image. Two helpful illustrations of this are found in the year 1967 – a particularly significant year, as Daiei's finances had started to flounder, and Katsu set up his own production company in order to continue making films with his regular crew and colleagues. Katsu was also an accomplished stage actor and singer, and he had started to perform 'Zatoichi's Lullaby' as a recurring theme tune (again, from 1967 onwards). However, Katsu and his colleagues would also vary their formula as much as possible, which led to some musical starlets often featuring in cameo performances. *Zatoichi's Cane Sword* (1967) included Kiyoko Suizenji as Oharu, the lead singer of a theatre troupe with which Ichi duets and hitches a lift. Famous for *enka* ballads and numerous stage, film and TV appearances, Suizenji is still performing to this day (as of 2022). Another popular performer was cast as a singer in a travelling troupe in *Zatoichi Challenged* (1967). Mie Nakao continues to perform on stage (as of 2022) and previously had a successful career from the 1950s to the 1970s as part of the Three Girls (who regularly released music and appeared in films together). Of course, in both films Ichi has to defend the troupe performers from nefarious *yakuza*. Thus, although popular singers would continue to be cast in later films and TV episodes, they were often damsels in distress that required saving.

After a failed comeback film in 1989 and Katsu's passing in 1997, Kitano's 2003 film would re-introduce the character to both Japanese and international film screens, with a much different costume. Converted from Japanese yen, the film made almost $24 million for distributor Shochiku, and it was Kitano's biggest domestic hit in Japan, in addition to winning the Silver Lion at Venice. Looking back upon these achievements now, it seems only logical that Kitano should be the filmmaker to do this, considering some of the career parallels he had with Katsu. Although not a musical performer or singer, his success was first found on stage as part of a *manzai* (duo) comedy act, The Two Beats. As his success grew through comedy routines and television presenting, Kitano soon turned to acting in the 1980s, and by 1989 he was also directing in between his busy schedule of TV appearances. Scriptwriting and editing followed soon after, as did parallel outputs in writing, radio presenting and canvas artwork, which were maintained even after a near-fatal motorbike accident in 1994. By 2003, Kitano seemed to have a larger-than-life star status due to these multiple facets of his career. This gave him both the reputation expected to fill a huge star's shoes, such as Katsu's, as well as the authority to bring such a radical visual change to the beloved blind swordman character. However, it could be argued that little else changed, in terms of the plot and characterisation expected of a *Zatoichi* film, especially when considering gender portrayals.

The film's plot is like many others – Ichi arrives in a town, befriends some locals, but also has to defend them against some violent and conspiratorial *yakuza*. This includes defending a brother and sister, disguised as *geisha*, who are trying to seek revenge against their parents' killers. The brother character in a *kimono*, Osei, could be seen as a progressive twenty-first-century step for both *jidai-geki* and *chanbara* films. But the character's significance is also found in the film's casting, specifically through the actor Daigoro Tachibana – whose only film acting credit is the 2003 *Zatoichi* film. This is because he is known primarily for his singing and acting on stage, specifically as part of a long tradition of *onnagata*, or female impersonators found in Japanese *kabuki* theatre. Tachibana may have been happy to be the butt of some jokes in a *chanbara* tale, having most likely starred in comedies, musicals and a variety of other on-stage productions. But Osei is frequently used to mock the notion of men wearing make-up, especially when he inspires a farmer (Shinkichi) to try doing the same. This mockery may be expected due to another casting choice, as the farmer is played by comedian Guadalcanal Taka. However, the film is directed by Kitano, with one of his most famous jokes being a V-shaped arm-salute alongside the phrase 'Comaneci!' as a reference to gymnast Nadia Comaneci's figure-hugging leotard. While he has not gained the womanising reputation of Katsu (documented in many news articles), Kitano's willingness to stereotype women as certain characters is demonstrated in his *Zatoichi* remake. An argument could be made about the limitations of the genre, but even after arming the *geisha* siblings with hidden swords, the film reduces them to damsels in distress that require saving, like many other female characters in the film.

Although the 2010 film, *Zatoichi: The Last*, attempted some significant changes within the formula, much also remains the same. Shingo Katori plays Ichi, most famous for being part of the popular boy band SMAP, which later disbanded in 2016. In 2010, his fame may well have been on par with Katsu's. This title was also funded by Toho, who had previously distributed some of Katsu's *Zatoichi* films from the 1970s onwards and had also attempted to cash in on 'ending' another franchise of theirs with *Godzilla: Final Wars* (2004), before reviving it in 2016. The studio therefore attempted to both provide a new interpretation of the blind swordsman and a definitive ending for the franchise, through the efforts of director Junji Sakamoto and (at the time) emerging scriptwriter Kikumi Yamagishi. Sadly, Japanese and overseas audiences seemed not to care. In 2010, *The Last* only made $3.68 million in Japan and was the 110th highest domestic and international release of the whole year. Despite the international profile of previous *Zatoichi* films (including *Ichi*), this title was not picked up for overseas distribution. The changes to the formula included introducing Ichi having a wife, Otane, only to have her killed off in the first few minutes, becoming part of the vengeful reasons forcing Ichi to draw his sword. However, Ichi ultimately is unsuccessful; for the first time on Japanese screens, he is shown dying on a beach at the end of the film (hence the word 'last' in the title). Despite this dramatic final scene, the film overall provided much fewer opportunities for proactive female roles on-screen, especially in comparison to *Ichi* (2008).

A brief history of the *Zatoichi* franchise has been necessary in this section, as it demonstrates how much Ayase's character from the 2008 film follows these established trends. At first, she seems to fulfil the role of a wandering and fearsome blind swordswoman, especially after dispatching the first few *yakuza* she encounters. However, her character becomes romantically involved with the male lead, while also needing to be rescued by him. Only after these plot points is Ichi able to tragically witness Toma's death and claim vengeance against the villainous Banki. Ultimately, the film ends with her travelling alone again, in the style of all films and TV episodes in the *Zatoichi* franchise. It remains that *Ichi* seems to require its protagonist to fulfil the stereotypical roles of romantic interest and damsel in distress, while also establishing her as a skilled sword fighter. This demonstrates how the history of the *Zatoichi* franchise, as well as its tendencies towards the representation of female characters and stars, ultimately shapes any later remakes, regardless of whether they attempt to stray from the expected formula.

## Conclusion

The actors who have starred as the blind swordsman on Japanese film and TV screens have often been established models, singers, presenters and/or actors, learning sword choreography for the role of Ichi. This chimes with a lot of existing research on Japanese screen stardom, such as Christopher Howard's analysis of Japanese idols (2014), who are simultaneously established as singers, actors and brands from a young age, especially when working for large agencies such as Amuse or Johnny & Associates. What is also clear from the various stars of the *Zatoichi* films is that Katsu's shadow still looms large over the franchise, and this extends to shaping gender and character portrayals within it. For instance, it was another male star, Kitano, who had most success with the franchise after Katsu. However, other stars failed to successfully establish their own interpretations of the blind swordsman, especially when the 2008 and 2010 films were so keen to reference previous portrayals.

The reasons for Ayase's and Katori's lack of success could be due to age, as well as their star personas and screen careers. Both actors were younger than Katsu and Kitano, in comparison to the years where they appeared on-screen as the blind swordsman. For instance, putting aside the number of films and TV shows from the 1960s and 1970s, Katsu and Kitano both played the character when they were in their fifties (in the 1989 and 2003 films). More significant, however, is the fact that Katsu and Kitano already had acted in several action films before their portrayals of Zatoichi. As mentioned earlier, for both Ayase and Katori, this was not the case. Ayase had begun to star in commercially successful romantic films and TV dramas after establishing herself as a model, and Katori had only just turned to acting after his successful music career. Their careers were much closer in comparison to supporting male and female actors brought into the *Zatoichi* franchise, especially over the period of Katsu's starring roles in films and TV episodes throughout the 1960s and 1970s.

What has been most prominent in this chapter is that, despite the efforts to frame Ayase as an action star within an established franchise, it was ultimately the history of the *Zatoichi* series and the memory of popular previous portrayals of the character that seemed to influence her character's portrayal on-screen in *Ichi* (2008). Ayase's own career also seemed to shape this to a certain extent. The characterisation of

Ichi parallels both the success of romantic dramas at the Japanese box office and Ayase's success within this genre. This chapter has allowed me to explore a different perspective on the blind swordsman franchise, in comparison to my book on its global influence, *The Paths of Zatoichi* (Wroot, 2021). The monograph concluded with the argument that the international history of this character demonstrated points made by Martinez and other scholars – that Japanese cinema and popular culture is enormously influential, and it is not static when it moves across national borders. However, on closer inspection regarding the portrayal of women and its influence on star personas within Japanese media, some aspects of the *Zatoichi* franchise remain largely fixed, in terms of gender stereotypes and action film protagonists. Since the release of *Ichi*, the most successful domestic and international *chanbara* films continue to be male-dominated – from *13 Assassins* (2010) to *Blade of the Immortal* (2017) and the *Rurouni Kenshin* franchise (2012–21). Until future Japanese productions move away from these stereotypical trends, it is likely that female characters will continue to be depicted in similar ways, regardless of whether they are sword-wielding protagonists.

## References

Anderson, A. D. (2001). Asian martial arts cinema, dance, and the cultural languages of gender. *Asian Journal of Communication*, 11(2), 58–78.
Brown, D. (2008). The changing charismatic status of the performing male body in Asian martial arts films. *Sport in Society*, 11(2/3), 174–94.
Butler, J. (1990). *Gender trouble: Feminism and the subversion of identity*. London: Routledge.
Clarke, R. C. (2009). Ichi. *Sight and Sound*, 19(8), 66.
Dyer, R. (1998). *Stars* (new ed.). London: BFI.
Howard, C. (2014). National idols? The problem of 'transnationalizing' film stardom in Japan's idol economy. In W.-F. Leung and A. Willis (eds), *East Asian film stars* (pp. 49–64). Basingstoke: Palgrave Macmillan.
Jenkins, D. (2009). Ichi. *Time Out London*. Retrieved from http://www.timeout.com/film/reviews/87344/ichi.html
Johnson, D. (2013). *Media franchising: Creative license and collaboration in the culture industries*. New York: New York University Press.Karlsson, M. (2015).
Karlsson, M. (2015). Setsuko Hara: Japan's eternal virgin and reluctant star of the silver screen. In A. Bandhauer and M. Royer (eds), *Stars in world cinema: Screen icons and star systems across cultures* (pp. 51–66). London: Bloomsbury.
Kono, K. (2010). *Romance, family, and nation in Japanese colonial literature*. Basingstoke: Palgrave Macmillan.
Lai, A. (2013). Reconfiguring the Japanese melodrama: Crying and return in 'Crying out love, in the center of the world'. *Film Criticism*, 38(2), 20–41.
Leung, W.-F., and Willis, A. (eds). (2014). *East Asian film stars*. Basingstoke: Palgrave Macmillan.
MacWilliams, M. (2014). *Japanese visual culture: Explorations in the world of manga and anime*. London: Routledge.

Maher, K. (2009). Ichi. *The Times Online.* Retrieved from https://www.thetimes.co.uk/article/ichi-7ntx29pbl3k
Malcolm, D. (2009). Fumihiko Sori stays clear of clichés. *London Evening Standard.* Retrieved from https://www.standard.co.uk/culture/film/fumihiko-sori-stays-clear-of-cliches-7415403.html
Martinez, D. P. (2009). *Remaking Kurosawa: Translations and permutations in global cinema.* Basingstoke: Palgrave Macmillan.
McDonald, K. (2015). *From book to screen: Modern Japanese literature in film.* London: Routledge.
Richie, D. (2005). *The Japan journals: 1947–2004.* Berkeley: Stone Bridge Press.
Shamoon, D. (2009). Misora Hibari and the girl star in postwar Japanese cinema. *Signs: Journal of Women in Culture and Society, 35*(1), 131–55.
Waddell, C. (2009, August). Ichi. *NEO Magazine, 61,* 74.
Wroot, J. (2021). *The paths of Zatoichi: The global influence of the blind swordsman.* Lanham: Lexington.

# Notes

1. Editors' note: In this chapter, Japanese names adhere to the Western convention of given name first, followed by family name.

Chapter 6

# Agency and Subjectivity of the Female Protagonists in Qiong Yao Films

*Xuelin Zhou*

A dominant genre in Taiwan cinema in the 1970s is the romantic drama. Of the Taiwanese romantic films produced over the period, nearly half were adapted from the local woman writer Qiong Yao's 瓊瑤 popular novels and stories. These youth romances, dubbed as Qiong Yao films, are known for the alleged commonalities that they share in characterisation, settings and thematic expressions. The conflicts that advance the narrative in the films are constituted primarily of those between male and female, old and young, traditional and modern. While Qiong Yao films boasted enthusiastic consumption in Chinese communities around the world, they remained under the radar of film scholars until recently. For many years during and after their production and exhibition, the so-called simplified approaches that Qiong Yao films adopted in characterisation and thematic expressions ignited (largely derogative) descriptions, such as evading social reality and escapism hiding in the shade of romantic fantasies and succumbing to patriarchal values (Li, 1997, p. 154; Qi, 1996, p. 164; Udden, 2009, p. 37). Although recent years have seen more attention given to these B-movies in the classical Taiwan cinema, overall, they have resisted a feminist reading.

One reason why Qiong Yao films have rarely been read from a feminist point of view is that most of them were directed by men. The gender relationships in the original novels, which were usually presented from a female perspective, were not infrequently re-configured in the process of filmmaking, to a male point of view. An early example is the adaptation of Qiong Yao's short-story 'Three Flowers' 三朵花 as *Love in Spring* 花落谁家 by the award-winning actor-director Wang Yin 王引 in 1966. After Qiong Yao had watched Wang's completed work, she felt that the film misrepresented what she meant to say in her original story. In the adapted film, the independent, self-reliant woman characters in 'Three Flowers' became men's fixtures – passive, ignorant and unreasonable –

and subjugated to the male gaze (Qiong, 1966, p. 9). When Qiong Yao brought her concerns to the director, the latter replied that her original story was too tragic in tone and that local audiences in Taiwan did not want to view a film of pessimistic tenor (Yang, 1966, p. 4).

Presumably in an attempt to have more control over the production of films based on her own fiction, Qiong Yao set up the Firebird Picture Company 火鸟电影公 in 1967. The company, however, was short-lived, churning out only two films before it ceased operation in 1970. Six years later, Qiong Yao established the Superstar (Hong Kong) Motion Picture Company 巨星(香港)电影公司. This time, her company was to produce the last thirteen Qiong Yao films, out of which ten were made by woman director Liu Lili 刘立立.[1] Unlike her male counterparts, Liu Lili was more sensitive to the female touches and sentiments portrayed in Qiong Yao's original stories.

This chapter will investigate a number of Qiong Yao films directed by Liu Lili in the late 1970s and early 1980s, relating them to the discussion of 'women's films' and observing how – from a feminist perspective – the female protagonists of the films display independent agency and subjectivity in building relationships with men. Although the films employ many Qiong Yao-esque generic elements, their narrative structure departs from the conventions and brings women's voices into play in interesting ways. The chapter seeks to explore these questions: To what extent was this emphasis on female agency and subjectivity tied to the industrial and socio-cultural context? How was it articulated, and how did it differ from traditional Confucian values? In discussing such questions, the chapter pays particular attention to two interrelated types of characters: the woman who directly challenges male stereotypes, and the woman who strives to gain greater control in heterosexual relationships. The discussion will make close reference to three Superstar products, *The Wild Goose on the Wing* 雁儿在林梢 (1978), *The Marigolds* 金盏花 (1980) and *Wells Up in My Heart* 却上心头 (1982).

Agency and subjectivity have long been the concern of feminist analysis and have been theorised from multidisciplinary perspectives by scholars. Sherry Ortner (2001) distinguished between two types of agency, 'one of which is closely related to ideas of power, including both domination and resistance, and another that is closely related to ideas of intention, to people's projects in the world and their ability to both formulate and enact them' (p. 78). In this chapter, the 'agency' refers to the latter type, which 'is not necessarily about domination and resistance', but 'about people having desires that grow out of their own structures of life' (p. 81). Female agency in Qiong Yao's work refers to the basic sense of power that every woman has at her disposal, the potential to act on her own behalf and to build (or at least seek to build) her 'own structures of life'. Two roles are especially important, the rescuer and the avenger – women who rescue men from conventional attitudes and/or save them from being lost in an emotional trauma, and women who wreak vengeance on the men who have caused women to suffer.

Film is the product of its time. The production of Qiong Yao films also speaks to the transformations that Taiwan underwent from an agrarian economy to an industrialised society during a span of twenty years, from the early 1960s to the early 1980s. The 1960s was a decade that saw political and ideological conservatism in Taiwan. Confucianism was reinforced by the Kuomintang regime as a means to help strengthen its legitimacy to govern. Within the Confucian-oriented ideology, family constitutes the foundation of society; the harmonious relationships of the family members define appropriate social and cultural behaviour. These relationships are marked by young members respecting the elders and women being inferior to men. Qiong Yao films produced during the decade, either by the state-run Central Motion Pictures Cooperation (CMPC) or the privately-operated Grand Motion Picture Company (GMP), celebrate familial hierarchy and gender distinction. In such men-directed films as *Four Loves* (婉君表妹, 1965) and *The Silent Wife* (哑女情深, 1965) from CMPC, or *Deep in the Mountain* 远山含笑 (1967) and *Love Eternal* (女萝草, 1968) from GMP, the female figures are often confined to inside the home as obedient daughters, faithful wives or/and self-sacrificing mothers. They play supportive and complimentary roles vis-à-vis their male counterparts. Their speech and conduct are governed and regulated by the Confucian principle of 'three obediences and four virtues'.[2]

The cinematic landscape in Taiwan underwent large-scale transformations in the 1970s. The business of the local film industry, especially in the private sector, was organised around a kind of vertical integration. The increase in the vertical integration of distribution and exhibition allowed some distributors to own cinema theatres and possess the power to decide what films were scheduled and for how long. Film companies churned out movies to appeal to the distributors, many of whom were poorly educated businesspeople lacking professional knowledge and sensitivity to market trends. Lack of vision led to lack of innovation, which in turn resulted in an excess of formulaic elements in film production. By the end of the decade, the Taiwan film industry was confronted by several problems, including insufficient investment, challenges from the vigorous Hong Kong film industry and political, social and cultural censorship (Rawnsley, 2016, p. 376). The three main types of local product that had dominated the film business – healthy realism, martial arts and youthful romance – all gradually faded away. The Taiwan film industry was running out of steam and begged for innovation in genre, subject and style.

On the socio-cultural level, despite the fact that Taiwan's overall political environment remained authoritarian and 'highly restrictive' (Ku, 1998) to the women's movement, awareness of feminist thought began to rise. Lü Hsiu-lien's (Annette Lü 吕秀莲) *New Feminism*, first published in 1973, criticised the Confucian-oriented prejudice against women and called for gender equality. Lü also toured university campuses and wrote for local newspapers to promulgate feminist ideas and to raise public awareness of the societal need for gender equality. Lü's commitment to women's self-awareness and self-realisation motivated others, including intellectuals, to join her. After Lü was arrested for undertaking political activities in the late 1970s, Li Yüen-chen 李元贞 and Ku Yenlin 顾燕翎, two like-minded university professors, moved on to launch *Awakening* (妇女新知), a monthly magazine devoted to spreading the ideas of women's 'self-consciousness', 'self-autonomy', 'independence' and 'growth'. The efforts of these pioneers in the autonomous women's movement helped to produce 'recognition of the need to create a gender-equal and gender-neutral Taiwan' (Rubinstein 2004, p. 271).

Therefore, by the time the Superstar Motion Picture Company was set up in 1976, Qiong Yao and her colleagues were confronted by the task of how to cater to the changing tastes of the market, through incorporating innovative elements (including feminist ones) in filmmaking in a novel industrial and socio-cultural context. The Qiong Yao films directed by Liu Lili feature a departure in their portrayal of the heterosexual relationship. This shift is in a sense embodied by substituting the pattern of 'one-woman-and-two-men' for the earlier narrative triangle of 'one-man-and-two-women'. The plotline of the film frequently developed the theme of rescue and salvation, but now the woman was the catalyst. Woman was not only intelligent and independent, but also played the leading role in building a relationship. The leading man usually had a successful career, but also displayed an arrogant personality. He was accompanied by another man suffering from some emotional problems. As the narrative advanced, both men were rejuvenated, thanks to the heroine's brilliance and intelligence. These strong-minded female characters transcended stereotypical roles in the Qiong Yao films of the previous decade.

In discussing the representation of women in the films of the early twentieth century, E. Ann Kaplan writes:

> It is significant that in general the woman's film, by virtue of being a resisting form, shows more sensitivity to social concerns than does the maternal melodrama, which situates itself more firmly in the terrain of unconscious Oedipal needs, fears, and desires. The woman's film on the other hand puts more stress on the cognitive/conscious level, often foregrounding sociological issues and dealing more frequently with social institutions. (Kaplan, 1987, p. 126)

*Wells Up in My Heart* and *The Marigolds* qualify as 'woman's film' for their 'resisting form' and 'sensitivity to social concerns'. Both films begin with the female protagonist being interviewed for a position by her male counterpart. The interviewing sequence is of symbolic meaning. The interviewee eventually manages to transform the interviewer into a 'better man' as the narrative advances. At the start of *Wells Up in My Heart*, Yinglan, the film's leading female character, is interviewed for a secretary's vacancy in a large corporation. On her first day in the company, she encounters Ah Qi, a self-proclaimed low-ranking employee with a cheerful and humorous personality. The two are attracted to each other, and their relationship continues to develop until one day another young man named Zhiwei appears. Zhiwei's arrival exposes Ah Qi's real identity as the youngest son of the general director of the company. He also reveals that the director's family has a tradition of targeting the company's young female secretary as their daughter-in-law. Yinglan feels betrayed and stops the relationship. Ah Qi's repeated attempts to explain and beg for forgiveness are rejected. Over the same period of time, Yinglan encourages Zhiwei, who has been traumatised by a failed relationship, to face reality and walk out of the shadows. At the end of the film, Zhiwei says to Yinglan: 'Thank you for rescuing me from a broken situation.'[3] However, the film's happy ending does not come until Ah Qi and his wealthy family change their attitude to many gender-related issues.

*The Marigolds* starts with Peiyin, the female protagonist, applying for the private tutor position to teach Qian Qian, the sole daughter of Zigeng, an outstanding achiever of high social status. Through tutoring Qian Qian, Peiyin soon comes to see that her pupil's interests (and talents) lie more in gardening and cultivating than in reading and writing. Zigeng, however, thinks otherwise. Conflicts arise between the family patriarch and the governess. Eventually, the father is convinced that it is not helpful to force Qian Qian to continue academic study. In the process, the widowed, middle-aged Zigeng is impressed by Peiyin's sharpness and independent thought, but before he can gain her hand, he must rectify his arrogance. Meanwhile, Peiyin must deal with another admirer named Songchao. When Songchao later falls into the trap set up by a seductive woman, he must rely on Peiyin to rescue him from emotional blackmail and to find him genuine love.

Yinglan from *Wells Up in My Heart* and Peiyin from *The Marigolds* come from working-class families, but they are both situated in a position to control their romantic relationships. They are spiritually strong and financially independent, not submissive to the patriarchal hegemony. 'I may be a nobody. But I have my dignity and my pride', as Yinglan says to Ah Qi in *Wells Up in My Heart*. She cannot accept the latter's dishonesty and believes that she has been treated as 'a shameless material girl'. When Ah Qi begs for forgiveness, she replies: 'This is not a question of forgiven or unforgiven but a matter of mutual respect'. Peiyin in *The Marigolds* also has the power to choose and to take responsibility in gender relations and, through dealing with the two men close to her, shows vision and perception. She not only successfully makes Zigeng, a noted solicitor in town, realise and rectify his pride and prejudice against women, but also facilitates Songchao's coming of age. The filmmaker's identification with Peiyin is revealed in the following exchange:

> Peiyin: What do you want your daughter to be like?
> Zigeng: Like you.
> Peiyin: What's good about me?
> Zigeng: You're independent and strong-willed. You're knowledgeable. You're eloquent in speech and quick in reaction. You're good at using one single case to bring out its bearings.

In the two films, the code of sexuality is associated with mutual respect and an equal relationship between the sexes. Instead of playing supportive and complementary roles vis-à-vis their male counterparts, the young women protagonists see no contradiction between 'romance' and 'career'. While building heterosexual relationships with men, each manages to create 'a place of her own'.[4]

Female agency is also central to *The Wild Goose on the Wing*, a film about a 'lady avenger'. Dan Feng is a graduate student majoring in drama at a British university. She learns from Jiang Huai, her would-be brother-in-law, that her elder sister has died of a heart attack. Upon graduation, Dan Feng returns to Taipei, suspecting that the real reason for her sister's death has been Jiang Huai's affair with another woman. She embarks on a revenge plot to seduce Jiang Huai. Meanwhile, she approaches Jiang Hao, Jiang Huai's younger brother, and dates him in the guise of Xiao Shuang. The film thus develops a plot hinging on the double identity of the woman. Xiao Shuang comes to appear in Jiang Hao's life, acting the part of a worry-free, tomboyish teenager, who instantly attracts the latter's attention. Each encounter draws Jiang Hao deeper into the relationship; and after each meeting Xiao Shuang mysteriously disappears from his life for a few days (during which time she is with Jiang Huai as Dan Feng, which drives Hao crazy). Her playing of this cat-and-mouse game is subtly expressed in a 'fishing' scene, where she is overwhelmed by the joy of catching a fish. (The scene is reminiscent of Audrey Hepburn fishing on a barge on the Seine in Stanley Donen's 1957 film *Funny Face*.) In the midst of her elation, she purposefully falls into the river. As she stays behind a rock to change her clothes, she warns Jiang Hao not to come closer. But she then bursts into screams, pretending that she sees a snake. Such experiences make the puzzled but fascinated Jiang Hao describe his newly acquainted girlfriend to his elder brother as 'a mixture of angel and devil' and 'the most dangerous animal in the world'.

There is a similar complexity to the character of Dan Feng, who also embodies a compromise of plainness and purity that finds an expression in many other female leads of Qiong Yao films directed by men. The film's pre-title sequence was allegedly influenced by Maya Deren's experimental *Meshes of the Afternoon* (1943) in setting up a dreamlike or nightmarish atmosphere. Sitting on a sofa shrouded by dim light, Dan Feng slowly turns the pages of a family album, cigarette in hand. She takes a drag, and a veil-like waft of smoke surrounds her, as if burying her in deep memories of the past. A number of point-of-view close-up shots of the album show the good relationship of the two sisters and their happy moments together, emphasised by the voice-over narration. This interior night scene then cuts to an exterior daytime sequence that shows Jiang Huai walking towards his car parked on the street. As he opens the door and sits in front of the wheel, some non-diegetic, sinister-sounding music is heard. All of a sudden, Jiang Huai sees, through the side mirror, a mysterious woman standing on the pedestrian walkway dressed in black from head to foot. He turns to look closer, but the woman has vanished. This enigmatic appearance-and-disappearance pattern, accompanied by the same menacing music, is repeated until the film's title comes up. A woman's revenge story is just about to unfold.

On one occasion in the film, Jiang Huai says to Dan Feng: 'I have never met such a tough woman in my life as you!' He continues: 'In a twinkle of eyes, you can change from a European black angel to a wild goose on the wing. You are such a changeable fairy spirit. Every time you change, you make me feel breathless'. The noir-ish atmosphere and the *femme fatale*-style deception in *The Wild Goose on the Wing* were admittedly unusual in Qiong Yao films. The film's narrative unfolds entirely from Dan Feng/Xiao Shuang's perspective. The heroine's ability to plot and to put her plans into action challenges the conventional gender (power) relationships. She is by no means an innocent 'fairy' or a 'goddess' unaware of sex and sexuality. As Dan Feng, and Xiao Shuang alike, she consciously employs femininity and sexuality as the means to challenge patriarchal power, by attracting men and then 'destroying' them.

The two roles of Xiao Shuang and Dan Feng in *The Wild Goose on the Wing* were played by Brigitte Lin Ching Hsia 林青霞. The eighteen-year-long popularity of the Qiong Yao films contributed several top stars to Chinese cinema, including Tang Baoyun 唐宝云, Wang Mochou 王莫愁, Zhen Zhen 珍甄, Gui Yalei 归亚蕾 and the 'two Chins and two Lins' 二秦二林 – namely Chin Han 秦汉, Chin Hsiang-lin 秦祥林, Lin Ching Hsia and Lin Fengjiao 林凤娇. Among these stars, Brigitte Lin was not only the most bankable but also the most noted one. She starred in one hundred films made in Taiwan (1970s/1980s) and Hong Kong (1980s/1990s). Lin was selected as the 'Filmmaker in Focus' by the 42nd Hong Kong International Film Festival in 2018. A special catalogue was also compiled by the Film Festival, which describes Lin as 'a key figure in the surging international popularity of Hong Kong cinema, earning acclaim for her stunning charisma and genderbending roles in dazzling *wuxia pian*' (Hong Kong International Film Festival Society, 2018, p. 123). The star's performance of gender-bending roles did not begin with *The Wild Goose on the Wing* and can be traced back to the 1977 Shaw Brothers' film *The Dream of the Red Chamber* 红楼梦 directed by Li Han-xiang 李翰祥. Brigitte Lin's ability to straddle two personalities with different mental qualities, as embodied in *The Wild Goose on the Wing*, suggests the multiple dimensions of femininity, which in turn reinforces a more complex approach to representations of women in the romantic drama genre in general and in Qiong Yao films in particular.

The popularity of Lin's films, with their strong-minded, unyielding female characters, is evidence of the changing attitudes to gender in Taiwan between the 1950s and the 1970s. Christian Metz remarks that cinema is an institution for the commodification of desire. The audience's desire to see the star image is the result of the 'perceptual passions' of narcissism, voyeurism and fetishism (1982, p. 58). Viewers gaze at the stars, desiring to relate to them through a process of identification. It is universally acknowledged that Lin's beauty was multidimensional, combining tradition and modernity, purity and sexuality (Hu, 2019, p. 64). Her physical attributes shaped her personality, which associated her with a specific kind of character in Taiwan romantic *wenyi* films. Different parts of her body, such as her black shoulder-length hair and her pure and innocent eyes, were given 'magic' qualities that produced different connotations among different groups of audiences. While female factory workers regarded her on-screen persona as a source of encouragement and inspiration, teenage students gained emotional satisfaction and a sense of beauty from the numerous romances in which she starred. Whereas conventional spectators consumed her beauty as an object to be gazed at, women with an awareness of feminist issues were struck by the intensity of the female agency and subjectivity in her screen roles. In Rawnsley's words, Brigitte Lin's stardom was closely associated with how Qiong Yao films were perceived and consumed (2014, p. 201).

The shifted representation of women and gender in the Qiong Yao films directed by Liu Lili both reflected social change and helped to encourage it. The films spotlighted – in Irina Makoveeva's words – 'a kind of awakening of female agency as a crucial moment in a woman's existence' (2017, p. 46). These films did not portray women's heterosexual relationships being complicated by parental pressures; neither did they delineate 'home' as an 'extension of the fatherland', an arena for the 'the rigidity of the fathers' law' and 'the saintliness of the mothers' (López, 1994, p. 260). The female protagonist now found herself in a position to take control of the pace and rhythm of gender relationships. In doing this, she was no longer the man's responsibility but her own. This construction of female agency embodied new forms of power and ways of relating to men.

It should be noted, however, that there are still conventional aspects to the portrayal of woman and romance in the Qiong Yao films of the Superstar era. The conventional view of female beauty still emphasises their physical attractiveness to men, their fair complexions and shapely bodies. Their identity remains limited to heterosexual relationships and, not infrequently, their stories lead to a traditional/conventional kind of happy ending. The young heroines of Qiong Yao films may have left behind the patriarchal definition of their roles as submissive and self-sacrificing, but they still embody contradictions as both the subject and the object of the gaze. Nevertheless, as the present chapter has shown, the generic codes and norms of Qiong Yao films underwent changes alongside situational shifts. Early Qiong Yao films of the 1960s incorporated qualities of self-sacrifice and submissiveness as the traditional signs of idealised femininity. But in the novel context of an increasing awareness of women's consciousness in an industrialised society of the late 1970s and early 1980s, producer Qiong Yao and director Liu Lili brought an innovative approach to popular culture, extending the range of the romance and the 'woman's film'.

Like other Qiong Yao films, the Superstar products were mainly addressed to female audiences and mostly driven by women's interests, dreams and desires. Unlike the earlier work by the male directors, these 'women's films' since the late 1970s opened the door to a variety of new possibilities. Other directors – both male and female – were quick to take them up, and the new perspectives on gender were to be carried to a further stage in Taiwan cinema. In the same year that Superstar produced the last Qiong Yao film, *Last Night Light* 昨日之灯, Taiwan New Cinema director Edward Yang 杨德昌 directed *That Day, On the Beach* 海滩的一天 (1983), a film about the problems that modern women experience in marriage. The next few years saw a series of local films tackling woman/gender-related issues from a more critical perspective. To a large extent, these films, such as *Ah Fei* 油麻菜籽 (1984), *Madam Yu Ching* 玉卿嫂 (1984), *My Favourite Season* 最想念的季节 (1985) and *Kuei Mei, A Woman* 我这样过了一生 (1985), mark a drastic departure from the dreamlike love. The women images portrayed in these films fostered realism rather than glitz and glamour. Collectively, these 'new wave' films removed their central female characters from romantic relationships, illusionary or otherwise, and reflected in a thought-provoking way the experience of women in contemporary Taiwan society. While the screen appearance of 'new women' proclaimed the beginning of a new phase in delineating gender roles in Taiwanese films, its presence was in a sense pioneered by the representation of the agency and subjectivity of the female protagonists in a number of Qiong Yao films of the late 1970s and early 1980s.

## References

Hong Kong International Film Festival Society. (2018). *The 42nd Hong Kong International Film Festival catalogue*. Hong Kong.

Hu, J. 胡晴舫. (2019). She defined 'super movie star' (她定义了"电影巨星"). In Li Zhuotao 李焯桃 and Chen Zhihua 陈志华 (eds), *Brigitte Lin, Filmmaker in Focus* 云外笑红尘 (pp. 64–67). Hong Kong: Hong Kong International Film Festival.

Kaplan, E. A. (1987). Mothering, feminism and representation: The maternal in melodrama and the woman's film 1910–40. In C. Gledhill (ed.), *Home is where the heart is: Studies in melodrama and the woman's film* (pp. 113–37). London: British Film Institute.

Ku, Y. (1998). Selling a feminist agenda on a conservative market: The Awakening experience in Taiwan. *Yam Women Web*. Retrieved from http://taiwan.yam.org.tw/womenweb/sell.htm

Li, T. 李天铎 (1997). *Taiwan cinema: Society and history* 台湾电影, 社会与历史. Taipei: Yatai tushu chubanshe.

López, A. (1994). Tears and desires: Women and melodrama in the 'old' Mexican cinema. In D. Carson, L. Dittmar, and J. Welsch (eds), *Multiple voices in feminist film criticism* (pp. 254–70). Minneapolis: University of Minnesota Press.

Makoveeva, I. (2017). Female agency in Svetlana Proskurina's *Remote access* (2004) and Vera Storozheva's *Travelling with pets* (2007). *Studies in Russian and Soviet cinema*, 11(1), 38–55.

Metz, C. (1982). *Psychoanalysis and cinema: The imaginary signifier*. Basingstoke: Macmillan.

Ortner, S. (2001). Specifying agency: The Comaroffs and their critics. *Interventions*, 3(1), 76–84.

Qi, L. 齐隆壬. (1996). The historical re-presentation of Qiong Yao film genre in the 1970s Taiwan 七零年代台湾琼瑶电影类型的历史再现. In Liu Xiancheng 刘现成 (ed.), *Chinese cinema: History, culture and re-presentation* 中国电影：历史、文化与再现 (pp. 159–69). Taibei: Taibeishi zhongguo dianying shiliao yanjiuhui.

Qiong, Y. 琼瑶. (1966, 9 May). On fiction and its filmic adaptation: The case of *Love in spring* 谈小说与改编电影 – 从《花落谁家》谈起. *United Daily* 联合报, p. 9.

Rawnsley, M. (2014). Stars as production: A case study of Brigitte Lin. In W. Leung and A. Willis (eds), *East Asian film stars* (pp. 190–204). Basingstoke-New York: Palgrave Macmillan.

Rawnsley, M. (2016). Cultural democratization and Taiwan cinema. In S. Gunter (ed.), *Routledge handbook of contemporary Taiwan* (pp. 373–88). London: Routledge.

Rubinstein, M. (2004). Lu Hsiu-lien and the origins of Taiwanese feminism, 1944–1977. In C. Farris, A. Lee, and M. Rubinstein (eds), *Women in the new Taiwan: Gender roles and gender consciousness in a changing society* (pp. 244–77). New York-London: M. E. Sharpe.

Udden, J. (2009). *No man is an island: The cinema of Hou Hsiao-hsien*. Hong Kong: Hong Kong University Press.

Yang, Y. 羊瑜. (1966, May 21). An artistic debate on film *Love in spring* 《花落谁家》艺术论战. *United Weekly* 联合周刊, p. 4.

# Notes

1. The shift to a male perspective is even visible in *Up to Rainbow*, also known as *Love Affair of Rainbow* 奔向彩虹 (1977), a product of her own company, but directed by male director Gao Shanlan 高山岚. In Qiong Yao's novel, the heroine was a country flower woman who was reluctant to be an object of the male gaze and sought to subvert the idealised, traditional Chinese image of woman. She went to the city to pursue self-reliance. In the adapted film, however, she was portrayed as little more than a beauty queen with a narrow mind. She became attracted by the urban glamour and sophistication and was eager to achieve Material success in her career as a fashion model. She ended up catering to the patriarchy and the established system.
2. The three obediences required a woman to be obedient to her father before marriage, to her husband after marriage and to her son in the case of the husband's death. The four virtues established the criteria that a woman was required to

meet in order to be called 'virtuous'. The virtues were morality, proper speech, a modest manner and diligence.
3. All exchanges taken from the films are my translations.
4. 'A place of one's own' (自己的天空) is an influential short-story by Taiwan woman writer Yuan Qiongqiong 袁瓊瓊. First published in 1980, the story narrates how a woman is betrayed by her husband for failing to bear him a (male) child and then gets divorced. The divorce turns her into an independent and successful businesswoman, who then develops a successful relationship with another man. The story has been read by many as an index of the social changes and the rise of feminism taking place in Taiwanese society at the time.

PART II

# CREATIVE LABOUR

Chapter 7

# Japanese Documentary Filmmaker Haneda Sumiko: Authorship and Gender Perspective[1]

*Alejandra Armendáriz-Hernández, Marcos Centeno-Martin and Irene González-López*

While Japanese cinema has inspired a vast amount of literature in the past half a century, women's contributions have yet to receive the attention they deserve. It is only in recent years that we are witnessing a growing academic and popular interest in the works of female Japanese filmmakers (González-López and Smith, 2018; Ikegawa, 2011; Laird, 2013).[2] There have been a limited number of women in positions of power within the industry, but another reason for this disregard is related to the fact that many women work outside the mainstream in fiction production – namely, in documentary which has traditionally been neglected by scholarly enquiry. Although Japan has one of the most important legacies of non-fiction filmmaking in the world (Murayama, 2010, p. 242), it is only in recent years that there have been serious attempts to explore the value of this enormous film culture (Centeno-Martin and Raine, 2021; Junpei, 2011; Murayama, 2010; Niwa and Yoshimi, 2012; Nornes, 2003). This chapter sheds light on women's contribution to Japanese documentary cinema by examining the work of Haneda Sumiko[3] (1926–), a pioneering female director whose trailblazing oeuvre remains hugely disregarded outside Japan. It examines Haneda's contribution to the development of new approaches to documentary filmmaking in post-war Japan in its intersection with women's cinema. It shows that her heterogeneous filmography defies categorisation but exhibits a sustained concern with the representation of women and gender dynamics. Also drawing on Haneda's writings and interviews, the following explores her approaches to authorship and to labels related to female authorship, complicating the use of the term 'women's cinema'.

## Becoming a Documentary Director: Early Inspirations at Iwanami

Haneda was born in 1926 in Dalian, in Northeast China. Between 1942 and 1945, she studied in Tokyo at the renowned Jiyū Gakuen [literally

'Freedom School'], a Christian school that provided an alternative education with emphasis on the arts. Under the recommendation of her teacher, Hani Etsuko – the daughter of Hani Motoko, the founder of the school and considered Japan's first female journalist, as well as the mother of director Hani Susumu – in 1950 Haneda joined Iwanami Productions (Iwanami Eiga Seisakusho), which became a sort of film school (Centeno-Martin, 2019b, 2021) for some of the leading figures of the post-war documentary scene. In Iwanami, Haneda was mostly influenced by two figures, Yoshino Keiji and Hani Susumu. Yoshino, the most veteran filmmaker at Iwanami, trained the young members of the company to make films with the scarce resources available, shooting on location with a reduced team of three people, and promoted a flexible environment where some filmmakers were quickly promoted without enduring the traditional extended training period (Haneda, 2014, p. 9). Impressed by Haneda's script for the short film *Ha* (*Tooth*, 1953), Yoshino invited Haneda to work as assistant director for Masuzawa Toshio (Haneda, 2014, p. 12). It was, however, the experience of working as Hani's assistant director in *Children in the Classroom* (*Kyōshitsu no kodomotachi*, 1954) that constituted a major turning point in her career (Haneda, 2014, p. 12). Commissioned by the Ministry of Education, the film was intended to showcase how education had changed after the war, but the resulting documentary instead concentrated on children's psychology and attempted to reveal their inner emotional world. At the time Hani was theorising about a new documentary method (Centeno-Martin, 2018, 2019a) based on filming 'protagonists who do not act' such as children and animals, rejecting impositions from scripts and montage (Hani, 1958), through patient observation (Hani, 1961a, 1961b), as well as technical asceticism and long takes (Hani, 1958), in order to explore the subjectivity of the characters filmed before the camera and to minimise the control of the filmmaker (Hani, 1959). Many of these ideas were tested in *Children in the Classroom*. To that end, the crew used a light 16mm Arriflex camera and telephoto lens to instantly capture spontaneous actions with the least possible interference. Rather than hiding the camera, they decided to make it visible. Since the equipment of the time was very noisy, Haneda made a cover from a futon, filled with cotton, to soundproof the camera. While at first the children were very excited about the cinematic apparatus, they quickly became familiar with it. In this way, Hani and Haneda devised a method to capture children's spontaneous behaviour, by moving the camera closer to the characters' world rather than moving the camera away.

## *Women's College in the Village*: Adding a Gendered Approach to Iwanami Filmmaking?

Haneda's first work as director was *Women's College in the Village* (*Mura no fujin gakkyū*, 1957), which was commissioned by the Ministry of Education; the ministry's Social Education Section was focused on promoting 'social education films' (*shakai kyōiku eiga*) on women's topics and particularly those concerned with rural areas. According to Haneda, villages still maintained feudal structures where peasants were subjugated by large landowners. In this environment, the most oppressed group were women. The Social Education Section designed a policy to improve their situation by creating 15,000 female schools and community centres across the country (Haneda, 2012, p. 241) and *Women's College in the Village* focuses on one of them.

Initially, Haneda was assigned as scriptwriter, and she chose Iwane village in Shiga prefecture, where women were very active in arranging activities. After reading her script, Yoshino suggested that she also direct the film (Haneda, 2014, p. 15). According to Haneda, this was a surprising decision, as the gender gap and sexism were widespread in the sector at the time, to the extent where it was unthinkable for a woman to become a director (Haneda, 2012, p. 242). However, the ministry's promotion of films on 'women's topics' created a favourable environment, and another woman, Tokieda Toshie, was also promoted to director a few months later to make *Town Politics: Mothers Who Study* (*Mura no seiji*, 1957). While it is quite remarkable that Iwanami promoted two young women to directors in the 1950s, no more female directors emerged from the company once the ministry stopped commissioning this kind of film. As Haneda noted, during the subsequent years, Iwanami increased its production of *PR eiga* ('PR films') sponsored by the leading sectors of economic growth, focusing on dams and factories, which were not regarded as appropriate topics to be depicted by women (Haneda, 2014, p. 16).

The shooting of *Women's College in the Village* started in January 1957. Haneda travelled to Iwane village with only one camera-person, Omura Shizuo, and producer Kudō Mitsuru, the person in charge of educational films at the ministry's Social Education Section – he became Haneda's husband five years later. Iwane exhibited strong patriarchal structures. The crew not only asked the mayor's permission, but also had to obtain consent from the women's families for the individual women to feature in the documentary (Haneda, 2014, p. 17). Once access was granted, Haneda managed to present this community from an innovative gendered perspective, by focusing on women's anxieties and dreams. What she filmed were not formal classes, but sessions in which women collectively discussed their concerns as mothers and their relationship to their children. This was a new documentary approach through which Haneda combined Yoshino's technical aestheticism with Hani's exploration of the protagonists' subjectivity that was allegedly not controlled by the filmmaker. Haneda claimed that, to do so, 'filming people and filmed people must establish a relationship of mutual confidence [. . .] Then, they reveal something that they have in their hearts' (2014, p. 20). To that end, the crew spent fifty days living in the village to familiarise themselves with the community and to develop a close relationship with the women attending the school. For instance, the crew would have meals with the women regularly, used their car to take the women to town when necessary and, after completing the film, Haneda continued corresponding with the women of the village for decades and visited the area several times (Haneda, 2012, pp. 246–51).

For Haneda, this was a kind of documentary grounded in strong interactions, through which filmmakers would impact the filmed people and the protagonists would also impact the filmmaker (Haneda, 2012, p. 251). A solid relationship of mutual trust allowed documentary film to become a tool for social change. Haneda recalls realising that through her films she could contribute to changing the 'feudal' mindset that oppressed women in Japan and proudly believed that the experience of participating in her documentary had had a life-changing impact on the women of Iwane (Haneda, 2002, p. 28). Even if Haneda acknowledged that such a close relationship was never reached in the subsequent documentaries (Haneda, 2012, p. 252), this closeness to female protagonists became a characteristic trait of many of her subsequent documentaries, as further explored in the following section.

To a certain extent, *Women's College in the Village* shows women's activities as requested by the ministry, but Haneda devotes most of the film to exploring characters' concerns and inner world (Figures 7.1a and 7.1b). While Hani used drawings and other creative works as gateways to access children's emotional universe, Haneda uses children's writings. In one scene, children are asked to write about their mothers in the classroom. These essays are distributed to their mothers in the women's college. The viewer hears the writings through the children's voice-overs which emphasise the bond between mother and child and heighten the emotional aspect of the sequence. Then, mothers talk about their feelings and worries after reading about their children's thoughts. Haneda's goal in dealing with the characters' emotional universe is also showing how

Figures 7.1a–b *Women's College in the Village* (screenshots). Copyright held by Kiroku Eiga Hozon Center

this inner world may change (Haneda, 2012, p. 246). To that end, she focuses on the relationship between a mother, Sonoda Sae, and her son. The first sequences depict the son giving Sonoda the silent treatment and show her still expression, followed by a scene in which the son gets angry at his parents at home. Sonoda gradually opens up in the session at the women's college, and the last sequence of the film features her and her son piling up wood together in the forest; on the way home, the boy cheerfully chats with his mother who at last smiles on screen.

This filmmaking method required close observation, during which Haneda follows Yoshino's approach and refuses the idea of 'directing' (*kanto*) according to a script, claiming instead to only 'produce' (*enshutsu*) the film (Haneda, 2012, p. 239). However, this method had inherent limitations. According to Haneda, she avoided imposing anything on characters and rather suggested topics to talk about (Haneda, 2012, p. 246). But even in observational proposals such as this, as opposed to the 'performative documentary' that emphasises its constructedness (Bruzzi, 2000, pp. 153–80), or the 'self-reflexive' documentary that points to its own process of production (Allen, 1991, p. 37), there are certain impositions that are given by the cinematic structure, such as editing and voice-over, as well as the mere presence of the filmmaker in the scene. This issue has been widely discussed over the past thirty years, in fields from visual anthropology over ethnography to newsreels and documentary studies, in relation to ethics, subjectivity, the filmmaker's responsibility, truthfulness and verisimilitude in non-fiction (Eitzen, 1995; MacDougall, 1992; Nichols, 2001). These critical contributions are helpful for understanding that even the documentary school that was being created at Iwanami was not completely free from any filmmaker's intervention. Haneda films situations that might have been proposed by her, and no one can assure that the actions she captures would have taken place had the crew not been there. Furthermore, Haneda gives meaning to those actions through editing. For instance, the selection and montage of shots in the closing sequence featuring Sonoda and her son recovering their relationship allows Haneda to give closure to a narrative with a sense of cinematic denouement (Figures 7.2a and 7.2b).

Haneda experienced other kinds of technical and personal difficulties in implementing this new documentary method, which required long takes so that meaning was mainly produced out of the shooting process rather than the montage. However, Haneda met the opposition of camera-person Omura, who, instead of cutting at forty seconds, as she had requested, systematically cut at a maximum of ten or twelve seconds (Haneda, 2014). Additionally, while Omura compromised with Hani in the usage of the light Arriflex, this time he insisted (against Haneda's will) on using a heavy 35mm Michele camera, which made it difficult to work on location, move quickly, shoot in reduced spaces and capture improvised actions. Finally, while Hani's film focused on children, Haneda's film required working with adult women whose spontaneous emotions were more difficult to capture (Haneda, 2014, p. 17). *Women's College in the Village* bears witness to the challenges that Haneda faced in trying to elaborate on the new approaches to documentary emerging from Iwanami. It also reflects her understanding of documentary film as a tool to address social issues, her concern with building solid relationships of trust with her subjects, her critical approach to gender dynamics and her interest in a vanishing Japan. All these elements would feature prominently throughout her career, and in the next section we

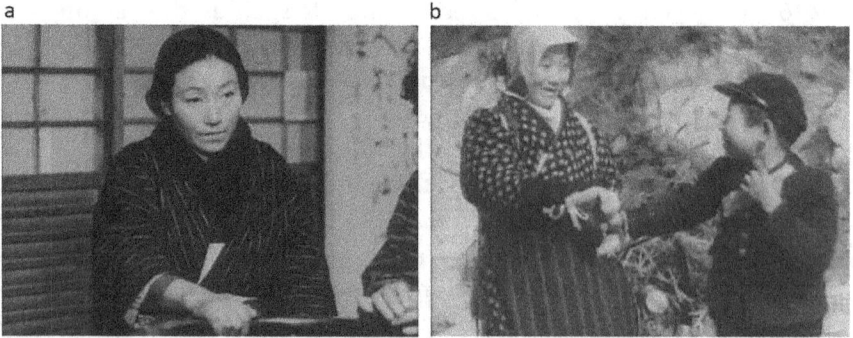

Figure 7.2a Sonoda Sae reading her child's letter (screenshot). Copyright held by Kiroku Eiga Hozon Center

Figure 7.2b Sonoda with her child in the closing sequence (screenshot). Copyright held by Kiroku Eiga Hozon Center

will explore how they intersect in her depiction of gender in an attempt to situate Haneda in relation to women's cinema.

## Female Authorship and Subjectivity in Haneda's Cinema

While at Iwanami, Haneda worked on approximately eighty documentaries (including those in which she was scriptwriter and/or assistant) until reaching the age of fifty-five – the mandatory retirement age for women in the company – in 1981. As if reacting against the restrictions in choosing projects at Iwanami, her first film as independent filmmaker was the experimental *Cherry Tree with Gray Blossoms* (*Usuzumi no sakura*, 1977), a mixture of social documentary and poetic art film. Since then she has worked hand in hand with her husband, the producer Kudō Mitsuru, and directed over fifteen film projects, most of them produced by their company Jiyū Kōbō ('Freedom Studio'). She has also received numerous awards, including the Education Minister's Fine Arts Award for *Ode to Mt Hayachine* (*Hayachine no hu*, 1982), becoming the first female director to win this prestigious award. Her documentary *And Then Akiko is . . . A Portrait of a Dancer* (*Soshite Akiko wa . . . aru dansā no shōzō*, 2012), directed at the age of eighty-six, stands as a testimony to her extraordinary energy and productivity.

Her filmography is extremely diverse, ranging from education films, PR films and documentaries on social issues, to science films, biographical documentaries, experimental artistic films and historical documentaries. Working in both cinema and television, she has made documentaries about Japanese traditional arts and creators, ageing society and care, the postwar disintegration of rural Japan, and social and political movements, among many other subjects. Her aesthetic style is as varied as her subjects, ranging from pragmatic austere productions of relative technical simplicity to highly sophisticated and innovative productions that challenge orthodox definitions of documentary, such as *Cherry Tree with Gray Blossoms* and *Into the Picture Scroll – The Tale of Yamanaka Tokiwa* (*Yamanaka Tokiwa*, 2004). This heterogeneity prevents generalisations about her cinema. It also distances her from the notion of the *auteur*, which is so central to the development of Japanese Film Studies; and this could partially explain why her work has often been disregarded in academia.

We argue that this diversity bears witness to Haneda's ability to adapt to different production contexts. Rather than in consistent stylistic traits, Haneda's authorial vision can be perceived in her approach to her subjects (and the ethical decisions that this entails) and through the material imprint of her persona in many of her films. Female protagonists occupy an important (albeit not completely dominant) place in her filmography. The involvement of women in the production, distribution and consumption of her films connects her work to women's cinema, which can be defined as 'films that might be made by, addressed to, or concerned with women, or all three' (Butler, 2002, pp. 19–20). Women's cinema is a contested term for its ambiguous and multiple definitions; its historical limitations as a prescriptive concept focused on certain Western understandings of feminism, authorship and cinema-viewing; and its potential threat of essentialising and pigeonholing films made by women. Nevertheless, it remains a fruitful site of debate where feminist theories and cinema practices are incessantly contested and from where critical interventions emerge (Butler, 2002; Wang, 2011; White, 2015). Authorship, which also remains a controversial subject, is of great importance to feminist film theories and to the notion of women's cinema, which is often associated with a cohesive and consistent authorial vision. In the following pages, we analyse Haneda's depiction of women and female subjectivity to shed light on her negotiation of establishing an authorial vision and foregrounding her subjects' voice, contextualising her work within women's cinema to then reflect on the limitations of this framework in defining Haneda's voice as filmmaker.

In depicting women as individuals and communities, Haneda often employs a biographical perspective through which to examine the everyday experiences, achievements and challenges of women in Japanese society. For instance, sharing the collective approach to women's lives of *Women's College in the Village*, the later *Women's Testimony: Pioneer Women in Labour Movement* (*Onnatachi no shōgen – rōdō undō no naka no senkuteki joseitachi*, 1996) explores the participation of women in the labour movement in Japan. Haneda also directed films centred on the life of exceptional women, such as the feminist Hiratsuka Raicho (*In the Beginning, Woman was the Sun: The Life of Hiratsuka Raicho* [*Genshi josei wa taiyō de atta – Hiratsuka Raichō no shōgai*], 2001) and the celebrated dancer Akiko Kanda (*Akiko – Portrait of a Dancer* [*Akiko – aru dansā no shōzō*], 1985, as well as the above-mentioned *And Then Akiko is*).

These films celebrate women's work, creativity and struggles, making a case for their recognition in the social history of Japan. In this regard, it can be argued that Haneda employs the biographical genre as a tool for women's history, leaving a visual trace of their bodies and everyday lives, preserving their stories and their commitment to arts and politics in the history of Japan. Haneda's depiction of women as historical subjects goes beyond their public persona, their body as spectacle, or their political cause to focus on their 'being in the world'. As Eric Cazdyn points out in reference to *Women's Testimony*, . . .

> [. . . t]he female body here does not allegorize anything; it is not appropriated in order to rethink labor history or present the women's movement. Instead, the representation is about the women themselves – women who are in front of the camera and who are the film. (Cazdyn, 2002. p. 260)

While Haneda has filmed women of all ages, the teenage girl (*shōjo*) occupies a central position in several of her films, as an autonomous character who guides the narrative. For example, her last documentary at Iwanami, *Dedicated Treasures of Horyuji-Temple* (*Hōryūji ken'nō hōmotsu*, 1971), which was commissioned to showcase the ancient artefacts displayed at the Tokyo National Museum, is structured around the presence of a teenage girl with a white blouse who gives a glaring look. Reflecting the production dynamics behind this educational film, as well as the gendered construction of knowledge regarding art and history, Haneda presents a double, gendered narrative. On the one hand, there is a male disembodied voice-over performing the typical 'voice of god' of the expository mode of documentary that narrates the official history of the artefacts. On the other hand, the film also features a female voice-over reading poetry and imagining how the original users of those objects felt and thought of them. Interspersed moving and still images of the girl observing the treasures and walking outdoors seem to suggest that it is her inner voice that we hear. In this way, the girl's presence evokes a feeling of timelessness, which unites us, the audience, with the past featured in the objects. Most importantly, on several occasions, the female voice takes over and silences the male voice, privileging the subjective knowledge and holistic engagement with art and history over the official (allegedly objective) history.

The female voices and the trope of the girl as an embodied meaning-construction technique was developed even further in *The Cherry Tree with Gray Blossoms*. In the film, a high-school girl recurrently appears and stares into the camera, sometimes inquisitively, other times reflexively, and yet other times distractedly as she freely moves through the rural landscape. A montage sequence introduces her, starting with the concatenation of three shots with a fixed camera of her in profile; the frame becomes tighter with each shot. The girl then looks back at the viewer as she sighs in a close-up. This shot is repeated twice and then again in a wider frame. This composition, used instead of a regular zooming in, may appear to objectify the girl into fragmented shots but,

116  Armendáriz-Hernández, Centeno-Martin and González-López

instead, it grants her a magnetic, empowering aura that arouses our curiosity, without any of the stereotypical sexualisation of the trope of the teenage girl (Figures 7.3a to 7.3d).

Her engaging gaze is combined with two female voice-overs that guide the viewer through the film, partially resembling the dichotomy played out in *Dedicated Treasures*. One of the female voices is typical of Japanese TV documentaries. It explains facts and customs relating to the magnificent tree, while the other is a husky and mysterious voice that speaks of the spiritual and transcendental questions that the long-standing cherry tree inspires. Together they conjure overlaying dimensions in which the tree simultaneously operates for those surrounding it, and they also bring into conversation different constructions of femininity operating in the popular imaginary.

The recurrent use of female voice-overs in Haneda's films increasingly became authorial inscriptions. As Haneda herself explains, 'I usually write the narrator's part, but I often asked another person to record it. However, recently I record it myself when I feel it's a film where I should use my own voice to express my thoughts' (in Kaneko, 2013). This (selective) urge to leave a material imprint of authorship and to

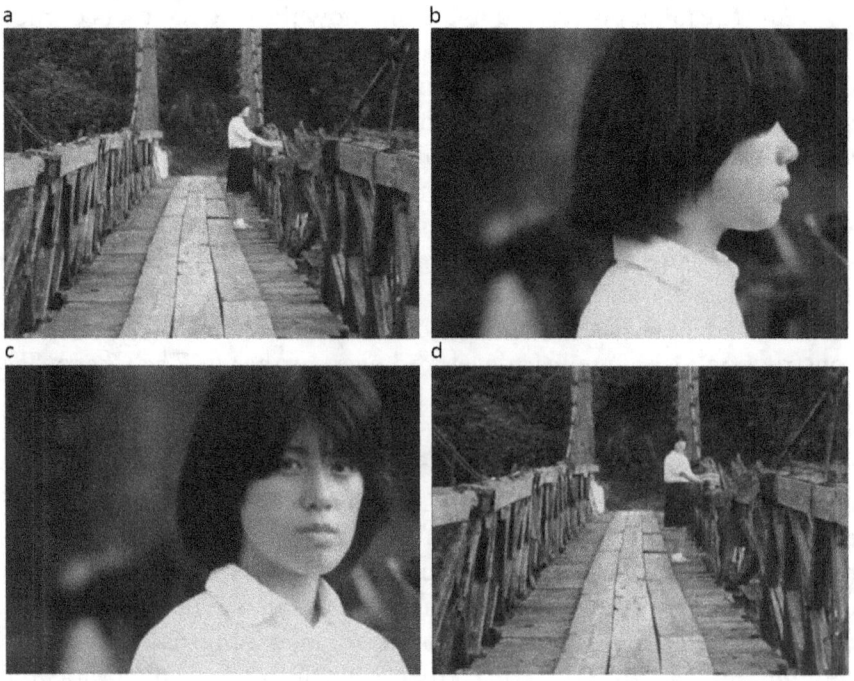

Figures 7.3a–d *The Cherry Tree with Gray Blossoms* (screenshots)

take responsibility for them is also visually highlighted in Haneda being featured at work in many of her films. For instance, in *The Life of Hiratsuka Raicho* she is shown searching for Raichō in old pictures (Figure 7.4), and in the beginning of *Women's Testimony*, she is filmed editing, while her voice-over explains the purpose of the material that we are about to watch (Figure 7.5). In this way, Haneda not only asserts her position behind the camera as filmmaker, but also shows the audience her personal engagement with the topics and the individuals she films.

Haneda's above-mentioned will to 'produce' (instead of 'direct') films where the subjects can take control over the narrative, as well as her commitment to building close relationships with her filmed subjects who are or become her own friends, remained unchanged throughout her career, because she believed that this intimacy was critical to depicting their inner universe. As an independent director, however, she increasingly chose themes that intersected with, and even reflected, her biographical persona. In fact, personal circumstances and connections are often there from the outset. For instance, Haneda was taking care of her elderly mother at home while filming the first part of the documentary on the elderly care system, *Welfare System Chosen by Residents in a Township* (*Jūmin ga sentaku shita machi no fukushi*, 1997) (Hori, 2011, p. 116). In another example, following her first documentary on Kanda (1985), Haneda and Kudō attended each of her new dance shows. The making of her second documentary on Kanda (2012), however, was triggered by her desire to record an opening show for her husband, who was sick and could not attend the event. Only after gathering some material did Haneda discover that Akiko was dying of cancer and reworked this project into a documentary (Haneda, 2014, pp. 115–16). In one of her latest documentaries, *Far-Away Home: Lushun and Dalian* (*Haruka naru*

Figure 7.4 *The Life of Hiratsuka Raicho* (screenshot)

Figure 7.5 *Women's Testimony* (screenshot)

*furusato: Ryojun Dairen*, 2011), Haneda returned to the town where she was born, Dalian, and visited the places where she grew up. This shift evidences not only Haneda's freedom as an independent filmmaker, but also a diversion from Hani's method, by establishing a candid dialogue with her subjects to reveal their inner universe in their own terms without denying but in fact stressing her control over the film.

Haneda's filmmaking methods and her personal involvement with her subjects are by no means limited to women; for example, she made a six-part documentary on kabuki actor Nizaemon Kataoka, *Kabuki yakusha Kataoka Nizaemon*, 1992–94. Nevertheless, given the invisibility of women's subjects both in male-dominated history and on film screens, her biographical approach and her attention to women's agency and subjectivity emerge as key aspects of her authorship. Moreover, her presence on screen, materialised through image and sound, makes it impossible to disregard the female authorship of her cinema. All these factors locate Haneda as an epitome of a women's cinema that underscores women's agency and subjectivity while critically depicting gender dynamics. However, when interviewed by Armendáriz-Hernández and González-López (2019), Haneda insisted on not identifying herself as female director and on never thinking of her work as 'some kind of women's movement'. Why not? Should we talk about Haneda as a 'feminist director', or even a 'female director'?

## Labelling Haneda

The number of female directors and the attention given to them by scholars, publishers and critics at film festivals, archives and other institutions has significantly increased over the past decade. This edited volume and the conference from which it emerged are among the many examples that highlight the impact of gender studies and transnational feminisms in the study of Asian cinema. Yet, filmmakers in Japan (and elsewhere) do not always wish to be labelled as 'female directors' (Armendáriz-Hernández and González-López, 2022). The case of Haneda offers an interesting example of this contradiction, which deserves further reflection. While her films and writings denote a critical consciousness about gender, Haneda always distances her work from a concise feminist ideology and emphatically rejects the label 'female director' (Armendáriz-Hernández and González-López, 2019, 2022).

In the previous section, we have examined how Haneda's depiction of women and authorship seems akin to a political understanding of women's cinema. Haneda's intention to distance herself from the concept of women's cinema seems further at odds with her involvement in women's film festivals in Japan and with the women who, for decades, have promoted women's cinema in the country. For instance, Takano Etsuko, previously manager of Iwanami Hall – historically Japan's most important venue for independent cinema – and the main organiser of the Tokyo International Women's Film Festival (TIWFF), is one of Haneda's biggest advocates. In 1977, she organised a screening of *Cherry Tree with Gray Blossoms* at Iwanami Hall, placing Haneda in the spotlight in this decisive moment of her career, as she released her first independent film. Years later, Takano encouraged Haneda to turn her work on Kanda into a feature-length documentary to be released at the first edition of TIWFF in 1985. As the only Japanese film screened at the festival, *Akiko* received great publicity, both in Japan and abroad. Since then, Haneda became a recurrent and central presence at the festival, regularly featuring in round-table discussions and press conferences – to the point that Ōtake Yōko, another key woman in Iwanami Hall and TIWFF, went so far as to declare: 'I think Haneda-san was the psychological support of the Women's Film Week [TIWFF]' (Takano et al., 1997, p. 5). Haneda also became a regular guest at Aichi International Women's Film Festival and part of the executive committee of the journal *Cinema Library* (2004–13) – an annual publication on films directed by women and released in Japan. Furthermore, through these women-led networks she helped other female directors, such as Hamano Sachi, who recalls in her memoirs that Haneda's support was instrumental in her decision to work outside the porn industry (Hamano, 2005, p. 58). Therefore, individuals promoting women's cinema in Japan have played an important role in Haneda's career and, conversely, she has become representative of those initiatives.

Haneda's work also benefited from the financial and creative support of women's organisations and audiences. Hori Hikari notices that her documentaries about ageing and the elder care system often circulated outside the routes of commercial distribution. Film screenings were frequently organised by local activists and held at community centres where audiences were encouraged to discuss the film and the issues it depicted. The audiences were primarily composed of women because, in Japan and elsewhere, they tend to function as primary care-givers for elderly family members (Hori, 2011, pp. 118–19). Similarly, *The Life of Hiratsuka Raicho* was born as the project of an association (mainly composed by women), dedicated to the memory of this emblematic Japanese feminist, supported by Takano and screened at TIWFF (Haneda, 2014, pp. 79–80).

In Haneda's opinion, however, it is natural that, with her being a woman, she would be interested in depicting other women and their history, but she underlines that it is not from a particular feminine point of view that she creates films, only a 'human' one (*ningen toshite*) (Armendáriz-Hernández and González-López, 2019). Haneda's rejection of the label of 'female director' hints at the threat of grouping all films made by women under one separate category, which is furthermore often associated with certain types of subjects, sensibilities and genres linked to alleged traits of femininity. In analysing Haneda's films and writings, it appears that this 'human' perspective to which she refers emerges from her personal lived experiences with which she engages from a critical stance, aware of her own positionality. In this way, stressing gender dynamics, challenging stereotypes of femininity, or celebrating women's achievements stems from the same motivation as that of depicting the personal and social implications of growing old, the experiences of the Japanese civilians left behind in Manchuria, the passionate determination of artists and the importance of understanding and preserving nature. We may label a director as feminist based on the disruptive and empowering readings that their films allow, regardless of how they identify themselves. Yet, it is now more important than ever to reflect on the contexts or instances in which we differentiate a filmmaker as 'female' and to what purposes.

## Conclusions

Despite being mostly unknown in the West, Haneda's works are essential to frame the renewal of Japanese documentary film since the 1950s. They anticipated a new approach to reality, based on close observation, an engagement with the protagonists' subjectivity, the rejection of scripts, and technical asceticism, which became the core of the Japanese documentary scene in decades to come. *Women's College in the Village* illustrates how Haneda pioneered a new filmmaking method that, while it was simultaneously theorised by Hani, emphasised crafting long-standing relationships of trust with the filmed subjects and reflected her critical approach to gender and the representation of women. Especially as an independent filmmaker, recurrent aspects in her filmography seem to align her work with women's cinema. These would include her focus on women's lives, her poignant depiction of gender dynamics, her recurrent physical presence on film and the productive synergies with other women and women's organisations. The framework of women's cinema also allows us to theorise Haneda's multiple approaches to authorship and the relationship with her filmed subjects.

At the same time, however, the case of Haneda fuels ongoing debates about women's cinema and the label of 'female director'. Haneda renders the female perspective of her work part of her human perspective, inseparable from it, yet not taking over other aspects of her identity. Her cinema stems from a self-reflexive exploration of her lived experiences and interests. As such, gender and female subjectivity constitute a decisive concern of many of her films, but always in their intersections with other elements that shape her positionality. Thus, Haneda's films and writings are key to illustrate the developments in the post-war documentary scene in Japan, while providing a fascinating contribution to ongoing debates around authorship and women's cinema.

# References

Allen, J. (1991). Self-reflexivity in documentary. In R. Burnett (ed.), *Explorations in film theory* (pp. 103–10). Bloomington: Indiana University Press.

Armendáriz-Hernández, A., and González-López, I. (2019). Interview with Haneda Sumiko. Online correspondence. Unpublished.

Armendáriz-Hernández, A., and González-López, I. (2022). 'Female director': Discourses and practices in contemporary Japan. In D. Desser (ed.), *A companion to Japanese cinema* (pp. 421–45). Wiley Blackwell Companions to National Cinemas. Hoboken: Blackwell Publishing.

Bruzzi, S. (2000). *New documentary. A critical introduction*. London: Routledge.

Butler, A. (2002). *Women's cinema: The contested screen*. London: Wallflower.

Cazdyn, E. (2002). *The flash of capital. Film and geopolitics in Japan*. Durham: Duke University Press.

Centeno-Martin, M. (2018). The limits of fiction: Politics and absent scenes in Susumu Hani's *Bad boys* (*Furyōshōnen*, 1960). A film re-reading through its script. *Journal of Japanese and Korean Cinema*, 10, 1–15.

Centeno-Martin, M. (2019a). Post-war narratives through avant-garde documentary: *Tokyo 1958* and *Furyō Shōnen*. In A. Lozano, D. Martínez, and B. Guarné (eds), *Persistently postwar: Media and the politics of memory in Japan* (pp. 41–62). New York, Oxford: Berghahn Books.

Centeno-Martin, M. (2019b). Legacies of Hani Susumu's documentary school. In M. Centeno-Martin and M. Raine (eds), *Developments in the Japanese documentary mode, arts* (pp. 53–64). Basel: MDPI.

Centeno-Martin, M. (2021). 1968 and rural Japan as a site of struggle. Approaches to rural landscapes in the history of Japanese documentary film. In *The Sixties: A Journal of History, Politics and Culture*, 1–18.

Centeno-Martin, M., and Raine, M. (eds). (2021). *Developments in the Japanese documentary mode*. Basel: MDPI.

Eitzen, D. (1995) When is documentary? Documentary as a mode of reception. *Cinema Journal*, 35(1), 88–102.

González-López, I., and Smith, M. (eds). (2018). *Tanaka Kinuyo: Nation, stardom and female subjectivity*. Edinburgh: Edinburgh University Press.

Hamano S. (2005). *Onna ga eiga o tsukuru toki* [When a woman makes movies]. Tokyo: Heibonsha.

Haneda S. (2002). *Eiga to watashi* [Cinema and I]. Tokyo: Shōbunsha.
Haneda S. (2012). '*Mura no fujin gakkyū* ga dekiteiru' [Making *Women's college in the village*]. In Y. Niwa and S. Yoshimi (eds), *Iwanami Eiga no ichi oku furemu* (pp. 239–54). Tokyo: Tokyo Daigaku Shuppankai.
Haneda S. (2014). *Watashi no kiroku eiga jinsei* [My documentary film life]. Tokyo: Iwanami Shoten.
Hani S. (1958). Jiyūna kamera [Free camera]. *Mita bungaku*, 48(16), 44–52.
Hani S. (1959). Gijutsu no ninmu [Duty of technique]. *Mita bungaku*, 49, 45–50.
Hani S. (1961a). Kiroku eiga to gekieiga: Dokyumentarī no hōhō o megutte [Documentary cinema and fiction cinema: On the documentary method]. *Shin Nihon Bungaku*, 16(5), 125–37.
Hani S. (1961b). Watashi no shinarioron [My script theory]. *Shinario*, 6, 56–59.
Hori H. (2011). Aging, gender, and sexuality in Japanese popular cultural discourse. In Y. Matsumoto (ed.), *Faces of aging: The lived experiences of the elderly in Japan*. Palo Alto: Stanford University Press.
Ikegawa R. (2011). *Teikoku no eiga kantoku Sakane Tazuko: 'Kaitaku no hanayome', 1943, Man 'ei.* [Sakane Tazuko, film director of the empire; *Brides of the Frontier* (1943, Man'ei)] Tokyo: Yoshikawa Kōbunkan.
Junpei Y. (2011). *Nihon tanpen eizōshi: bunka eiga, kyōiku eiga, sangyō eiga* [History of Japanese short films: culture films, educational films and industry films]. Tokyo: Iwanami Shoten.
Kaneko Y. (2013, June 14). Dokyumentarisuto no me 7: Haneda Sumiko kantoku intabyū. Interview with Haneda Sumiko. *Neoneo*, online version. Retrieved from http://webneo.org/archives/9515
Laird, C. (2013, May). Imaging a female filmmaker: The director personas of Nishikawa Miwa and Ogigami Naoko. *Frames Cinema Journal*. Special issue: 'Promotional materials'. Retrieved from http://framescinemajournal.com/article/imaging-a-female-filmmaker/
MacDougall, D. (1992). Whose story is it? In P. Claford and J. Simonsen (eds), *Ethnographic film aesthetic and narrative tradition* (pp. 25–42). Aarhus: Aarhus Intervention Press.
Munroe Hotes, C. (2022). *Women behind the scenes*. Online database. Retrieved from https://sites.google.com/site/japanesewomenbehindthescenes/
Murayama H. (2010). Kiroku eiga no hozon to genjō [Current situation on preservation of documentary film]. In T. Satō (ed.), *Shirīzu Nihon no dokyumentarī 4. Sangyō, kagakuron* (pp. 240–46). Tokyo: Iwanami Shoten.
Nichols, B. (2001). *Introduction to documentary*. Bloomington: Indiana University Press.
Nornes, A. M. (2003). *Japanese documentary film: The Meiji era through Hiroshima*. Minneapolis: University of Minnesota Press.
Niwa Y., and Yoshimi S. (eds). (2012). *Iwanami Eiga no 1-oku furēmu* [Images of postwar Japan: The documentary films of Iwanami Productions]. Tokyo: Tōkyō Daigaku Shuppankai.
Takano E., Ōtake Y., and Kotoda C. (1997). The tenth year of International Women's Film Week. *TIWFF Catalogue*, 4–6.
Wang, L. (ed.). (2011). *Chinese women's cinema: Transnational contexts*. New York: Columbia University Press.
White, P. (2015). *Women's cinema, world cinema: Projecting contemporary feminisms*. Durham: Duke University Press.

## Notes

1. This text is part of a research project titled 'Japanese Documentary Filmmaker Haneda Sumiko: Authorship and Gender Discourses', sponsored by the Sasakawa Foundation, the Japan Foundation and Birkbeck Research Committee Strategic Funds led by Marcos Centeno and co-organised with Irene González-López, Alejandra Armendáriz-Hernández and Ricardo Matos, including two international symposia hosted at Japan Research Centre, SOAS University of London, in July and September 2021.
2. Other important initiatives include the online databases 'Women behind the scenes' led by Catherine Munroe Hotes (2022) and 'Women Pioneers in Japanese Cinema' (Nihon eiga ni okeru josei paionia) (2022) hosted by Kyoto University website, as well as events such as the series on 'Japanese Women Directors' (Nihon josei kantoku) organised in 2019 by the National Film Archive of Japan.
3. Editors' note: In this chapter, Japanese names adhere to the traditional order of family name first, followed by given name.

Chapter 8

# A Challenge on Every Page: Female Screenwriter-Directors in the South Korean Film Industry

*Monika Kukolova*

Following the boom period of Korean cinema in the 2000s and its growing international popularity, directors including Hong Sang-soo, Park Chan-wook and Bong Joon-ho have been hailed as the leading film auteurs of the new generation of Korean cinema.[1] The auteur label is a valuable recognition of the highly distinctive film styles of these filmmakers; nevertheless, it eclipses the creative labour that assisted the directors in establishing themselves on the global film scene. While the above auteurs often take on multiple roles during the production and post-production stages, they still have long-term collaborators who also shape those films, many of whom are women.[2] Although this may appear as a minor matter of publicity, it becomes more significant when we consider that female film professionals face an uphill battle to be recognised as equals in the Korean film industry. Furthermore, by paying attention to the way in which focusing on the auteur bypasses female creative labour, it is possible to clarify why so few Korean women receive the kind of international attention garnered by their male peers. As I go on to show, historically, women have had a strong presence as directors, screenwriters and producers across both film and TV industries in Korea, yet this has not quite been replicated in the international profile of Korean cinema.

The attention paid to female creatives' work varies depending on the socio-cultural context in which their films are exhibited. The London Korean Film Festival has a strand of programming dedicated to women's voices, while the 2019 BFI London Film Festival screened four films by Korean women out of a total of five Korean films that year. As valuable as these efforts are, their impact is limited to the particular audiences who seek out film festivals and audiences in the English capital and those who have a certain type of socio-economic privilege. However, when it comes to general cinema releases, so far no films by Korean women have seen anything like the scale of release for Park Chan-wook's Vengeance Trilogy (*Sympathy for Mr Vengeance* [2002], *Oldboy* [2003] and *Lady Vengeance* [2005]), for instance, which have seen release theatrically and repeated home media iterations. The likelihood of a Korean film's general cinema release in the UK depends closely on its success on the film festival circuit, as was the case for *Oldboy* which won the Grand Prix in Cannes in 2004. And yet, films by women that have had success in the domestic (Korean) film circuit and made it onto the international festival circuit have not been acquired for general cinema release – this was the case for Yim Soon-rye's *Little Forest* (2018). In fact, it is more likely that a female filmmaker's work will receive a general cinema release in the UK if she is not in the director's seat.

The following chapter will consider creative professionals in the Korean film industry whose work has gone largely unrecognised in commercial markets outside of South Korea, due to the bias towards directorial auteurship. For many of the women screenwriters discussed below, their craft has gone unacknowledged internationally unless, or until, they make a transition into directing roles. Therefore, this chapter will emphasise the value of screenwriting as a creative act by highlighting industry connections between film and television, where screenwriters hold similar power to directors, and by analysing the impact of the screenplay on character and theme development in the case-study films. I will examine two films by Lee Kyoung-mi, a screenwriter-turned-director, in order to illustrate the impact of her screenwriting experience on her work as a film and television director.

One of the reasons why so few Korean women filmmakers are known internationally may be related to a limited understanding of the word 'filmmaker', which also correlates with a director-led approach in both the global film industry and in the academic discourse on Korean cinema. Perhaps we need a broader definition of a filmmaker as someone involved in any of the key stages of making a film, instead of the dominant perception that only the director is a filmmaker. This current interpretation of the word serves as a crucial marketing tool in film distribution and exhibition, especially for non-franchise releases and arthouse cinema. In academic discussions, the equating of filmmaker and director can help to reveal thematic tendencies and stylistic categories across history and in contemporary cinema. For instance, Kim Mee-hyun (2007, pp. 402–12) drafts an 'aesthetic topography of Korean cinema' that classifies Korean filmmakers into four groups: film buffs or the supporters of minor genres

(Park Chan-wook, Bong Joon-ho and so on); intimists (Hong Sang-soo, Kim Ki-duk and so on); expanded realists or national realists (Im Sang-soo, Im Kwon-taek and so on); and mainstream currents (Kang Je-gyu, Kim Sang-jin and so on). Such a framework illuminates some of the most persistent concerns in Korean cinema, as well as giving an intriguing insight into Korean film culture, and yet it is starkly devoid of women.

If we broaden the definition of 'filmmaker' to include producers and screenwriters, Kim's proposed map of Korean cinema opens up to include several women. To begin with, the list might mention Park Chan-wook's long-time collaborator and screenwriter Jung Seo-kyoung, who has co-written five of his films – namely, *Lady Vengeance*, *I'm a Cyborg But That's Okay* (2006), *Thirst* (2009), *The Handmaiden* (2016) and *Decision to Leave* (2022). Also on the list could be Park Eun-kyo who co-wrote *Mother* (Bong Joon-ho, 2009) and Kwak Sin-ae who produced *Parasite* (Bong Joon-ho, 2019). Next, the prolific Im Kwon-taek has collaborated with Kim Mi-yeong who wrote *Beyond the Years* (2007), Song Yoon-hee who penned *Revivre* (2014) and Bang Eun-jin who co-wrote *Salut d'Amour* (2015). Finally, Kim Sang-jin's hit comedies *Attack the Gas Station* (1999) and *Kick the Moon* (2001) were co-produced by actress Kim Mi-hee. These are just a few examples based on some of the directors mentioned in Kim's list, but they effectively demonstrate how auteur culture in the global film industry undermines and undervalues the collaborative nature of filmmaking, which disproportionately affects women in filmmaking professions.

A potential critique of the above suggestion to broaden the meaning of the term filmmaker comes from the auteur camp, which argues that the creative vision and overall control of the film project rests overwhelmingly with the director. Darcy Paquet (2005, p. 46) acknowledges that, 'in terms of film-making practices, profound differences [between Korea and Hollywood] remain in the screenwriting process, as well as in the degree of influence a director holds during the shooting of a film (in Korea it remains much higher)'. He further expands upon this topic in an article for *Korean Cinema Today*, abbreviated for *Acta Koreana* as follows:

> [I]n Korea, directors usually write their own screenplays. [. . .] The notion of the auteur who develops an original idea, writes a screenplay and then directs a film is widespread in Korea, even for commercial films. Indeed, there is an unspoken assumption that directors will write their own scripts if they wish to be taken seriously. There is a practical side to this as well. For the multitudes of young directors hoping to make their commercial debut, the most promising road lies in writing a good screenplay. (Paquet, 2011, p. 29)

There are a couple of ideas in Paquet's analysis that I would like to discuss in more detail. The initial impression seems to be that screenwriting is not a respected profession in the Korean film industry, that it only has value in its connection to the visual element of a film, via the director's persona. Yet, Paquet's words reveal a slightly different situation, one where 'a good screenplay' has the power to attract funding and launch a director's career. Paquet (2011, p. 30) admits as much, concluding that . . .

> . . . well-written screenplays have simply become more noticeable than they were in the past. Although producers lament that it is difficult to find financing in the current environment, they will also readily admit that an outstanding screenplay can very quickly attract investors.

While this difference in the status of film screenwriting may have appeared negligible to Paquet in 2010, when he wrote the original article, it has gained larger significance in recent years, especially in relation to the funding opportunities offered by international streaming platforms. Netflix, in particular, has shown the potential to narrow the value gap between screenwriting for film and for television. I will return to this argument later in the chapter.

Before discussing the substance that screenwriting has in the filmmaking craft, I would like to highlight the fact that the Korean film industry has undergone serious developments over the past thirty years and that the role of the screenwriter has not always lacked the industry's respect. In the late 1980s and early 1990s, Hollywood production companies set up local branch offices in Korea, following the sixth revision of the Motion Picture Law that allowed foreign-owned film companies to operate in Korea. Following their establishment on the Korean market, Hollywood companies lobbied for a nationwide model of distribution rather than a regional system, essentially marginalising local film companies and producers in their own market. In order to prevent Hollywood's domination, film producers invited Korean conglomerates known as *chaebol* to invest in the film industry, offering lucrative profits in the form of video and television rights to films in return (Cho, 2019, p. 55). The *chaebols* introduced a more corporate style of film financing, with tight accounting practices and market research, which resulted in a push towards a more cost-effective, commercial cinema. Several film producers met these demands by developing 'planned films' which closely relied on screenwriters crafting the script in response to interviews and surveys. The most commercially successful[3] 'planned film', *Marriage Story*

(Kim Eui-suk, 1992), famously employed eight screenwriters responsible for sixteen rewrites of the script.

As a profession and a workplace, however, filmmaking (in the broadest sense of the word) in the Korean film industry was not a welcoming space for women. According to Minja Kim Choe (2006, p. 293), it has only been since the industrial developments in the 1970s and 1980s that levels of education for women began rising, with women rarely able to find work beyond the sales and service sectors before then.[4] Writing in the mid-2000s, Choe (2006, pp. 293–94) observed that Korean women were slowly pivoting towards career-oriented jobs but they were facing 'social norms and institutional habits such as hiring practices and employment conditions [. . .] dominated by attitudes of older members of the society'. The effects of such a traditional, patriarchal environment across Korea's institutions can be seen in the wide gender gap in employment among the university-educated population – it is over three times the average in OECD countries (Brinton and Choi, 2006, p. 310). Given that many of the creative jobs in film and television industries generally require a university degree and therefore contribute to this gender gap, it becomes clear that budding women filmmakers have faced a hostile working environment. Additionally, both Choe (2006, p. 300) and Brinton and Choi (2006, p. 313) show that marriage and childcare further complicate women's employment status, resulting in high proportions of university-educated women not marrying (Choe, 2006, p. 300). These data strongly suggest that jobs requiring university degrees continue to be unsustainable for women who wish to have a career as well as the option to marry and have children.

In light of these gender inequalities in employment, the career of Kim Soo-hyun,[5] one of Korea's most prolific television and film screenwriters, seems like an unlikely paradox. Kim, who earned a degree in Korean language and literature, started her career at MBC (Korean television and radio network), writing for television dramas.[6] However, before her first drama *Rainbow* even premiered in 1972, Kim had already written scripts for at least eight films, several of which were collaborations with director Jeong So-yeong. These early films share themes of sexual violence and abuse of both married and widowed women, as well as the struggles of single mothers and working women in a strict, Confucian society. For instance, her 1970 film *Pilnyeo* (dir. Jeong So-yeong) places its protagonist in a coal mine, where she decides to work after the death of her husband. *Pilnyeo* received critical acclaim at the Blue Dragon Film awards in 1971, winning Kim the award for best screenplay. The screenwriter's film career spans from the 1970s until the early 2000s

(Korean Movie Database, 2018), when she moved exclusively into television writing, adapting her skills in the melodrama genre to both film and television. She came close to making a comeback in the film industry in 2010, when she wrote an adaptation of the 1960 film *The Housemaid* (Kim Ki-young) and recommended director Im Sang-soo to the film's producer. However, this collaboration was not meant to be, due to Kim and Im's disagreement over the script (Lee, 2009), so Kim eventually left the project, which ended up in competition for the Palme d'Or at the 2010 Cannes festival.

Kim's decades-long career across the film and television industries shows that the works based on her screenplays have found audiences in both media formats. Without attempting to draw too broad a correlation, Kim's traversing between the small and big screens hints at the fact that both types of audiences place some value on the genre stories she writes, as well as on the exploration of similar themes. At the same time, of course, film and television audiences and the expectations that they bring with them differ in quite crucial ways. Consider, for example, Cho Junhyoung's point about the impact of television on Korean film audiences in *A brief history of Korean cinema*, observing that . . .

> . . . the first type of audience group that stopped going to theaters with the emergence of television was middle-aged women and families. However, films remained a cultural event for youth. Therefore, new waves of South Korean films were created in the 1970s for the youth population. (Cho, 2019, p. 49)

Cho suggests that the primary audience for television content were middle-aged women and families, while younger people sought out a different form of entertainment (and possibly privacy) in cinemas. Cho (2019, p. 48) also remarks that, while the global film industry competed with television through the inclusion of sexually explicit and violent images, the Korean film industry did not have the same option. In 1972, the Korean government essentially became a dictatorship under Park Chung-hee, which meant, among other changes, tighter film censorship under the newly amended Motion Picture Law. Therefore, film and television content faced the same restrictions, narrowing down at least some of the choice for audiences.

The staple, then, of 1970s Korean film and television production was melodrama, a genre adept at evoking strong emotional thrills without necessarily needing to depict violence or sex. One attraction of melodrama, indeed one of its defining features according to melodrama scholar Ben Singer (Stewart, 2014, p. 5), comes from its narrative structure, which is crafted into a precisely balanced rhythm of emotional and moral upheavals.[7] These narrative events, in turn, shape character development until all narrative tension is resolved at the end. Both narrative structure and character development are the primary responsibilities of the screenwriter, and so a large part of a melodrama's appeal to the audience relies on the quality of the script. It does not mean that the role of the director is in any way diminished; in fact, their guidance of the actors is crucial in achieving the desired emotional intensity of a melodrama. What I am suggesting, however, is that the melodrama film wave of the 1970s was substantially powered by the creative labour of screenwriters such as Kim Soo-hyun. Furthermore, the melodrama genre has been a consistent source of revenue in Korean cinema since 1955 (Kim, 2005, p. 185), and its relatively low cost of production has carried the film industry through some of its darkest times (Paquet, 2007, p. 37). The 1970s saw cinema audience numbers plummeting,[8] along with the number of local films and imported productions. Still, throughout the decade melodramas consistently featured in the top ten of bestselling films, with both *The Woman I Betrayed* (1978) and *The Man I Betrayed* (1979), written by Kim Soo-hyun and directed by Jung So-Young, becoming some of the bestselling films of the 1970s (Koreanfilm.org, 2012).

It would seem that, with the changing tastes for Korean cinema both at home and abroad, the screenwriters' craft that was so clearly showcased during the height of 1970s melodrama lost some its utility in contemporary Korean commercial cinema. Choi Jinhee (2010, pp. 181–82) and Paquet (2011, p. 20) both suggest that a slick aesthetic, or visual imagery, is a more important factor driving the domestic and international demand for Korean films. With political changes that consequently opened South Korea up to investment by American studios, the trends in commercial Korean filmmaking have shifted towards genre spectacles with ever-growing budgets (Cho, 2019, pp. 56–58). Abroad, a specific taste for Asian cinema has also developed. The UK-based distribution company Metro Tartan, for example, launched its 'Asia Extreme' label in 2001, 'targeting the cult "fan-boys" but soon incorporating the art-house audiences (or world cinema patrons) to its niche' (Shin, 2009, p. 86). The films distributed under this label placed emphasis on visual and thematic provocation, which can overshadow the quality of the screenplay and draw attention wholly to the director and cinematographer.

Still, the demand for aesthetically appealing cinematography does not spell the end for film screenwriters, even if their role may currently be less valued than that of the cinematographer or director. As I mentioned at the beginning of this chapter, there are a couple of high-profile women screenwriters working in the Korean film industry today who have so far sustained their careers by working mostly in film. Among them, Jung Seo-kyoung and Park Eun-kyo have built a rich portfolio of scripts through both independent work and collaboration with established film directors, and both have recently forayed into television writing. Additionally, the two women (along with Park Chan-wook) collaborated with Lee Kyoung-mi on the screenplays for her first and second feature films *Crush and Blush* (2008) and *The Truth Beneath* (2016), and I will look at these films more closely in the following section. It is worth noting that Lee Kyoung-mi started her career as a screenwriter for *Lady Vengeance* and then moved into directing films, for most of which she still at least co-writes the scripts – her latest writing/directing project is the adapted Netflix series *The School Nurse Files* (2020). Lee's move into directing appears to be a common strategy among film screenwriters in Korea; other women who have combined screenwriting with directing include Jeon Go-woon, Bang Eun-jin, Lee Jeong-hyang and Hong Ji-young. These professional migrations suggest that, while the position of the screenwriter is an undervalued one, it may be a much-needed source of experience for budding female film directors.

## *Crush and Blush* and *The Truth Beneath*: Reading Beyond the Lines

Although director Lee's debut feature film *Crush and Blush* and her second feature *The Truth Beneath* belong to different genres and do not have the same visual themes, they share similar concerns expressed through a tightly controlled narrative. To begin with, the emphasis that director Lee places on the screenplay is evident from the credits alone: both films have screenwriting teams of no fewer than three people (Lee herself, Park Eun-kyo and Park Chan-wook on *Crush and Blush*; Lee again with Park Chan-wook, Jung Seo-kyoung, Kim Da-young and Jeong So-young on *The Truth Beneath*). The involvement of Jung Seo-kyoung and Park Chan-wook in the script for *The Truth Beneath* is especially noteworthy, since the influence of the creative duo can certainly be felt in the film's narrative pace, as well as in its exploration of a character's breakdown and ultimate revenge. In fact, both films observe their protagonists' roads towards revenge and redemption, but they do so in ways that are different from each other and from Park Chan-wook's Vengeance trilogy.

*Crush and Blush* follows an unpopular high-school Russian and English teacher Mi-sook (Gong Hyo-jin), who has a long-term crush on her former teacher and now colleague Jong-cheol (Lee Jong-hyuk).

Sensing that Jong-cheol, who is married, may be having an affair with her more popular colleague Yoo-ri (Hwang Woo-seul-hye), Mi-sook establishes an unlikely partnership with Jong-cheol's daughter Jong-hee (Seo Woo). The two allies orchestrate an elaborate social media scam targeted at Yoo-ri but, as their plan is eventually discovered by Jong-hee's mother (Bang Eun-jin), Mi-sook and Jong-hee have to face the choices they have made and what they really found in each other. The film adopts a distinctive three-act structure, and the finale, a reckoning between all the key players in the marital affair, is staged in a language classroom. This scene, in its resemblance to a courtroom hearing led by Jong-hee's mother, forces the viewer to acknowledge the standpoint, motivations and regrets of each character and thus demonstrates to both the viewer and Mi-sook why she should stop seeking Jong-cheol's affection and accept herself as she is. Even though the theme of self-acceptance might be well-worn in female-led dramas, the *Crush and Blush* screenwriting team use the final 'courtroom' act in the language classroom to suggest that the character's self-acceptance can only be reached by listening to others and herself in equal measures. This experimentation with the format of narrative resolution in the finale demonstrates the significance of the screenwriters' input.

In addition to the three-act structure of the narrative, the film also anchors Mi-sook's character development in a specific dramatic reference that further highlights the status of the screenplay. In order to avoid drawing attention to the increasing time they spend plotting against Yoo-ri, Mi-sook and Jong-hee sign up to perform at the school's festival. Mi-sook chooses an excerpt from Samuel Beckett's *Waiting for Godot* (1954), and she practises the play with Jong-hee every night, while they write salacious online messages to Yoo-ri under Jong-cheol's name. Mi-sook's choice of *Waiting for Godot*, an absurdist play that resists a clear-cut interpretation, adds another layer to how the viewer can perceive her character development. From the beginning of the film, Mi-sook's only goal in life seems to be a relationship with Jong-cheol; more fundamentally, she wants to be noticed and appreciated. Yet, even when she manages to spend the night with drunk Jong-cheol, she does not find satisfaction – the heteronormative lifestyle she aspired to does not work for her. Like in Beckett's play, the character's expectations never quite materialise in the form that she imagines. When their scheme is discovered in the final act and Mi-sook chooses her friendship with Jong-hee over her crush on Jong-cheol, the film concludes with the two friends smiling as they perform in front of a jeering crowd of students. Mi-sook realises that she cannot disregard everyone and manipulate her dream into existence, that she can be happier treating her life more as a game, echoing some of the themes in *Waiting for Godot*. This subtle incorporation of the play into the character development in *Crush and Blush* spotlights the filmmaker's knowledge of the craft of writing.

Like *Crush and Blush*, Lee's second feature *The Truth Beneath* also utilises a tightly structured screenplay in order to continue Lee's exploration of her female protagonists' defiance and self-reinvention. *The Truth Beneath* considers the insidious effects of gender roles in a heterosexual marriage and briefly also maps this onto the political patriarchy in Korea. Kim Yeon-hong (Son Ye-jin) dedicates all of her time to support her husband Kim Jong-chan (Kim Joo-hyuk) in his run for a seat in the National Assembly. One day before the start of the campaign, their daughter Min-jin (Shin Ji-hoon) goes missing, which threatens Jong-chan's election manifesto built on his promise to protect the younger generation. Faced with her husband, his team and the police's reluctance to investigate her daughter's disappearance, Yeon-hong follows the clues left behind by her daughter to uncover the truth beneath her picture-perfect family.

Although the film's genre is decisively in the thriller category, there are multiple scenes punctuating the film's pace that open it up to be read as a character study, too. These scenes, which often obscure dialogue in favour of an oppressive *mise en scène* and Son Ye-jin's performance, generate a conversation between the film's intensely propelled thriller narrative and moments of the protagonist's emotional overload. For instance, after the discovery of Min-jin's body, Yeon-hong's simultaneous grief and anger is shown through her wordlessly stomping her feet at the police station, the close-up of her face fading into the close-up of Min-jin on the morgue table, then cutting to Min-jin's funeral as Yeon-hong observes the press swarming around her husband's performed mourning. The sequence focuses solely on Yeon-hong's emotional state, her face appearing in most of the shots and the echo of her stomping feet interrupted by a voice-over reporting on how this tragedy will likely get her husband elected. This oscillation between a fast-paced narrative and quiet moments of intense emotion pays homage to the melodramatic tradition in Korean cinema, and crucially it is also the guiding narrative structure of many contemporary Korean television dramas. In fact, director/screenwriter Lee replicates a similar narrative framework in her Netflix series *The School Nurse Files*, in which the fantasy genre also makes way for the protagonist's subdued contemplation of her identity. It is intriguing to see comparable narrative structures and the use of melodrama across Korean film and television, indicating a considerable transferability of directing and screenwriting skills between the two media formats.

Furthermore, *The Truth Beneath* makes use of recurring dialogue motifs, a practice that is widely used in contemporary Korean television dramas because it accentuates narrative continuity and rewards viewers who watch all of the episodes in a series. In the film, when Yeon-hong finds her daughter's only school friend Choi Mi-ok (Kim Soo-hee) and asks her what her parents do for a living, Mi-ok answers that her father is a driver who 'loads shit in the back and drives it around'. In that moment, Yeon-hong and the viewer understand Mi-ok's father's profession at face-value; she thinks that her father is a sewage truck driver and that Mi-ok was stealing expensive items from her daughter. Yeon-hong's behaviour and accusation of Mi-ok in this scene conform to the deeply ingrained principles of class and privilege in Korean society: the characters' interaction is based on their superficial perceptions of each other. The second time this reference to Mi-ok's father's job appears in the film, Mi-ok is being investigated at the police station in connection to Min-jin's murder. Yeon-hong realises that Mi-ok's father is her husband's driver, and she confronts the family for betraying her trust and disrespecting Jong-chan. The meaning behind Mi-ok's words changes, as does the relationship between the two characters: Yeon-hong drops the veneer of politeness informed by her class status when she understands that Mi-ok does not respect her on the basis of her carefully crafted middle-class femininity. Mi-ok's words make their third and final appearance in the lyrics of her and Min-jin's song, and the significance of the initial expression shifts yet again now that both the viewer and Yeon-hong are aware of the full scale of her husband's betrayal. The barrier of class between Yeon-hong and Mi-ok, which manifested through their lack of semantic comprehension, disappears and Yeon-hong embraces Mi-ok as if she were her deceased daughter. The recurring rhetorical association of men and their jobs with excrement in the film makes use of a screenwriting device commonly used in television drama to develop narrative over the course of multiple episodes. However, in this case, the dialogue motif weaves in ideas about the effects of class on female solidarity, thus building further links with the concerns of contemporary Korean television drama.

Considering these cross-media writing and directing techniques, it is no surprise that director/screenwriter Lee, alongside some of the previously mentioned women, made her most recent project a transition into television streaming. Moreover, Lee, Jeon Go-woon, Park Eun-kyo, Park Hyun-jin and Jung Seo-kyoung[9] have all written and/or directed their latest projects (2019–22) as Netflix originals – produced and distributed internationally via the streaming platform. This 'cross-pollination' of media is less the case in the other direction – namely, female television screenwriters/directors venturing into the film industry; other than its reputation, the film industry currently does not offer financial or other practical incentives for women screenwriters to make the transition. There are exceptions here, too. Kim Eun-hee, the screenwriter of the internationally popular Netflix series[10] *Kingdom* (Kim Seong-hun, 2019), has written a film prequel to the series, *Kingdom: Ashin of the North* (Kim Seong-hun, 2021), also produced by Netflix – this film is presented as both a special episode of the series and a feature film on Netflix, additionally blurring the boundaries between the two formats. Likewise, the career of screenwriter/director Park Hyun-jin points in the direction of Netflix: Park started as a writer for Im Sang-soo's *The Old Garden* (2006), moving into writing and directing her debut *Lovers of Six Years* (2008) before switching into television writing (koreanfilm.or.kr, 2017) and, most recently, directing the Netflix original *Love and Leashes* (2022). Although these examples are quite recent and the impact of Netflix on Korean television and film industries is a matter of ongoing development, it appears that the platform offers multiple doors to Korean women screenwriters/directors that provide better access to the international market.

The Korean film industry has been and continues to be a tricky workplace for screenwriters and women. This chapter has examined some of the reasons for the current unenviable status of screenwriters in Korean film, finding that the issue is compounded by institutionalised patriarchy and a seemingly market-driven prioritisation of cinematography over scriptwriting. In addition to these domestic factors, the international film festival circuit, film distribution, curation and even film scholarship have played a role in diminishing the creative labour of Korean women screenwriters as well as directors. Although the new waves of Korean filmmaking, along with the cinema's increased international exposure, looked like equitable opportunities for women screenwriters and directors to make their mark (Paquet, 2005, p. 48), the promise did not altogether materialise. Over the past five years, film festivals including the London Korean Film Festival and the BFI London Film Festival, have been rectifying this neglect of Korean women directors – many of whom write their own films – but there is much less done in the effort to distribute their films to audiences outside of the film festival. As for the labour of screenwriters, it remains obscured by a narrow understanding of authorship in both film industry and film studies. The work of women screenwriters (some of which are budding directors) is repeatedly hidden in plain sight, by a film industry either blind to or actively sustaining the cult of the male auteur.

From a cursory glance, the craft of screenwriting seems to be more recognised in the Korean television industry, with a number of film screenwriters transitioning into television work. However, in this chapter I have suggested that the television and film formats have been subject to similar trends in the past and that the ongoing oscillation of screenwriters and directors between the two industries points to the transferability of their skills and techniques. As both a film and television content provider, the global streaming platform Netflix is ideally placed to recognise the porous boundaries between Korean film and television, and it has recently been placing its bets on several women screenwriters and directors. The next few years will show whether Korean women screenwriters will truly be able to start a new chapter.

## References

Brinton, M. C., and Choi, M. (2006). Women's incorporation into the urban economy of South Korea. In Y. Chang and S. H. Lee (eds), *Transformations in twentieth century Korea* (pp. 310–44). London: Routledge.

Cho, J. (2019). A brief history of Korean cinema. In S. Lee (ed.), *Rediscovering Korean cinema* (pp. 34–64). Ann Arbor: University of Michigan Press.

Choe, M. K. (2006). Modernization, gender roles, and marriage behavior in South Korea. In Y. Chang and S. H. Lee (eds), *Transformations in twentieth century Korea* (pp. 291–309). London: Routledge.

Choi, J. (2010). *The South Korean film renaissance: Local hitmakers, global provocateurs*. Middletown: Wesleyan University Press.

Kim, M. (2020). Women-made horror in Korean cinema. In A. Peirse (ed.), *Women make horror* (pp. 133–44). New Brunswick: Rutgers University Press.

Kim, M. H. (2007). *Korean cinema: From origins to renaissance*. Seoul: Korean Film Council.

Kim, S. (2005). Questions of woman's film: *The maid*, *Madame freedom*, and women. In K. McHugh and N. Abelmann (eds), *South Korean golden age melodrama: Gender, genre, and national cinema* (pp. 185–200). Detroit: Wayne State University Press.

Koreanfilm.org. (2012). *1970–1979*. Retrieved from http://www.koreanfilm.org/kfilm70s.html

Koreanfilm.or.kr. (2017). *People directory: Park Hyun-jin*. Retrieved from https://www.koreanfilm.or.kr/eng/films/index/peopleView.jsp?peopleCd=20110969

Korean Movie Database. (2018). *Kim Soo-hyeon*. Retrieved from https://www.kmdb.or.kr/eng/db/per/00006333

Lee, H. (2009, November 2). Jeon Do-yeon cast in *The housemaid*. *The Korea Times*. http://www.koreatimes.co.kr/www/news/special/2009/11/178_54726.html

McHugh, K. (2005). South Korean film melodrama: State, nation, woman, and the transnational familiar. In K. McHugh and N. Abelmann (eds), *South Korean golden age melodrama: Gender, genre, and national cinema* (pp. 17–42). Detroit: Wayne State University Press.

Nam, I. (2007). Korean women directors. In M. H. Kim (ed.), *Korean cinema: From origins to renaissance* (pp. 161–68). Seoul: Korean Film Council.
Paquet, D. (2005). The Korean film industry: 1992 to the present. In C. Shin and J. Stringer (eds), *New Korean cinema* (pp. 32–50). Edinburgh: Edinburgh University Press.
Paquet, D. (2007). *Christmas in August* and Korean melodrama. In F. Gateward (ed.), *Seoul searching: Culture and identity in contemporary Korean cinema* (pp. 37–54). Albany: State University of New York Press.
Paquet, D. (2011). An insider's view of a film industry in transition: Darcy Paquet's meditations on the contemporary Korean cinema. *Acta Koreana*, 14(1), 17–32.
Shin, C. (2009). The art of branding: Tartan 'Asia Extreme' films. In J. Choi and M. Wada-Marciano (eds), *Horror to the extreme: Changing boundaries in Asian cinema* (pp. 85–100). Hong Kong: Hong Kong University Press.
Stewart, M. (2014). Introduction: Film and TV melodrama: An overview. In M. Stewart (ed.), *Melodrama in contemporary film and television* (pp. 1–21). Basingstoke: Palgrave Macmillan.

# Notes

1. In the Korean language and society, it is unusual to refer to 'South Korea', or '*namhan*', with many people preferring to see the peninsula as a Korean nation, '*hanguk*', although divided. For this reason, the author chooses to identify the South Korean film industry in the chapter title but refers to Korean filmmakers in the rest of the text.
2. For instance, Son Yeon-ji edited a number of Hong Sang-soo's films since 2017, while Bong Joon-ho's breakout hits *Memories of a Murder* (2003) and *The Host* (2006) first went through Kim Sun-min's editing suite. Both women have also edited films for directors outside of Korea.
3. The film, partially funded by Samsung, topped the box office upon release (Cho, 2019, p. 55).
4. There were exceptions: for example, Hong Eun-won entered the film industry in the late 1940s, working as a screenwriter and assistant director for fifteen years before her directing debut *A Woman Judge* (1962) (Nam, 2007, p. 161). Hong wrote articles about the sexual harassment she endured while working in film (Kim, 2020, pp. 136–37).
5. Kim Soo-hyun is the pen name of Kim Soon-ok.
6. MBC TV was established in 1969, in response to a steep increase in television penetration in Korea (Cho, 2019, p. 48), so Kim would have been one of the first television screenwriters hired by the company.
7. This is a broad genre definition. For more discussion of the cultural specificity of Korean melodrama, see Kathleen McHugh's chapter 'South Korean film melodrama: State, nation, woman, and the transnational familiar' (2005, pp. 23–25).
8. Total admissions steadily dropped from 166 million in 1970 to 66 million in 1979; 209 films were produced locally, and sixty-one were imported in 1970, while in 1979 the quantity of local films decreased to ninety-six local films and thirty-three imports (Koreanfilm.org, 2012).
9. Jung's adaptation of *Little Women* (Kim Hee-won, 2022) into a television series is the only exception here – it is produced by the television network tvN but will be airing internationally on Netflix. The series director's previous work with tvN and Netflix reached the top five of all TV shows on Netflix in April 2021.
10. *Kingdom* is Netflix's first Korean series original.

Chapter 9

# The Film Star and Her Husband: The Collaboration between Takamine Hideko and Matsuyama Zenzō

Till Weingärtner

The opening chapter of Japanese film star Takamine Hideko's (1924–2010) 1970s collection of autobiographical essays focuses on Shige, her aunt and foster mother.[1] Suffering from brain damage following encephalitis, the elderly Shige must relearn to read and write. She is taking great pride in her slow progress in memorising the basic Japanese syllable alphabet. When calling for her foster daughter, Takamine, she calls her 'mother' (okā-san) (Takamine, 1998a, p. 13). This may seem a curious place for Takamine to begin her look back on a career that spanned fifty years and roughly 300 films, from her debut as a child actor in 1929 to her retirement from acting in 1979. The reader might expect her to start her narration with an episode from the post-war years, during which she played a number of the iconic roles that she is best remembered for today. In *Twenty-Four Eyes* (*Nijūshi no hitomi*, 1954; dir. Kinoshita Keisuke) – which some critics regard as 'the greatest Japanese antiwar film' (Orr, 2001, p. 110) – she explored the role of individual responsibility in wartime through the character of countryside primary school teacher Ms Oishi. In the films of Naruse Mikio (1905–69),[2] she portrayed a series of lower-middle-class women, working mothers, writers and middle-aged bar proprietors. Or perhaps Takamine could have focused on her second career as an essayist, through which she remained in the public eye after retiring from the screen. I would argue, however, that Takamine's very identity as a film star and the creation and reception of her films are intrinsically linked to the narrative which she is offering here and which had been constructed over the course of her career. In that, the relationship to her foster mother is central.

First, as an overall role-reversal between (foster) mother and daughter, it is an end point of a narrative that has Takamine's search for agency and control over her own life at its heart. Takamine's early career, starting during her early childhood and adolescence, is characterised by other people making decisions for and about her. Takamine recalls the physically hard and mentally draining work of being a child actor – her inability to even understand what was going on and her just doing what she was told to do. She disliked the hard work and describes how the life of a child actor made it impossible for her to attend school on a regular basis, despite her wish to do so (Takamine, 1998a, p. 44), or to just enjoy the comforts of a 'normal' family home life (Takamine, 1998a, p. 50). There is a clear contrast to the depiction of Takamine's 'motherly' role in supporting Shige as she enjoys her studies. In hindsight, Takamine is aware that not only did she provide the means of income for the family to make a living, but she also hints at the fact that Shige might have projected her own dreams of a career in the world of film on the little girl – the pseudonym Takamine Hideko was the same Shige had used in an earlier attempt at a career as a *katsudō benshi*, or silent film narrator (Takamine, 1998a, p. 20). Now, Takamine is not only in control of her own life, but also Shige's, providing her with a very different kind of home environment.

Second, writing about the home environment with Shige gives Takamine the opportunity to introduce another important character in her narrative: her husband, the film director and script writer Matsuyama Zenzō (1925–2016). At this point, with the focus on Shige's health, the reader is provided with a brief but very relevant piece of information: Shige is calling him 'father' (*otō-san*) (Takamine, 1998a, p. 13). Not only does Takamine play her part in a role reversal, but her husband is also complicit in the creation of a new quasi-parental relationship with Shige. It is as if, in caring for Shige and looking after her together in this way, the couple is pulling in the same direction to address the demons from Takamine's past.

However, is there any evidence that this narrative is relevant to the public perception of Takamine Hideko as one of the most celebrated 'stars' of twentieth-century Japanese cinema? Did it contribute to her immense popularity as an actor?[3] Previous writings about Takamine have focused more on what the films in which she has appeared did for her profile, arguably at the expense of what Takamine's personal profile brought to those films. For example, Anderson and Richie present an early English-language assessment of Takamine's popularity and image in Japan, in which she appears almost as a cipher. Writing in 1959, they state: 'Always, to the movie-going public, she is completely representative of both their problems and their hopes' (Richie and Anderson, 1982,

p. 408). The nature of Richie and Anderson's work more widely suggests that the assessment is mostly based on the characters whom Takamine played within the films and the works of the film directors chosen for discussion. Furthermore, the concept of a singular 'movie-going public' neglects the fact that the image of a film star cannot only be different for different audiences, but that it also changes over the course of time.

Takamine's biographer, Kida Shō, also contextualises the appeal of Takamine as a star, chiefly in relation to her films. At the beginning of his biography, he sets out the conditions that constitute an 'actress representative of Japanese cinema': (1) her appearance in both silent and sound films, (2) her appearance in famous films, and (3) 'being used' by different leading film directors (Kida, 2012, p. 2). Takamine is ticking all these boxes for Kida. Although 'being used' sounds less harsh in Japanese than it might appear here in the English rendition, Kida's account reflects an approach which considers that the director bears, as the *auteur*, the main responsibility for the artistic result of the film, thereby also shaping the success of the actors involved.

This approach to cinema, which is rooted in auteur theory (cf. Hayward, 2006, pp. 27–33), has been elemental in English-language academic engagement with and recognition of Japanese cinema. For example, the case-study chosen by Mitsuhiro Yoshimoto to demonstrate the relevance of Japanese film for the establishment of film studies as an academic discipline in the United States is that of director Kurosawa Akira (Yoshimoto, 2000). This focus on key directors is also apparent in, for example, the way in which Japanese films are included and presented in the international canon. Films by directors such as Kurosawa Akira or Ozu Yasujirō constantly appear near the top of the lists of important or favourite films, such as the British Film Institute's famous list of the 'greatest films of all time', which has been published once every decade since 1952 ('The Greatest Films of All Time', 2012). Such approaches, however, arguably treat actors as mere tools of the director, pawns he or she can arrange and move around on screen to express his or her artistic version. The agency and back-story of the actors are then easily overlooked. In this context, an actor presenting an autobiography with a focus on her own agency poses a challenge, not only to the people or institution involved in limiting her decisions, but also to the perception of actors in film criticism in general.

Within the literature, the challenge comes from the star studies approach that emerged from Richard Dyer's seminal study *Stars* which first appeared in 1979 (Dyer, 1998). Here, Dyer introduces the star's image as a text in and of itself, the product of different 'media texts', such as 'promotion, publicity, films and criticism and commentaries' (Dyer 1998, p. 60), alongside the films in which the actor appears. With filmic and nonfilmic discourse, such as interviews, media reports, fan letters and promotion material contributing to the star's image, it should be understood and analysed as intertextual, intermedia and open-ended. This image is also referred to as the 'star text' and is read by audiences in conjunction with any given film text. Taking such an approach, we can ask several questions in relation to Takamine's star text. What does Takamine represent to different audiences? How does she participate, consciously or not, in the construction of her public image? What is the impact of that image on the films in which she appeared throughout her life? In this chapter, I will focus on the representations of Takamine's increasing agency, both in relation to her directors and in her life away from film. I argue that the filmic and nonfilmic discourses within her star text are mutually reinforcing and offer important perspectives on the films in which she appeared. These discourses are nowhere closer than in the films in which she is directed by her real-life husband, Matsuyama Zenzō, which I will then move on to explore in greater detail. Here I aim to demonstrate how the off-screen relationship between actor and director is also referenced and reflected in the relationships between the characters whom Takamine embodies and the men around them. In this context, we will also consider how questions of agency are illuminated by the female characters whom Takamine and Matsuyama create together.

Going back to Takamine's opening autobiographical essay, the key narrative that she is promoting about herself – her contribution to her personal star text – is, I argue here, her personal story of taking control of her life. This idea is at the heart not only of the depiction of her changed relationship with her foster mother, Shige, but also in how she describes her relationship to the most important male film directors in her post-war career – namely, the directors Kinoshita Keisuke (1912–98), Naruse Mikio (1905–69) and her husband, Matsuyama Zenzō. Although less commonly fêted as a director, Matsuyama's relationship with Takamine is particularly interesting in this regard and will be explored further below. Takamine presented Kinoshita as an ally when she decided to become a freelance actor in 1949 (Takamine, 1998b, pp. 174–77). She made this decision after learning more about the financial arrangements between different film studios, here in the context of a film directed by Kinoshita. The decision to break away from a contractual relationship with one studio was unusual at the time and reported in the media (Tanimura, 1949). Takamine links the decision to leave studio Shin-Tōhō with a new approach to decision-making: 'From now on I myself will take responsibility for my actions. It was wrong that I entrusted others' (Tanimura, 1949, p. 43). Her work with Kinoshita flourished after this quest for agency: Takamine describes Kinoshita as a big supporter, encouraging her to make her own decisions, while also promising her films with scripts specifically tailored to her (Takamine, 1998b, p. 175). Indeed, some of her most celebrated and well-remembered films of the 1950s were directed by Kinoshita, such as *Carmen Comes Home* (*Karumen kokyō ni kaeru*, 1951) and *Twenty-Four Eyes* (*Nijū-shi no Hitomi*, 1954). In both films, the main characters (played by Takamine) struggle with questions of personal agency and responsibility in the face of societal pressures.

Her collaboration with Naruse, however, is described more often through concrete events taking place during the shoot, by Takamine herself, as well as by other actors and scholars. Takamine's presence and behaviour on the set had an impact on her fellow actors and affected the end-result. For example, Takamine's co-star in *A Wanderer's Notebook* (*Hōrō-ki*, 1962), Takarada Akira (b. 1934), describes how he felt that Takamine and Naruse almost teamed up to bully him, criticising his performance while refusing to give clear instructions. Infuriated, he finally expresses the emotion for which Naruse was looking in the next take (Takasai, 2011, pp. 22–23). Actor Nakadai Tatsuya (b. 1932) praises Takamine's artistic sense as displaying the insight of a film director, always being aware of the shooting process, the importance of close-ups, the specific demands of film acting, and how a film is put together 'like a puzzle' (Kasuga, 2017, S. 150). Catherine Russell, too, quoting Takamine, emphasises the active role that Takamine had in the production of Naruse-directed films:

> Takamine Hideko claims that starting with *Lightning* (*Inazuma*, 1952) she worked on the scripts herself with Naruse, mainly cutting out lines of dialogue that she 'didn't want to say', presumably replacing them with performance elements of gesture, posture and eye movement. (Russell, 2008, p. 16)

These reports of Takamine's work with Kinoshita and Naruse highlight her increasing agency in her films. However, much less attention has been paid to her collaboration with her husband, the less-celebrated director Matsuyama Zenzō. Although Matsuyama's prominence in Japanese post-war cinema should not be under-estimated (as a scriptwriter, he worked on such seminal films as Kobayashi Masaki's trilogy *The Human Condition* [*Ningen no jōken*, 1959–61]), it is fair to say that the films he directed are not well remembered. After his directorial debut in 1961, he shot a small number of films starring Takamine, but at the time of writing this article, only his first work, *Happiness of Us Alone* (*Na mo Naku Mazushiku Utsukushiku*, 1961), is publicly available. Throughout his career, Matsuyama was often perceived as being, first and foremost, the husband of the famous film star, an image he seemed happy to accept and embrace. Remembering Takamine in 2010, he not only refers to her as an actor and his wife, but also as a 'master' when it comes to films (Matsuyama, 2010). This image persists – for example, a recent book with a portrait of Matsuyama on the cover is titled *The Man Takamine Hideko Loved* (Saitō, 2012).

Despite the more limited appeal or artistic merit of the films they made together, I argue that the marriage between Takamine and Matsuyama, their partnership and how it was presented to and perceived by the public nonetheless plays a central role in the formation and evolution of Takamine's star image. On and off the screen, the relationship appears in striking – almost pointed – contrast to her depiction of her experiences as a child actor under the control of Shige. Shige brought a young Takamine to her first audition and, as she herself would proudly tell journalists, carried her on her back to the next shoot ('Sutā no haha', 1949, p. 14), an experience that Takamine herself compared to that of being a 'performing monkey [*saru mawashi no saru*]' (Takamine, 1998a, p. 37). While Shige is always associated with Takamine's lack of agency, Matsuyama is presented as instrumental for Takamine exercising her agency. In this context, it makes sense for Shige to see him as *father*, taking his place at Takamine's side in a quasi-parental role.

After getting to know each other on the set of *Twenty-Four Eyes*, where Matsuyama served as assistant director under Kinoshita, Takamine and Matsuyama married in 1955. Although the couple remembers that the director introduced Matsuyama as a marriage candidate and encouraged them to date, the media narrative at the time clearly focused on Takamine's actions in choosing a marriage partner. An article in the magazine *Shūkan Sankei*, for example, introduces Matsuyama to its readers under the headline 'the man chosen by Takamine Hideko' (Kusano, 1955, p. 14). Kinoshita is quoted describing his role as intermediary and adviser, but he emphasises that ultimately Takamine's choice was the decisive factor (K. [*sic*], 1955, p. 69). Takamine's image as a woman making her own decisions is constantly emphasised. Reacting to puzzled questions from the media that query the prominence and income of Matsuyama, Takamine declares that she is not interested in rich and successful men (K., 1955, p. 68). She is also making clear that she is not interested in a marriage that would affect her taking responsibility for her own life. Indeed, the same articles mention Matsuyama's small monthly income of 14,000 yen and Takamine's intention to continue her career ('Karumen kon'yaku su', 1955). When Takamine writes in the 1970s that the marriage happened despite Shige's reservations, she points to the central role of marriage in her narrative of agency-finding. In hindsight, it is presented as a key moment when she stops simply complying with the demands of her foster mother.

Indeed, married life with Matsuyama is often referred to in Takamine's writings as a contrast to her former life with Shige. Matsuyama is presented as the ideal partner with whom she can overcome a difficult early life dominated by Shige. Matsuyama can support Takamine when necessary, as a partner; moreover, he is shown as not just respecting, but also appreciating Takamine's leading role. Matsuyama's appeal is described by Takamine when she recalls their first date in a French restaurant, which she had chosen. Matsuyama appears unfamiliar with the right dining etiquette and unable to afford visits to expensive Western-style restaurants himself. She describes Matsuyama as not being shy to show her his own ignorance, asking her about the correct use of cutlery and to demonstrate the correct way to eat (Takamine, 1998b, p. 321). The idea that Matsuyama could learn from Takamine is also expressed in an interview he gave in the year of their marriage. Although admitting Takamine's tendency to be stubborn, he links this to her long experience in the film world. Matsuyama indicates that he is happy to be on Takamine's side and to escort her through her career ('Karumen kon'yaku su', 1955, p. 78). The husband is presented as happy to play the subordinate role. Presented in this way, the marriage feeds the image of Takamine as an actor who makes her own decisions. In a magazine article published in the second year of their marriage, Takamine reflects on her earlier wish to leave her acting career behind, feeling the frustration of being used by her foster mother and the industry, with no ability to make decisions for herself. Takamine goes so far as to call her feelings for her work 'disgust' and recalls her wishes to go 'astray', especially at times when her film career prevented her from attending school. Takamine avoids personal blame but does say that her foster mother was 'over-protective'. At this point in her life and career, Takamine summarises her attitude: 'You can only take responsibility and think for yourself!' (Takamine, 1956, p. 88). Rereading the publications from the time of their wedding and Takamine's later recollections, her marriage to Matsuyama – at a time when marriage for female stars was more likely to bring the end of a career and a sacrifice of agency – plays a central role in a narrative that sees Takamine exercising her own agency. By choosing a man who is unable to financially support her, Takamine's decision to continue her career is framed as both a necessity and personal choice. Five years after breaking free of the studio system, Takamine's marriage sees her doubling down on her independence rather than relinquishing it.

From the beginning, Takamine and Matsuyama seem to have been active in shaping the public narrative about their relationship. Indeed, the announcement of their marriage, as part of possibly the first press release of its kind, is chiefly intended to forestall any possible gossip about their relationship, which would feel, in Takamine's words, 'filthy' ('Karumen kon'yaku su', 1955, p. 79). In her autobiographical writings, Takamine presents the domestic life of the couple as redressing the imbalances in her earlier life: the lack of home comforts and educational opportunities, as well as the resultant anxieties. In one of her autobiographical essays, Takamine writes about her desire as a newlywed to prepare a typical new year's soup with rice cake for her husband. Eating the soup in the warm and cosy setting of a family home was something she had always missed as a child, when she was ferried by Shige from cinema to cinema to greet the audiences during this busy time of the year. Takamine admits that she had no idea how to make a delicious soup and was only able to prepare it with help from the maid. When Matsuyama, to Takamine's joy, eats her first ever soup without any complaints, he is presented as a kind and grateful partner who is happy to receive what Takamine brings into the marriage (Takamine, 1998a, p. 52). Indeed, the couple's shared life of discovery – cooking, eating and travelling together – is part of Takamine's narrative of finding agency rather than subjugation to the state of marriage. This shared domestic life becomes an essential part of how the couple is portrayed in the media and in later book publications. The image of Takamine as nourished and thriving in her domestic life and relationship becomes part of Takamine's persona, which goes hand in hand with her search for agency and emerges in contrast to her life as a younger star.

Depictions of Takamine and Matsuyama's life outside the home can also be contrasted with her earlier life with her 'over-protective' foster mother, who prevented her from gaining an education and attending school with her peers. The couple enjoyed a wide circle of social contacts, among them artists and intellectuals, such as the writer Tanizaki Jun'ichirō (Takamine, 1998a, pp. 175–78) and the painter Umehara Ryūzaburō (Takamine, 1998b, pp. 238–51). Takamine's growing confidence, here with the support of Matsuyama, to move in such circles despite her self-proclaimed lack of education is exemplified in an episode that she recounted in her memoirs. When Takamine was intimidated by the prospect of an upcoming meeting with an intellectual admirer, Shinmura Izuru, the editor of the renowned *Kōjien* dictionary, Matsuyama is described as supportive and reassuring, successfully calming her down. The nervous Takamine, in her own depiction, hardly knew how to use a dictionary at the time. The episode of the meeting itself is told as a humorous story: Shinmura's household turned out to be full of Takamine memorabilia, and the scholar likely found the meeting with Takamine just as intimidating as she did (Takamine, 1998a, pp. 174–87). A photo taken later shows a serious-looking Shinmura in the middle, with Takamine sitting to his right and his wife sitting to his left. Matsuyama stands in the background, the only one not sitting, but attracting attention with a big smile on his face ('"Kōjien" no hensha wa chāmingu', 2021). With Matsuyama's support, here literally smiling in the background, the young Takamine gains more confidence, and her entrée to the intellectual world becomes less daunting. These connections enrich the lives of the couple outside the professional circles of the film business. The detail of Shinmura being such a devoted fan of Takamine, and probably equally impressed by her, suggests that she was now living a life that her fans could understand as rightfully hers – even if it took Matsuyama's support for her to get there. This opening up of Takamine's world through marriage, and the opportunity it presented to surpass the limitations placed on her by her early life, is perhaps counter to what one might expect in terms of patriarchal understandings of marriage. I would argue, however, that this is a key part of her star text: a star text which she and Matsuyama created together through artistic and personal collaboration, and a star text that audiences would read when watching the films in which she appears.

In a photo used to advertise a series of film screenings dedicated to both Takamine and Matsuyama in 2017 ('Matsuyama Zenzō Takamine Hideko', 2017), the focus is on their shared professional background in the film industry and hints at their collaborative endeavours on a number of films. In the photo, the couple is engaged in examining rolls of celluloid films. At the front edge of the photo, one can see a number of reels stacked on top of one another. Matsuyama appears to be setting up a device for cutting and editing. Takamine, on the right-hand side of the picture, is examining a short strip of film from a reel that she is holding in her hand. The protective glove she wears on her right hand and with which she touches the celluloid seems to emphasise that she is not just a casual visitor, but actively engaged in the work of reviewing and editing the material on the reels. The couple's concentrated looks can be read as a clear indicator that they are seriously and collaboratively engaged in the creation of a film, particularly when comparing this photo to the more typical pictures of them in domestic settings with big smiles on their faces. Although being foremost an actor, we can see how Takamine is presented as a collaborator in the filmmaking process. Matsuyama might be the director of the film, but the film that the two are preparing here is *their* film (Figure 9.1).

Matsuyama was most active as a scriptwriter, writing the script for a number of films starring Takamine, such as *Yearning* (*Midareru*, 1964), *Hit and Run* (*Hikinige*, 1966) and *The Twilight Years* (*Kōkotsu no hito*, 1973). It would be interesting to explore how the partnership between Takamine and Matsuyama might have impacted these scripts, but I want to use the remainder of this chapter to look at several examples in which Takamine and Matsuyama collaborated on films as actor and director, respectively: the above-mentioned *Happiness of Us Alone* (1961) and the films *Burari Bura-bura Monogatari* (1962), *The Bridge Between*[4] (*Sanga ari*, 1962) and *Dark the Mountain Snow* (*Rokujō yukiyama tsumugi*, 1965). These last three are currently unavailable for home viewing.[5]

Figure 9.1 Photo of Matsuyama Zenzō and Takamine Hideko (courtesy of Saitō Akemi)

*Happiness of Us Alone* focuses on the hardships of a couple with hearing impairments in the post-war years: Akiko (Takamine) and Michio (Kobayashi Keiju). Working from his own script, Matsuyama Zenzō depicts the suffering of the couple through traumatic wartime events (including the death of Akiko's first husband), which would be relatable to a post-war audience. Over the course of the film, Akiko develops more agency after initially being just the subject of the decisions made by the people around her. For example, the family of her first husband decides to send the young widow back to her mother, and we see her own family discussing her future, knowing that she is not even aware of what is being talked about. Within her relationship with Michio, Akiko develops the strength to speak out and make decisions for herself. Because Akiko only lost her hearing at the age of three, she is able to speak more easily with hearing people – for example, taking charge of communicating with the innkeeper on their honeymoon. She comes to the fore in the relationship and becomes the voice of the couple speaking to the outside world on their behalf. Several scenes illustrate the idea that only in such a partnership of equals can Akiko be properly understood. The couple are pictured conversing in noisy environments or next to a busy train track, situations where hearing couples would be unable to communicate. In one of the most striking scenes of the film, Akiko and Michio communicate through opposite windows at the end of the two cars of a commuter train while the train is moving. Michio assures her that he will always be at her side. Framed by the window, and thereby resembling actors speaking from the silver screen to the audience, the couple reassure each other of their love and ongoing support. The audience are at the same time both witness to and, through having to rely on the written translation, distanced from the intimate scene. *Happiness of Us Alone* manages to portray a couple with a strong bond forged through shared hardships which – although their precise circumstances and challenges will differ – will be familiar to an audience still marked by the war and post-war years. Critics were impressed by the drama and the moving depiction of the love between Akiko and Michio, calling their communication through sign language 'beautiful' and praising the way in which the film takes their unique circumstances to show experiences that are universal and relatable (Kusakabe, 1961).

*The Bridge Between* is another of Matsuyama's films that displays a pacifist message by framing the suffering of its character in the context of war. This film is on a more epic scale, with a narrative spanning several decades and the Pacific Ocean. It tells the story of Japanese immigrants making their home in Hawaii before getting caught in the crossfire of the Pacific War. Takamine plays Kishino, the mother of two sons born in Hawaii. She desperately tries to keep the family alive and together after her husband, upset by a fight with his son over loyalty to Japan, dies of a sudden heart attack. Returning the ashes of her husband to their homeland, Kishino and her accompanying son are surprised by the outbreak of the war. The son is imprisoned and tortured by the Japanese authorities in a prisoner of war camp. The film appears designed as a perfect vehicle for Takamine, possibly giving her the opportunity to repeat her memorable performance in (and the great success of) *Twenty-Four Eyes*. Both films showcase Takamine's ability to age on screen from a young woman to a more mature and disillusioned person who is prematurely aged, war-torn and marked by suffering and loss. Although both characters marry and have children, marriage plays a far more important role in *The Bridge Between*. Many of the decisions made by Takamine's character are motivated by her role as a wife, widow and mother, and she is unable to rely on the decisions of others after losing her husband. When she sings a Hawaiian song to her son, who is homesick for his birthplace, the viewer might briefly feel the longing for Hawaii: a lost paradise for the characters of the film, but a holiday destination known to be enjoyed and favoured by Matsuyama and Takamine.

*Burari Bura-bura Monogatari* depicts Takamine as the fraudster Komako, who pretends to be a victim of the atomic bomb to trick people out of their money. Although presented in a comedic narrative, it is interesting to consider the film's take on 'acting' to make financial gains in a dishonourable manner. Komako is an independent woman tricking her victims by herself. The prospect of marriage, however, is connected to the possibility of leaving the world of deception behind: when fellow fraudster Junpei, played by Kobayashi Keijiu, confesses his love for Komako, she seems to agree to marry him, on the condition that they leave their criminal past behind, demanding that Junpei find a job. Ultimately, however, Komako is not interested in relying on a husband for her income. Staying true to her ways, not only does she not marry him, but she steals his money. Later, the pair reunite and join efforts to help two small, abandoned children, putting their talent for fooling others to better use. Komako does not seem able to leave her talents behind her.

Ine, Takamine's character in *Dark the Mountain Snow*, does, however, leave her career as an entertainer – a geisha – behind when marrying a son of the well-off Rokujō family. The married bliss does not last long because her husband commits suicide soon afterwards and leaves her alone in a power struggle with a suspicious and cold-hearted mother-in-law, who despises Ine as a gold digger. Ine's interests in marriage are, just like Takamine's, not of a financial nature: motivated by her husband's love for the family business in the regional tradition of silk production, Ine dedicates herself to keeping the tradition and business alive. Flashbacks show how Ine engaged with her husband in studying different aspects of the family business. Here, we might see a reflection of real life: Takamine working with her husband to leave certain aspects of her acting career behind to find something else that they would work on together as a shared endeavour. One specific scene in flashback shows Ine and her husband together, inspecting large prints of silk patterns. It bears a marked resemblance to the photo in which Matsuyama and Takamine work on a film, with Takamine holding a strip of film rather than silk.

In that sense, the film celebrates the shared passion of a married couple for a joint enterprise or profession, with the spouse who is left behind eager to honour the deceased fictional partner. In addition, the film bears a number of other parallels to the real-life couple. There are two mother figures, Ine's sceptical mother-in-law and Ine's own mother (in a brief but striking performance by Sugimura Haruko). Ine's mother appears unable to accept her choice to get married, quit the geisha business and leave her behind. Both mother figures make Ine's life more difficult and painful, reminding us once again of the impact of Shige's overwhelming presence on Takamine's life. Another way in which the film resonates with real life is Ine's painful experience of being watched and being the subject of scandal, a reminder of Matsuyma and Takamine's shared fear of gossip. In her attempts to change the traditional silk business, Ine is supported by Jirō (Frankie Sakai), a young man whom Ine's husband had saved from homelessness in his childhood and who feels obliged to support her. This arouses suspicion both in the Rokujō family and the wider community, where the watching eyes and voices gossiping over what is perceived as an affair between Ine and Jirō are put onto screen in surreal, if not horror-film, style, with overlapping speech and close-ups of eyes peering through windows, cracks in the wall and tears in the paper of the *fusuma* (vertical rectangular) sliding doors. Jirō's final efforts to put an end to the gossip might be just another love declaration from Matsuyama, acknowledging the hardships of his film-star wife and the pain of being constantly under public scrutiny. Ine, however, discovers her own agency and becomes strong enough to make her own decisions through a bond with her late husband. Ine worked with spools of silk and Takamine with reels of film.

We see that the depictions of the couples in the films on which Takamine and Matsuyama collaborated display a rich accumulation of themes that relate to the marriage of the two artists. The films appear to tell stories that are relevant and important to the couple, and the viewing experience was undoubtedly enriched by the public perception of the marriage. Takamine Hideko's star text comprises her own early career and her subsequent disavowal of it, media coverage of the financial aspects of her marriage and the idea that the partnership of marriage can support women in developing their own agency. Takamine's role in these films can be interpreted as much more than just giving voice to the director's vision: her life with Matsuyama off screen brings resonance to what audiences see on screen, experiencing a truly collaborative product of actor and director.

## Acknowledgement

I wish to express my gratitude to the Japan Foundation for their generous financial support during my stay in Japan in late 2022. Their backing was instrumental to my research while working on this paper.

## References

Bock, A. (1985). *Japanese film directors* (new ed.). Tokyo: Kodansha International.
Dyer, R. (1998). *Stars (new edition): With a supplementary chapter and bibliography by Paul McDonald*. London: British Film Institute.
Hayward, S. (2006). *Cinema studies: The key concepts* (3rd ed.). London: Routledge.
K., S. [*sic*]. (1955, March 13). Deko-chan tsui ni kekkon. Kono hiroi sora no shita ni ita danna-san. *Shūkan Yomiuri*, 68–69.
Kasuga, T. (2017). *Nakadai tatsuya ga kataru nihon eiga ōgon jidai*. Tokyo: Bungei Shunjū.
'Karumen kon'yaku su': Matsuyama Zenō-Takamine Hideko no bāi. (1955, March 3). *Shūkan Asahi*, 78–79.
'Kōjien' no hensha wa chāmingu?! Mago no yoru denki 'Kōjien wa naze umareta ka'. (2021, August 13). *Asahi.com*. Retrieved from https://book.asahi.com/jinbun/article/13616644
Kida, S. (2012). *Takamine Hideko: Onna toshite joyū toshite*. Tokyo: Asahi Shinbun Shuppan.
Kusakabe, K. (1961, 18 January). Utsukushii kaiwa ni miryoku: Kandō saseru fūfu ai. *Mainichi Shinbun*, 5.
Kusano, E. (1955, 13 March). Takamine Hideko no eranda dansei: Matsuyama Zenzō to iu jokantoku. *Shūkan Sankei*, 14–15.
Matsuyama, Z. (2010). Joyū-Tsuma-Shi. In A. Saitō (ed.), *Takamine Hideko* (pp. 190–93). Tokyo: Kinema junpō-sha.
Matsuyama Zenzō Takamine Hideko. Fūfu de ayunda eiga jinsei. (2017). *Cinenouveau*. Retrieved from http://www.cinenouveau.com/sakuhin/matsuyama-takamine/matsuyamatakamine.html
Orr, J. (2001). *The victim as hero: Ideologies of peace and national identity in post-war Japan*. Honolulu: The University of Hawai'i Press.
Richie, D., & Anderson, J. L. (1982). *The Japanese film: Art and industry* (expanded ed.). Princeton: Princeton University Press.

Russell, C. (2008). *The cinema of Naruse Mikio: Women and Japanese modernity*. Durham-London: Duke University Press.
Saitō, A. (2012). *Takamine Hideko ga ai shita otoko*. Tokyo: Hāsuto fujin gahō.
Sutā no haha: Kokuchiban. (1949, 23 March). *Asahi Gurafu*, 14.
Takamine, H. (1956, September). Jibun no koto wa jibun de kangaeru shō ga nai. Aru shitashii tomo to no taiwa. *Bessatsu Chisei*, 88–89.
Takamine, H. (1998a). *Watashi no tōsei nikki V.1*. Tokyo: Bungei Shunjū.
Takamine, H. (1998b). *Watashi no tōsei nikki V.2*. Tokyo: Bungei Shunjū.
Takasai, T. (2011, April). Takarada Akira ga kataru: Jibun o sasaeta 'Hōrōki' no genba ni okeru Takamine Hideko-san no hitokoto. *Kinema Junpō, 1580*, 21–23.
Tanimura, K. (1949, November). Takamine Hideko to nihon eiga kai. Kanojo wa okotta. Soshite. *Zaidan*, 42–43.
The Greatest Films of All Time. The Results. (2012). *Sight and Sound*, 22(9), 39–71.
Yoshimoto, M. (2000). *Kurosawa: film studies in Japanese cinema*. Durham: Duke University Press.

# Notes

1. Editors' note: In this chapter, Japanese names adhere to the Japanese convention of family name first, followed by given name.
2. On Takamine's role in Naruse's films, see Bock (1985, p. 113); Russell (2008).
3. I am using the term 'actor' for Takamine as a person who acts, regardless of gender. In quotes from other authors, including in Japanese when indicating the gender-specific term *joyū*, however, I am using the term 'actress'.
4. This film has also been shown under the English title *Mother Country*.
5. I would like to express my thanks to Kataoka Ichirō, who helped me gain access to these three films from the archive of a private collector. The films I had access to were recordings from television broadcasts on Japanese cable television.

# Chapter 10
# Angie Chen: Hong Kong Film Pioneer

*Andy Willis*

Less acknowledged within critical and academic circles than her contemporaries Ann Hui and Mabel Cheung, filmmaker Angie Chen is in many ways their equal in terms of being a pioneer within the Hong Kong film industry. Like Hui and Cheung, Chen also studied abroad, initially in the International Writing programme at the University of Iowa, before undertaking film-based training at the prestigious and influential University of California Los Angeles (UCLA) film school, alongside future feature film directors such as Alex Cox. Following her return to Hong Kong, Chen directed feature films for the major production companies of the day, Shaw Brothers (*Maybe It's Love*, 1984 and *My Name Ain't Suzie*, 1985) and Golden Harvest (*Chaos by Design*, 1988), during the period now widely labelled as the Hong Kong 'new wave' in the 1980s. The poor critical and commercial reception of *Chaos by Design* saw Chen move away from making fiction features and into the field of directing commercials. In that arena she established her own company, Scorpio Films, and became an award-winning director, creating advertising campaigns for high-profile clients such as Proctor and Gamble. More recently, Chen has worked on a series of personal, and once more award-winning, documentary feature films: *This Darling Life* (2008), *One Tree, Three Lives* (2012) and *I've Got the Blues* (2017). In 2019, I curated a short season of Chen's work at HOME in Manchester, as part of that venue's year-long celebration of women in global cinema (see Hayward and Willis, 2022). In preparing that retrospective, I was able to see examples of Chen's fiction and documentary work from across the various chapters of her career in close proximity. Seen together in this way, I became more convinced of the ground-breaking nature of a body of work that is only just now gaining the critical acknowledgement it deserves. The retrospective also offered the opportunity to speak to the director at length about her work. These conversations underpin this chapter.

## Outside In

A number of influential filmmakers within the Hong Kong film industry spent time studying abroad. For example, the above-mentioned Ann Hui and Mabel Cheung attended the London Film School and New York University, respectively. Other key new-wave figures also spent time abroad, such as Tsui Hark who attended the University of Texas. This was an important factor as it enabled these filmmakers to bring a more international perspective to their work when they returned to Hong Kong. This was particularly influential in their approaches to film form. As David Bordwell put it, . . .

> By the 1980s virtually all Hong Kong films were in Cantonese, and a new generation of directors came to the fore. Often trained in the west and in television, less tied to Mainland traditions than older hands, these young filmmakers [ . . . ] reshaped Hong Kong cinema into a modern and distinctive part of the territory's mass culture. (2000, p. 4)

Angie Chen's background is also an example of this trend. She took undergraduate and postgraduate courses at the University of Iowa, the latter in the prestigious International Writing Programme which was led by Hualing Nieh Engle and Paul Engle and aimed at bringing writers from around the world into dialogue with each other. Chen would use her relationship with Hualing Nieh Engle to form the basis of her 2012 documentary *One Tree, Three Lives*. Following her time in Iowa, Chen attended the world-famous UCLA film school. There she studied filmmaking alongside future directors such as Alex Cox. This international experience opened Chen up to the influence of a variety of global filmmaking styles and production techniques. She would return to Hong Kong marked by these practices and would eventually attempt to implement them in various ways within her own filmmaking.

It was during her time at UCLA that Chen made the award-winning short documentary, *The Visit* (1980). At its core, this is a film about her strained relationship with her father. *The Visit* follows Chen as she reconnects with him during a period in his life when he is living in Bonn, then the capital of West Germany. The film also reveals that at the time he was suffering from cancer. An emotionally driven piece, the style and approach of this early work foreshadows Chen's later documentary method. From the outset it places the director as an active participant in the events that unfold before the camera. Rather than assuming the classic documentary position of an objective observer, Chen, as a participant, and her camera are clearly emotionally involved. This emotive engagement at times has a clear impact on the shape of what appears on screen. As in her later documentary features, Chen appears unapologetically close to her subject and, in doing so, joins the likes of Nick Broomfield in rejecting the dominant, distanced, observational perspective adopted by many factual filmmakers. In doing this, her work seems to exist between what Bill Nichols describes as the 'participatory' documentary – that is, films in which 'the filmmaker becomes a social actor (almost) like any other (almost because the filmmaker retains the camera and with it a degree of potential power and control over events)' (2001, p. 139) – and what he labels as 'performative' documentaries, ones where the film focuses on the maker's involvement and interaction with their subject. In various ways Chen's subsequent documentary work can be seen to fruitfully negotiate a space between Nichols' two categories. However, before returning to the documentary film, Chen would establish herself as an innovative fiction film director within the Hong Kong film industry.

Chen's career in fiction filmmaking has its origins at UCLA. While studying there, she was introduced to the Taiwanese composer and director Liu Chia-chang. This led to her being invited to assist him in the development of a project that was going to be partly made in the USA. While Chen's involvement in this venture did not lead to anything substantial, it was through Liu that she was introduced to Jackie Chan and his manager/producer Willie Chan. This, in turn, opened up a road to filmmaking that led back to Hong Kong. Chen states that she was not planning a move back to Hong Kong at this time, but rather contemplated staying in the United States and trying to forge a career there. However, Jackie Chan subsequently invited the young filmmaker back to Hong Kong to act as his assistant director on *Dragon Lord* (1982), a film in which he would star, as well as direct and co-write the script. An offer that was difficult to refuse, this large-scale project took Chen to South Korea and Taiwan during its lengthy shoot and placed her firmly within the Hong Kong film industry.

Having been invited back to work in Hong Kong, what followed for Chen was a period when she began to establish herself in that male-dominated business of the early 1980s. She began to do this by continuing to work as an assistant director to some of the most high-profile figures in the local film industry. One of these was Po Chih Leong, with whom she worked as an assistant director on the thriller/horror hybrid *He Lives by Night*, which was released in 1982. This film was made for the Cinema City production company through which Chen was able to make professional contacts with some of the most influential figures in the Hong Kong cinema of the period, such as Eric Tsang. With her experience as an assistant director providing inside knowledge of the way in which the Hong Kong film industry operated, Chen would begin to work towards making films in her own right.

## Shaw Brothers

Following her experiences as an assistant director, and at the height of Hong Kong cinema's 'new wave' of the 1980s, Chen would begin to establish herself as a filmmaker. Her opportunity came after being introduced to Mona Fong, who since 1973 had been head of the production department at the Shaw Brothers studio. In 1981 Fong became a member of the board of directors of the company and, according to Chen, was keen to support the development of women filmmakers. This is reflected by the fact that during this period Ann Hui directed *Love in a Fallen City* (1984) and Mabel Cheung made *The Illegal Immigrant* (1985) for the studio. As Sek Kei notes, she also oversaw a number of directors associated with the Hong Kong cinema's 'new wave' make films for Shaw Brothers, such as Patrick Tam, Eddie Fong and Alex Law (2003, p. 47). During this same period, Chen was offered a three-film directing contract with Shaw Brothers. This was made up of two guaranteed films, with an option to be extended for a third. Certainly, such a deal was rare for a female director in Hong Kong at that time.

The first result of Chen's Shaw Brothers contract was *Maybe It's Love*, released in 1984. The film starred the popular Shaw Brothers contract star Cherie Cheung and is something of a whodunnit, which Chen has suggested was conceived as an homage to Alfred Hitchcock's *Rear Window* (1954). With plenty of suggestions of voyeurism within a small village, the film uses its conventional suspense structure to include some tentative feminist ideas, somewhat compromised by the studio's need for scenes that play well with young male audiences, such as those of Cheung doing aerobics. According to the website the Hong Kong Movie Database (HKMDB), the film proved to be a surprise success at the local box-office, making HK $5,765,303 during its theatrical run from 9 to 21 March 1984. This box-office success meant that Shaw Brothers was willing to allow Chen's next project to be one to which she felt particularly committed.

Chen followed up *Maybe It's Love* with *My Name Ain't Suzie* in 1985 – a film that can be read as a riposte to the images of Hong Kong women that circulated in Western popular culture, most directly Hollywood's 1960 adaption of Richard Mason's 1957 novel *The World of Suzie*

*Wong*. The director remembered seeing the film as a child: 'I watched *The World of Suzie Wong* when I was 12, and it left a profound impression on me [. . . it is] a film seen from a male and western perspective'. Chen goes on to recall that she was determined to challenge this point of view:

> Many years later, returning to Hong Kong from America, I decided to tell the story from a female and a Hong Konger's angle, to try to delve deeper into the psyche of a prostitute working the sailors in the 1950s and 1960s. You can say it was my reaction to *The World of Suzie Wong*, hence the title *My Name Ain't Suzie*. (Chen, 2019b)

Chen's film looks at the lives of a group of bar girls in the Hong Kong district of Wan Chai. In addition, *My Name Ain't Suzie* follows a young mixed-heritage man's search for his father. Chen consciously constructs the film in a manner that makes the bar girls 'real' people with a range of issues impacting their lives, rather than the background stereotypes of Western representations. As she put it, '[i]t was about struggle, hardship, love and abandonment. It was a story about women' (Chen, 2019b). In making the film, Chen wanted to use an approach that would deliver a sense of realism to the project. This certainly aligns her with the wider aspirations of the Hong Kong 'new wave' filmmakers to bring a fresh stylistic method to their work. To this end, Chen remembers:

> We managed to rent an abandoned building in Wan Chai, built the main bar's facade, recreated Wan Chai in the 50s, and shot on actual street locations [ . . . ] some of the vintage costumes were acquired in second-hand shops in London which was actually cheaper than making them in Hong Kong. We searched diligently for vintage props including rickshaws which were an icon of the time and are now extinct in Hong Kong. (Chen, 2019b)

This search for authenticity also extended to the casting of the film. The production team held extensive auditions in their search for an actor to play the young mixed-heritage character. Rather than cast a Shaw contract player, they decided on an inexperienced actor called Anthony Perry. They selected him because 'he was Eurasian, and he was fatherless and desperately searching for his father. The male character Jimmy was also Eurasian, an angry young man, abandoned by his Caucasian father' (Chen, 2019b). Perry would go on to become a major star of Hong Kong cinema under the name Anthony Wong.

Initially, Mona Fong, who had begun her entertainment career as a dancing hostess before becoming a singer in a cabaret, was a strong supporter of the project. Chen suggests that this was one of the reasons why they were able to attempt to make such an authentic film. However, during post-production her enthusiasm waned, and the studio became less keen on supporting the film's release. The film would prove a disappointment at the box office, and the option for Chen to direct a third film for Shaw Brothers was not taken up.

## Golden Harvest

Following her release from Shaw Brothers, Chen's third feature film, *Chaos by Design* (1988), a romantic comedy set in the Hong Kong fashion industry, was made for another of the key Hong Kong production companies of the period, Golden Harvest. Starring a pair of rising actors, Cherie Chung and Cecilia Yip, and with an almost farce-like plot, on the surface one can see *Chaos by Design* as something of a typical, almost run-of-the-mill Hong Kong film of the period. However, the film's significance is not contained in its plot; it lies in its inclusion and representation of LGBTQ+ characters, something that in the context of mainstream Hong Kong cinema of the period is exceptional. This aspect of Chen's work had appeared in *My Name Ain't Suzie* in the costume selected for Deannie Ip's character Wong Ying. Whenever she appears, she challenges the overtly sexualised 'female' attire of the bar girls by smoking small cigars, sporting short, slicked back hair, male-styled shirts and a white suit with a shirt and bow tie.

As in *My Name Ain't Suzie*, in *Chaos by Design* sexuality and the blurring of gender boundaries are shown without presenting them as an issue to be focused on and explored. Rather, in Chen's films, from the outset the characters just exist as part of the community represented on screen.

This is certainly the case in *Chaos by Design*. Here, in the opening sequences that introduce the film's central character Abel Sang as he leaves his Japanese fashion school, we see him briefly wrestling with his Japanese best friend who then hands him a photograph of himself dressed as a geisha to remember him by. Abel accepts the keepsake without being shocked or surprised. This quietly and without sensation suggests that seeing his friend dressed in such a manner is not out of the ordinary in their milieu. Here, Chen normalises and makes everyday something that in the context of other mainstream popular culture in the late 1980s would likely be represented in a cinematically more hysterical manner, in order to ridicule the image of the friend or use it for comedic effect. The fact that this is not done in *Chaos by Design* indicates

Chen's intention to avoid such hyperbole in her representation of the film's characters.

Following this sequence, Abel returns to Hong Kong, and the film introduces the audience to the fashion house where he is seeking (and will shortly find) work. This world also offers Chen the opportunity to further present a range of gay and lesbian characters. Once again, rather than the more common single gay character who is a side-kick or comedic supporting player, Chen offers a range of characters, enabling an avoidance of simplistic stereotyping. The inclusivity of the world represented on screen is solidified early in this section of the film. Once we have been introduced to a number of characters who are variously signified through the film's *mise-en-scène* and the actors' performances as gay, one of the fashion house employees states: 'We are a big family here, Abel Song'. A family that is clearly comfortable embracing difference. This tone continues when a celebratory sequence follows Abel on his first social encounter with his new work colleagues, a party celebrating the 'marriage' of two gay friends. The opening sections of the film also create an 'is he, is he not?' series of questions about Abel's sexuality. Many workers wonder about Abel's preferences, with one woman confidently asserting that 'he's one of us'. Chen subtly reinforces these aspects of the film through several cultural references, such as the inclusion of a clip from a Warner Bros cartoon, which appears on television and shows a cross-dressing Bugs Bunny, and at a party the cross-dressing performance of a Chinese Opera character by fashion house boss Derek, a form traditionally linked to males playing female roles.

While, following these striking opening sections, *Chaos by Design* settles into being a more conventional heterosexual romantic comedy, reminding us how mainstream the film was designed to be, the acceptance and positive images of Hong Kong's gay community remain a vital backdrop to its story. Ultimately, what is perhaps most striking about the positive representation of Hong Kong's gay community in *Chaos by Design* is that it is present in a film that was released in the territory in 1988, three years before the Hong Kong Legislative Council passed a law decriminalising homosexual acts between consenting men aged twenty-one and above in private on 10 July 1991 (Suen, 2021). Her ability to create images that 'naturalise' the presence of LGBTQ+ characters and communities in 1980s Hong Kong films further stresses the significance and ground-breaking nature of Chen's work. In this way, once again, it is possible to argue that here we have the career of a pioneer figure within the Hong Kong film industry.

## Commercials

Following her disillusionment with Shaw Brothers' handling of the release of *My Name Ain't Suzie*, the commercial failure of *Chaos by Design* and a feeling that she did not want to direct the projects she was subsequently offered, Chen began to move away from the mainstream Hong Kong film industry. Her disenchantment was further exacerbated by her feeling that, as a woman and as someone who had trained in the USA, she was an outsider. This was something which she had felt in the male-dominated environment of Cinema City and which had been brought home to her at Shaw Brothers. Indeed, Chen often tells an anecdote regarding the practices she observed at the studio and how in her own small way she rallied against them:

> Women weren't allowed to sit on the equipment cases on sound stages because that would bring bad luck. They would really scream at you, the crew. When they would see a woman, anyone, the cast or an extra or anybody who just wanted to sit on a case, it was 'Butt out'. So I witnessed that, but I didn't say anything at the time. When I got my own film, I did an experiment. On the set, I saw this case, and I sat down. And then I waited for a response. Nobody said anything. (Eagan, 2019)

In 1987, Chen was approached to make a commercial for a company called Take 3, and this opportunity would take her career in a different direction. Director Po Chih Leong – with whom, as noted earlier, she had worked as an assistant director – had also worked with the company; hence, Chen felt that it was a legitimate offer that would, as she put it, challenge her to tell a story in thirty seconds. She was reasonably happy with the result and found that she enjoyed the environment, thus was happy to take the resulting assignments that followed. What is more, with her ability to speak Cantonese, Mandarin and English, she was in a position to take on shoots in Hong Kong and Taiwan, as well as in the rapidly developing markets in Mainland China. As a result, Chen became one of the few Hong Kong-based women directors working in high-end advertising.

In 1990, in order to take greater control of her career, Chen established her own production company, Scorpio Films. This allowed her to avoid some of the bureaucracy associated with the advertising industry at the time, and it gave her the ability to be more in control of her assignments by saying no to projects. From 1990 until 1997, Chen would work on high-profile and award-winning campaigns for agencies such as J. Walter Thompson and clients including Proctor and Gamble, Peugeot, Ford and Apple. Alongside this work, Scorpio Films also made promotional works for the Hong Kong government. For example, they made films that contributed to projects such as road safety campaigns. This work would see Chen collaborate with new emerging talents within the Hong Kong film scene, such as cinematographer Christopher Doyle. Following the end of Scorpio Films as a company devoted to work within the advertising industry in 1997, Chen returned to freelancing. This period of Angie Chen's career is often overlooked, but it is significant, as once again it reveals a filmmaker willing to challenge a male-dominated industry. Her success in this arena, combined with her feature film work in the 1980s, reveals a career that is both significant in terms of its output and ground-breaking in its variety and willingness to challenge patriarchal industrial structures.

## Three Documentaries

In the twenty-first century, Angie Chen would revive Scorpio Films, this time as a production company to develop documentary films and support her work as a factual filmmaker. The director had grown tired of making commissioned work for other people, feeling that she wanted more control and input into her projects. In an interview with Ronny Agustinus for the Yogyakarta Festival Film Dokumenter (FFD), she stated that...

> ...when you make a TV commercial, they tell you what to do, what they want. And I just want to do a film of my own and at that time I thought the fastest, easiest way to do it was to make a documentary because you don't need a big crew, you don't need a lot of money. (Agustinus, 2018)

Since the decision to return to more personal subjects, Chen has completed three documentary features: *This Darling Life* (2008), which explores the lives of dog owners from various segments of Hong Kong society; *One Tree, Three Lives* (2012), which returned Chen to the world of the Iowa writing programme and explores the life of her teacher Hualing Nieh Engle; and *I've Got the Blues* (2017), which sees her intellectually sparring with Hong Kong painter, art director, blues musician and activist Yank Wong Yan-kwai. Chen's immersive approach meant that each of her documentary features took a significant amount of time to be realised. She observed that, in contrast to her features and commercial work, ...

> ...with my documentaries, in average each film has taken three years from beginning to completion. It's a long process because I follow the subject for

a long time. Because I think you have to follow in order for the interesting things to emerge. (Agustinus, 2018)

This lengthy production and post-production schedule reflects the director's participatory approach, which sees her directly engaging with her subjects over time.

Chen's first feature documentary after her return to the form, *This Darling Life*, began as a study of dog owners in Hong Kong. In her choice of subject, the director, in retrospect somewhat typically, decided to focus on something close to her. She was, and still is, a dedicated dog owner who was coming to terms with the fact that her pet, Baby, was coming close to the end of its life. The subsequent documentary film offers images of a wide cross-section of dog owners, from a homeless man who lives under a bypass with his dog, to a woman who single-handedly runs her own shelter with over a hundred dogs. Each has a close relationship with their canine charges, and Chen's camera brings the human aspects of their relationships to the fore. As Maggie Lee notes in her *Hollywood Reporter* review, 'Chen infuses the film with her own subjective and poetic images of Hong Kong, making it both meditative and confessional' (Lee, 2008). In Chen's hands, the film becomes about how people interact with their dogs and what their interactions reveal about their humanity. The intimacy of this aspect of the film is driven by the fact that it also returns to the subject of her first documentary short, *The Visit*, her relationship with her father. Lee observes:

> The director explores her own feelings about her 15-year-old four-legged companion Baby's impending death, which segues into conversations with her brother about their estrangement with their father, interspersed with home-movie footage of his life with his Caucasian partner. The project underlines her quest to find the capacity in herself to forgive her father through witnessing unconditional love from Baby. (Lee, 2008)

Lee's comment on the film is insightful, as it reflects Chen's argument that the film is 'about love, life and death' (Korbecka, 2019). What is most striking is the way in which Chen's documentary films are able to move deftly from what seems to be the subject of the film to a more thoughtful, introspective reflection on the filmmaker herself.

This approach is utilised again with Chen's next documentary feature, *One Tree, Three Lives*. The film returns to a significant and inspirational figure in Chen's life, the writer and educator Hualing Nieh Engle, who described herself as 'a tree, with roots in China, the trunk in Taiwan, and the many leaves in Iowa, USA'. In response to this, the film explores its subject's life and movement from China to Taiwan to the USA where she was central in the development of the International Writing Programme with her husband Paul Engle. Covering each location of her life, the film explores the impact she had on those around her, through a series of interviews with now established writers such as Mo Yin and Pai Hsien-yung. In addition, the film explores how Nieh Engle's work reflected her life's journeys. Chen has stated that *One Tree, Three Lives* 'is about the love between Nieh Hualing and her husband, as well as a selfless love for literature' (HKIFF, 2018). It is also a film about migration and creativity. Chen herself has experienced such a life, variously living and working in China, Taiwan, Hong Kong and the USA, and this experience gives her a particular understanding of the feeling of exile that Nieh Engle suggests she has felt.

Chen's last feature to date is another documentary, *I've Got the Blues*. Once again choosing a subject close to her own life, here the focus is on Hong Kong painter, art director, blues musician, photographer and activist Yank Wong Yan-kwai. The director had known Wong for many years, as he had contributed to some of the government projects that Scorpio Films had made in the 1990s. However, in interviews at the time of the film's screening at the 2018 Hong Kong International Film Festival, Chen made it clear that, '[w]hen I started, I didn't know him that well' (HKIFF, 2018). However, in Wong she found a subject that offered a similar uncompromising approach that had marked the subjects of her previous documentary films. She stated that she was drawn to 'Yank's passion [ . . . ] for artistic creation', as well as his uncompromising approach to his various artistic endeavours. She stated: 'He has never made any sort of compromise for his art. He has always been pure. An art director for more than 30 films, Yank never worked on a project for the money' (HKIFF, 2018). However, as with her previous documentaries, Chen places herself inside the film, and in doing so draws out other aspects that elevate it above being simply a profile of its subject.

Through a series of often interrupted interviews Chen uses her (occasionally elusive) subject as a starting point for a meditation on personal and social issues related to contemporary Hong Kong people and society. Chen has said about the project: 'I have sought to bring the vibrant underground art scene to the forefront, to introduce Yank and his friends', while significantly acknowledging that she wanted to 'make this film not only about Yank, but also about Hong Kong and its people' (Chen, 2019a). By focusing on the relationship between filmmaker and subject, *I've Got the Blues* also ultimately captures the fleeting nature of creation, in this instance on both sides of the camera. In doing so, the film seems typical of Angie Chen's documentary practice.

## Conclusion

When one draws the various aspects of Chen's career together, it quickly becomes apparent that hers is a unique career within the context of the Hong Kong film industry since the 1980s. Her international experiences and perspective have meant that within her work she is always willing to challenge negative representations that were perhaps more acceptable within the Hong Kong film industry of the 1980s and beyond, striving to find great human warmth within her subjects, be they fictional or factual. Her pioneering career is only now becoming acknowledged as important, and as such Angie Chen offers a model for those women (and men) who want to make films that have something to say about the world we live in – and make them on their own terms.

The year 2019 would prove to be an important one in terms of positioning Angie Chen as a significant figure in the history of Hong Kong cinema. In addition to the retrospective at HOME in Manchester, where she was present for two Q & A sessions following screenings of *My Name Ain't Suzie* and *I've Got the Blues*, Chen's work was screened as part of two other key events. In April, at the influential Udine Far East Film Festival in Italy, there was a screening of *My Name Ain't Suzie* with the director present. In his review of the festival, Chris Berry said that he was 'privileged' to see the film, which he labelled 'a hard-hitting exposé' (2019). In August and September 2019, the Metrograph cinema in New York ran a season of films titled 'Shaw Sisters'. This brought together work by women who had worked for the studio, and Chen's *Maybe It's Love* and *My Name Ain't Suzie* played alongside work by Ann Hui, So Jing-man, Angela Mak and Mabel Cheung (Gilman, 2019). The fact that the programmers of the season picked both of her Shaw Brothers films for inclusion also indicates that a reassessment of her contribution to Hong Kong cinema is ongoing. As it does, it can only reveal a noteworthy figure whose pioneering status needs much more recognition, as the history of Hong Kong cinema is re-negotiated in order to acknowledge the importance of those once marginalised.

## References

Agustinus, R. (2018). *Interview with Angie Chen, director of* I've got the blues. Retrieved from https://ffd.or.id/revpro/en/interview-en/interview-with-angie-chen-director-of-ive-got-the-blues/

Berry, C. (2019, July). A vintage year – The 21st Far East Film Festival. *Senses of Cinema, 91*. Retrieved from https://www.sensesofcinema.com/2019/festival-reports/a-vintage-year-the-21st-far-east-film-festival/

Bordwell, D. (2000). *Planet Hong Kong: Popular cinema and the art of entertainment*. Cambridge: Harvard University Press.

Chen, A. (2019a). Director's statement. *Hong Kong Fringe Club*. Retrieved from http://www.hkfringeclub.com/en/whatson/1466-Screening+and+discussion+of+I%E2%80%99ve+got+the+blues.html

Chen, A. (2019b). *My name ain't Suzie*: Reflections. Retrieved from https://www.fareastfilm.com/eng/archive/catalogue/2019/my-name-aint-suzie-riflessioni/?IDLYT=31711

Eagan, D. (2019). A bigger voice for women: Angie Chen on directing features in the 1980s. *Mubi Notebook*. Retrieved from https://mubi.com/notebook/posts/a-bigger-voice-for-women-angie-chen-on-directing-features-in-the-1980s

Gilman, S. (2019, August 23). The Shaw Brothers' sisters: Filmmakers at a fallen studio. *Mubi Notebook*. Retrieved from https://mubi.com/notebook/posts/the-shaw-brothers-sisters-filmmakers-at-a-fallen-studio

Hayward, R., and Willis, A. (2022). Celebrating women in global cinema: Curating a year-long programming initiative at HOME, Manchester. In L. Tsitsou, H. Rana, and B. Wessels (eds), *The formation of film audiences: Conference proceedings*. Retrieved from https://www.dhi.ac.uk/books/film-audiences/celebrating-women-in-global-cinema/

HKIFF. (2018). *Strolling with Yank Wong under water – Interview with Angie Chen at 42nd HKIFF*. Retrieved from https://industry.hkiff.org.hk/en/index.php?route=news/detail&news_id=37

HKMDB. (n.d.). *Maybe it's love*. Retrieved from http://hkmdb.com/db/movies/view.mhtml?id=6557&display_set=eng

Korbecka, M. (2019). Angie Chen interview: 'A documentary film needs to be honest and ethical, yet creative and open'. *easternkicks.com*. Retrieved from https://www.easternkicks.com/features/angie-chen-interview-a-documentary-film-needs-to-be-honest-and-ethical-yet-creative-and-open/

Lee, M. (2008, April 8). *This darling life*. *The Hollywood Reporter*. Retrieved from https://www.hollywoodreporter.com/movies/movie-reviews/darling-life-126123/

Nichols, B. (2001). *Introduction to documentary*. Bloomington: Indiana University Press.

Sek, K. (2003). Shaw Movie Town's 'China dream' and 'Hong Kong sentiments'. In W. Ain-ling (ed.), *The Shaw screen: A preliminary study* (pp. 37–47). Hong Kong: Hong Kong Film Archive.

Suen, Y. (2021, July 10). When will Hong Kong fully protect its LGBT community from discrimination? *South China Morning Post*. Retrieved from https://www.scmp.com/comment/opinion/article/3140330/when-will-hong-kong-fully-protect-its-lgbt-community-discrimination

## Chapter 11

# Her Own Feminism: Authorship and Editing in Ning Ying's Filmmaking Practice

*Francesca Young Kaufman*

This chapter will explore the independent cinema of Chinese director Ning Ying in the context of institutionalised challenges to women filmmakers in the 1990s and early 2000s. Against a backdrop of significant restrictions in both the domestic and international markets, Ning Ying worked independently to produce a series of ethnographic and experimental films chronicling the social implications of China's urban expansion. Her practice is unusual for combining the roles of director and editor, maintaining a high degree of personal control over the finished film. A closer examination of her work reveals the extent to which control of the editing enabled a resistance to the norms governing both Chinese 'women's film' (films made by women directors) and the representation of female characters and experience. Through considering Ning Ying's creative responses to the twin restrictions placed on women filmmakers and female representation, this chapter will contribute to current scholarship on feminist cinema by re-emphasising the importance of authorship for women working in a non-dominant position in the Chinese film industry.

Ning Ying trained as part of the first intake of students to the Beijing Film Academy (BFA) when it re-opened in 1978 after the end of the Cultural Revolution (1966–76). Unlike her colleagues Chen Kaige and Zhang Yimou, she left the BFA after only two years and moved to Italy to study at the Centro Sperimentale di Cinematographia. After completing her training in editing, she went on to work with various directors, including Federico Fellini, and was an assistant director to Bernardo Bertolucci on *The Last Emperor of China* in 1987. In the early 1990s, Ning Ying returned to China and made a triptych of innovative films about Beijing, her home city. *For Fun* (找乐, *Zhao le*, 1993), *On the Beat* (民警故事, *Minjing Gushi*, 1995), and *I Love Beijing*, or *Hot Summer Nights* as it is sometimes translated (夏日暖洋洋, *Xia Ri*

*Nuan Yangyang*, 2001), combined a loose, ethnographic filming style and the use of amateur actors with carefully structured and highly creative editing. Ning Ying went on to use more directly observational and experimental methods in a documentary about migrants (*Railroad of Hope*, 希望之旅, *Xiwang zhi lü*, 2002) and in *Perpetual Motion* (无穷动, *Wuqiong Dong*, 2005), a drama exploring the tensions and conversations between four middle-aged elite urban women in Beijing. *Perpetual Motion* received mixed reviews, and in the later 2000s Ning Ying moved into commercial filmmaking, although she continued to be actively involved with every element of the production process. Ning Ying's early films have often led to her being associated with the 'sixth generation' of directors, a group including her brother-in-law Zhang Yuan, whose work utilised the technical innovations of the 1990s, such as MiniDV cameras to create an exploratory realist style and semi-independent practice. This chapter will explore one of Ning's films from this period, *I Love Beijing*, and consider her directorial approach and the role that editing plays in constructing a uniquely creative aesthetic. Set against the institutional barriers faced by many Chinese female directors in the 1990s and early 2000s, this chapter will propose that personal authorship defines Ning Ying's filmmaking and offers an alternative way of conceptualising feminist practice in China.

## Institutional Context

By the late 1990s, when Ning Ying was making *I Love Beijing*, the Chinese film industry was well advanced in a process of fragmentation that had been taking place since the beginning of the decade. In the late 1970s and 1980s, Chinese female directors such as Zhang Nuanxin, Huang Shuqin and Hu Mei had benefited from an institutional structure that ensured access to production and distribution networks for their work (Cui, 2003). It was also within the state studio system that Ning Ying's BFA contemporaries Chen Kaige, Tian Zhuangzhuang and Zhang Yimou made the films that became internationally recognised as China's cinematic New Wave. But lesser-known directors working on more mainstream productions were also able to take advantage of the security afforded by an established production system, in concert with a cultural atmosphere strongly in favour of artistic experimentation (see Zhang, 2007). In the 1990s, however, the shift to a market-led culture industry dramatically changed the environment within which directors needed to work. By the end of the decade, the Chinese film industry had broken into three uneasily co-existing strands. The state-studio system, no longer a bastion of cinematic innovation under the aegis of liberal-minded professionals such as Xie Fei, was in dramatic decline, losing support from the state as it failed to compete internationally with a series of didactic and derivative flops. In its place, a rising commercial sector was producing increasingly competitive mainstream films focused on patriotic themes and unambivalent genres, such as Feng Xiaogang's wildly popular new year comedies. In parallel with these developments, a third cinema industry was producing and promoting independent Chinese filmmaking to an audience primarily located on international film festival boards and screened at global venues such as Cannes, Sundance and the Berlinale. This independent practice was dominated by a handful of significant directors who had achieved international recognition and who were able to utilise their cultural cachet to negotiate a precarious position for themselves within the recognition and tolerance of the state (Braester, 2005).

These shifts in the Chinese film industry disproportionately affected women directors. Having previously received significant support within the state studio system, female filmmakers found themselves increasingly marginalised in the 1990s, as those same studios were progressively privatised in an effort to compete with the commercial and independent sectors (see Brady, 2008). Many of the challenges experienced by filmmakers generally in this period were exacerbated for women directors, due to the problematic status of 'women's cinema' in China. In 1986, the China Film Art Research Centre, a state-led institute for promoting the development of domestic cinema, hosted a symposium on 'women's cinema' led by 当代电影 *Dangdai Dianying* (the Chinese *Contemporary Cinema* journal). The views of leading film scholars and critics were published in a subsequent edition of the journal. Analysing their statements in 1988, Chris Berry identified a consensus coalescing around the idea of 'women's cinema' as a specific phenomenon (Berry, 1988). He found that institutional attitudes towards female directors in China were inflected by a set of implicit assumptions about their gender and how this would affect their work. It was expected that films made by women would have a clearly social focus and engage in some way with the psychology of their female characters. Women filmmakers were praised for their sensitivity in depicting the interiority of their subjects, but simultaneously critiqued for lacking the depth of maturity evident in their male colleagues' work. These gendered categorisations of female filmmaking produced a highly limiting definition of women's cinema, as films made by women, depicting women and for an audience of women. The limitations experienced by women in the domestic film industry were compounded by the challenge of breaking into lucrative overseas markets through the global art cinema network. By the 1990s, particular narratives and visual styles were increasingly expected by Western cinema audiences. The preference for lush, expansive epics, ideally with a flavour of political disaffection to them, or alternatively the new, gritty 'realism' of the urban fable, privileged a particular body of directors and limited the opportunities for already marginalised women filmmakers to take advantage of overseas capital and distribution (Pickowicz, 2012). Female directors were thus simultaneously marginalised within a reforming industry that did not view women's cinema as a genre that could compete in new markets and restricted to directing a certain type of cinema for which they were believed to be essentially suited.

The challenging position of female filmmakers within the Chinese industry had its roots in the representational modes that had long dominated the depiction of women on screen. From the early days of Chinese filmmaking, the medium became an effective tool for highlighting China's socio-political position as a semi-colonised nation lacking a unified and effective government. The opportunities inherent in cinema as a medium of mass communication were quickly identified by agents of all political colours. Within this highly politicised discourse, the figure of woman on screen came to be dominated by the need to represent the nation and its plight cinematically. Inter-war films such as *Street Angel* (马路天使, *Malu Tianshi*, 1937, dir. Yuan Muzhi) and *The Goddess* (神女, *Shennü*, 1934, dir. Wu Yonggang) positioned their female protagonists as victims and martyrs, selfless women who bore physically and emotionally the scars of China's historical and cultural trauma (Cui, 2003). Even after the communist victory in 1949, when the gendered dichotomy of male and female was gradually replaced by a gender-neutral ideal labouring subject, the female form was still used to promote national progress. The bodies of women engaged in healthy, active and productive labour for the state were presented as models for emulation to both men and women. Films such as *The Red Brigade of Women* (红色娘子军, *Hongse Niangzi Jun*, 1961, dir. Xie Jin) consciously suppressed all aspects of sexual difference (and, indeed, sexual desire) between the characters in order to use its female protagonists as an educative motif, communicating correct revolutionary doctrine to the viewing public (Silbergeld, 1999). To a large extent, the new 'women's cinema' that was under discussion at the *Dangdai Dianying* symposium in 1986 arose as a reaction against this occupation of the female subject by nationalist and state discourse. Films such as *Sacrificed Youth* (青春祭, *Qingchun Ji*, 1986, dir. Zhang Nuanxin), made in the aftermath of the Cultural Revolution (1966–76) and influenced by the atmosphere of liberation and repudiation that permeated the early days of reform, deliberately used cinematic techniques to counter the desexualisation of women that had dominated representation in the 1960s and 1970s. In *Sacrificed Youth*, Zhang Nuanxin used voice-over, point-of-view shots, extreme close-ups and visual metaphor as ways in which to explore female subjectivity and to highlight a unique women's experience. The tropes that were shaping attitudes to women's film in the late 1980s and 1990s were therefore born from a revolutionary new aesthetic aimed at communicating distinct female voices on screen. Nonetheless, the filmic representation of gender and gendered divisions continued to be limited by the heritage of representational tropes in which women could only be imagined in certain ways.

## Ning Ying's Approach

In Western scholarship, Ning Ying is generally approached as a chronicler of China's urban change, with academic interest focused on the Beijing Trilogy and what it reveals about the social implications of economic reform (Braester, 2010; Cui, 2007; Veg, 2010). This positioning is in part a function of the trend for urban studies research on China in the last fifteen years. Ning Ying's films appeared around the same time as a host of other work in both the cinematic and visual art realms responding to the visceral transformation of Chinese cityscapes. *I Love Beijing* compares well, for example, with Lou Ye's *Suzhou River* (苏州河, *Suzhou He*, 2000), and *For Fun* might profitably be viewed alongside Zhang Yang's *Shower* (洗澡, *Xizao*, 1999). Analysis of Ning Ying's depiction of gender has, by contrast, been generally dismissive and at times highly critical. With the notable exception of a recent article by Bérénice M. Reynaud (2019), *Perpetual Motion* has been viewed by scholars as Ning Ying's only attempt to produce a piece of feminist filmmaking, where earlier work including the Beijing triptych is often approached as lacking evidence of gender awareness. Cui Shuqin's observation is a classic example of this position:

> Although Ning Ying is an important female director, her early films neither focus on woman's issues nor show explicit feminist interest. When her camera finally frames gender relations against the urban milieu, it does so through the male protagonist's perspective. (Cui, 2007, p. 242)

It is interesting to see how the dominant scholarly position continues to frame gender through a limited model relying on the foregrounding of women's issues and subjectivity. I find this approach problematic, seeming to imply that, for a female director to be recognised as feminist, she must produce work centred on women's experience, and do so in such a way that the interior worlds of the subjects are highlighted. It also appears to disregard the institutional settings and challenges that contextualise a female director's practice and the impacts that these may have. As Wang Lingzhen (2021) notes, 'an individual woman's artistic agency along with the historical significance of her filmmaking is contingent on and embedded within dynamic interactions among geopolitical, socioeconomic, cultural, and individual forces' (p. 6).

It will be helpful, therefore, before considering *I Love Beijing* itself, to discuss Ning Ying's own view of her filmmaking, as well as to explore what can be meant by feminist filmmaking in a Chinese context. It is noticeable, and highly unusual, that Ning Ying credits herself as both director and editor on *I Love Beijing*. While filmmakers usually have close collaborative relationships with their editing team, Ning Ying goes further by declaring herself an active participant in the editing process. Perhaps more than any other function in a film's production, editing structures the storytelling and generates meaning. The choices that are made about ordering and altering shots tell the audience how to follow the plot and give considerable insight into a filmmaker's intent. As Tasker (2010) notes, in a wider filmmaking discourse in which women's contributions are typically marginalised, for a female director to so deliberatively stamp her creative identity on a key element of the production stands out as significant. In conversation with Louisa S. Wei (2010), Ning Ying said: 'My motivation to make films is to depict people I can identify with. You can say that every film of mine starts out from a relatively impersonal approach to history' (p. 67). We see expressed here a filmmaking practice that, by taking a detached, observational position in relation to the subject, seeks to produce an ethnographic cinema of detail, capturing what might otherwise be overlooked as too quotidian or every day for mainstream cinema (White, 1997). Of particular significance is Ning Ying's elision of any obvious interpretative framework or meta-narrative, an approach that runs counter the dominant representational modes shaping Chinese film since the 1920s. In the same way, a subjective camera deviates from the didacticism and collective ideological messaging that the Chinese state strongly encourages in all cultural forms, an approach that was re-emphasised after 1994 with the launch of the nationalistic Patriotic Education campaign (Volland, 2011). 'My camera does not lie', even though a questionable statement when considering the curated process of filmmaking, became something of a motto for the independent directors of the 1990s, with whom Ning Ying was possibly most in alignment at this point in her career. The assertion of a personal vision was a method by which directors could express themselves as artists and even present versions of China's social condition that were at odds with the mainstream, without coming into direct conflict with the vicissitudes of state politics. Ning Ying's ownership of the editing process makes visible the formal methods by which she asserted that vision and her own authorship.

Taken more broadly, the pursuit of a distinctive personal voice is often an act of resistance in a system that requires conformity. Janet Staiger (2003) observes that, 'authorship matters, especially to those in non-dominant positions in which asserting even a partial agency may seem to be important [ . . . ] or where locating moments of alternative practice takes away the naturalised privileges of normativity' (p. 27). In the same way, Stephanie Donald (2012) pertinently comments that 'female authorship is undervalued in cinema generally, and Chinese language cinema especially' (p. 883). As Felicia Chan (2016) reminds us, successful women directors tend to be regarded as both exceptional and unusual, held up as anomalies within a male-dominated industry. The pursuit of authorship and a subjective creative vision may therefore offer an alternative framing for Chinese feminist practice in filmmaking, when existing models seem to fall short. Where filmmaking itself is situated within a system promoting didacticism and female directors find themselves further hemmed in by essentialised expectations based on their gender, authorship and the assertion of a unique artistic voice is an act of resistance to both representational and institutional norms. In this sense, authorship as a mode of feminist practice reflects values similar to those identified by Wang Lingzhen (2021) as the hallmarks of Chinese socialist feminist filmmaking before the 1990s, in which deliberate challenges to gender essentialisms went hand in hand with a refusal to conform to institutionalised expectations of a woman's capacity to direct. These approaches resonate with Wu and Dong's (2019) description of contemporary and historical C-Fem, or 'made-in-China feminism'. Highlighting the deeply contextual nature of C-Fem, they observe that disruption of patriarchal societal norms is its defining feature, with the intersection of gender and class, and the ways in which women can resist this, forming the key concern. In the same way, I argue that Ning Ying's self-positioning as the author of her films and a privileged observer of her subjects is a disruptive act, and one that constitutes a feminist assertion within the boundaried industry of Chinese filmmaking. As she described in a panel discussion in 2009, quoted by Sebastian Veg (2010), 'women's films were a way of standing outside the system, in which there were only male directors, to look at characters who were outside the lens angle of other people's camera' (p. 9). Thinking about authorship as feminism therefore requires us to examine the focus of Ning Ying's camera and her storytelling, in order to notice these disruptive moments of resistance to institutionalised norms.

## Disruptive Filmmaking

*I Love Beijing*, the third film in Ning Ying's triptych, explores the experiences of Feng Dezi, a taxi driver in the rapidly changing city. Floating between women and romantic entanglements, Dezi's story is structured around his taxi journeys through Beijing's complex network of ring roads. The narrative is punctuated by lengthy driving sequences accompanied by an heteroglossic soundtrack from the cab radio and passengers. After being divorced by his wife in the film's opening sequence, Dezi goes in search of the ideal romantic relationship. In turn, Dezi visits his mistress Xiaoxue, picks up an attractive librarian who takes him home, is introduced by the librarian to a young migrant woman who wants to get married, is called back to the home of Xiaoxue who has committed suicide, drives a middle-aged radio host who invites him to an exclusive club, and leaves the bar later with a very drunk party-girl. The film concludes with Dezi on the cusp of yet another romantic encounter with a beautiful passenger in his taxi. The overall structure of the film is episodic, mirroring the chaotic nature of Dezi's encounters with different women, and the editing enhances the fragmentary effect through an extensive use of jump cuts and montage. In the opening scene, the camera fades in on an aerial shot of a traffic jam developing at a road intersection, jump-cutting forward in time to view the progressive pile-up. Having established the audience's privileged position of viewing Beijing life from a distance, the film then dives straight into the middle of Dezi's divorce proceedings. From behind the camera, we watch the couple seated opposite us conducting increasingly frustrated and irate conversations with an off-screen voice. Jump cuts are again used to create chronological syncopation, with the only indication that multiple interviews are taking place being the couple's changing clothes. For an audience used to the stable structures of genre cinema, this beginning is counter-intuitive, particularly as the divorce does not act as a preamble to a new narrative but is instead revealed to be simply one in a series of loosely connected vignettes. Ning Ying's approach has the effect of privileging the audience as participants in the narrative process, responsible for making connections and deriving meaning for themselves. Ambiguity and an observational perspective that elides didactic messaging therefore act to disrupt audience passivity, instead folding them into the meaning-making process.

Ambiguity and resistance to representational norms are enhanced in the film through a progressively gestural aesthetic that amplifies Dezi's sense of personal dislocation and confusion. Berry (2014) highlights the role of gestural cinema, with its emphasis on the body and embodied communication, in resisting social patterns that can be reinforced through conventional narratives. By centring audience experience in the physical, gestural cinema invites reflection on the process by which people are labelled as either conforming or nonconforming, instead highlighting the body as a space of both discomfort and shared connection. This approach is in marked contrast to the emphasis on model individuals promoted by the Chinese state as educative tools. PRC (People's Republic of China) culture is intended to be mimetic, presenting the population with idealised representations of revolutionary citizenship which, in turn, generate a society-wide practice of copying and internalising the new social norms (see Pang, 2017). Model individuals, such as the notorious Lei Feng who dominated youth culture in the 1960s, were chosen as the embodiment of state values and could easily be revived or rewritten as those values shifted. Their mimetic qualities are intended to generate 'docile bodies' (Lu, 2007), who respond to the changing needs of state politics and social concerns through internalisation and replication. By contrast, gestural cinema gives physical expression to that which is excluded from model narratives. In *I Love Beijing*, gestural qualities emphasise Dezi's emotional disintegration, as he encounters a radically modernising city in which he feels adrift. At the climax of the film, Dezi attends a party at a high-end club, mostly populated by foreigners talking in English about the horrors of Beijing. As Dezi drinks himself into a stupor, so too the behaviour of the other patrons becomes progressively surreal. A number of them are fast asleep in chairs around the room, despite the blaring music, and several others are on the dance floor dancing by themselves. As Dezi is removed from the club by the staff, a girl who has been sleeping on the stage at one end of the room totters after them and climbs into his taxi. They drive off in search of 'another party'. Suddenly Dezi pulls up by the side of the motorway and climbs out to vomit. Having collapsed on the ground, the camera films from his point of view, as the girl screams with excitement and turns up the music in the cab before climbing out to dance beside the road, as if she were in a club (Figures 11.1 and 11.2). She leans into the camera looking over the top of her dark glasses to ask if Dezi is all right, while

Her Own Feminism 175

cars rush past on the motorway beside them, their headlights saturating the back of the shot. The scene has been edited to remove every third or fourth frame, which creates a visual stutter, a series of minute disruptions in the frame rate that echoes the gestural qualities of the scene by forcing the viewer to notice a physical sensation of discomfort as their eyes adjust.

*I Love Beijing*'s detachment from linear editing and formulaic narrative styles allow the film to offer alternative articulations of gender

Figure 11.1 The party girl dances beside the motorway (screenshot from *I Love Beijing*)

Figure 11.2 Dezi sobs in the foreground as the girl continues to dance (screenshot from *I Love Beijing*)

than would be expected in a more mainstream production. The very diversity of female characters who float in and out of Dezi's life runs contrary to cinematic norms, both in terms of their failure to leave a lasting impression on the protagonist's narrative and the rich way in which different social experiences are expressed. Dezi's mistress, Xiaoxue, is a rural migrant working in a faux-Turkic restaurant where the Han Chinese waitresses pose as members of the Uighur minority to serve the clientele. She lives in a tiny flat in a former *hutong* area that is mid-reconstruction, with building rubble and cinderblocks piled on either side of the crowded street, and her apartment is filled with extended family, all of whom have travelled from the countryside to look for work. When we first meet Xiaoxue, she is lively and affectionate with Dezi but also experiencing profound anxiety about her future in Beijing and his lack of availability. In the course of conversation, it becomes clear that Dezi is paying for her apartment and that her financial future is dependent on him, a reworking of the relationship he had previously played out with his wife before the divorce. We also learn that she left her home in order to escape an abusive situation, but there are indications that her family's arrival in Beijing has triggered old traumas. The next time Xiaoxue appears it is after Dezi has been summoned to her flat by the police. He is escorted upstairs to identify her body. Xiaoxue lies slumped against the wall, surrounded by broken glass and pooling blood (Figure 11.3). In a series of abrupt single-second shots in extreme close-up, the camera captures a broken bottle top, Xiaoxue's feet with one sandal half-off,

Figure 11.3 Xiaoxue's body in her apartment while the police look on (screenshot from *I Love Beijing*)

her knee with a fly on it and then her lolling head. Particular emphasis is given to the scene through an abrupt change in the soundscape, from the catatonic layering of multiple tracks that characterises much of the film down to a sudden quiet, punctuated by the whirr of a camera shutter as the police photographer records the scene. As Dezi is questioned about Xiaoxue, the camera focuses past him on the policemen, two of whom are lighting cigarettes in the hall, while another goes through her collection of cassette tapes before pocketing the best ones (Figure 11.4).

The depiction of Xiaoxue's suicide resists a more traditional aesthetic that has often informed both classic Chinese literature and film. Historically valorised as a powerful act of agency, the higher than global average female suicide rates in China became the focus of campaigns by the Chinese state in recent decades. Nonetheless, the trope of the virtuous or noble suicide still regularly appeared in Chinese films well into the 1990s, utilised as a way to propel a narrative forward by offering a model female character prepared to sacrifice her own life for her beliefs or agency (see Chow, 2007). By contrast, Xiaoxue's death in *I Love Beijing* only highlights the everyday indignities of her short life. The camera's focus on mundane details and the sordid police examination emphasise her marginalised social position in the city. Similarly, no wider interpretative framework is offered to place Xiaoxue's suicide in context. The episodic structure of the film means that Dezi appears to experience no catharsis or transformative moment after witnessing his mistress's death; she simply vanishes from the narrative without leaving

Figure 11.4 A police officer looks through Xiaoxue's cassette collection (screenshot from *I Love Beijing*)

an imprint. Normative conventions in Chinese mainstream cinema typically require an arc of character development for the protagonist, as well as clearly defined heroes and villains, in order to communicate unambiguous social messages to the audience (Pang, 2017). The women whom Dezi encounters, however, are neither constrained within nor essential to the progress of his narrative as protagonist. Dezi therefore has no opportunity to perform the role of rescuer or educator to the women, or to be corrected and to develop himself socially. Indeed, the film concludes with Dezi on the cusp of yet another romantic entanglement.

Despite having a male protagonist at the core of the story, *I Love Beijing* consistently turns its attention toward Dezi's interactions with the women he meets in order to observe and undermine his perspective. Rey Chow (2007) notes that, 'in socialist Chinese cinema, the tendency was to downplay the gendered specifics of women's agency, so that differences and tensions between women and men became consistently invisible, or at least were made negligible, under a genderless collectivity' (p. 211). By contrast, Ning Ying allows gender conflict to be made visible through observing Dezi's own internalised patriarchal attitudes and highlighting the ensuing tensions that emerge as he encounters the limitations of being marginalised himself. In an escort club, for example, Dezi's view of the girls is captured in a classic rendering of the male gaze. Extreme close-ups and tight framing focus on disjointed body parts: breasts, shoulders, necks and profiles, thighs, a hand on a glass. Each shot lasts no more than two seconds, abruptly jump-cutting between

Figure 11.5 The camera catches Dezi's gaze at the women in the escort club, before . . .

images in a montage that suggests the roaming of Dezi's eyes around the room (Figure 11.5). However, the camera also returns to him, revealing in a series of low-angle shots his position within the group of men whom he drove to the club as his clients (Figure 11.6). He sits slightly out of their circle, and lower, hunched awkwardly in his seat, not speaking but laughing with them at their lewd jokes. Dezi is disregarded by all of them, and the audience witness his uneasy social position as a tolerated outsider, not part of the new Beijing rich or even its underclass. In the same way, after chatting up a young intellectual and spending the night with her, in what appears initially to be a classic one-night stand in which Dezi holds the power, he is later confronted by her own agency when she rejects further contact with him and instead introduces him to a 'more suitable' young migrant who is newly arrived in the city and looking for someone to marry. In this way, Ning Ying foregrounds a confrontation between her protagonist's masculine ideals and a more complex reality in which class and gender intersect.

Schaffer and Song (2007) observe that, while Western definitions of feminism have often been rejected within China, female artists across disciplines have nonetheless engaged in a search for an indigenous feminism that refuses to conform to the boundaries set within male-dominated institutions. Women in China's film industry in the late twentieth and early twenty-first centuries were projected into particular modes of working, based on institutionalised norms and gender-based limitations. By maintaining a clear authorial voice in her films, one which elided the restrictions on both content and filmmaking style being

Figure 11.6 . . . returning a critical gaze at him (screenshots from *I Love Beijing*)

imposed on female directors, Ning Ying pushed back at 'women's film' as an institutional practice that might limit her creative expression or career progress. Control of the editing process allowed for a disruptive observational aesthetic within which hegemonic social norms could be revealed and critically assessed, without coming into direct conflict with the state. Intersections of class and gender permeate Ning Ying's early films, making gendered conflict and diversity visible in a cultural milieu that typically flattened difference and encouraged linear progressive character arcs and stable heteronormative social relations. Ning Ying's filmmaking has not typically been approached as an example of feminist directorial practice. Informed by narrow definitions of feminism, scholars have overlooked work made by female directors working within specific cultural and institutional contexts that limit agency and have instead looked for universalist tropes to define what may and may not be articulated as a feminist act. When recontextualised within local industrial norms, however, it is possible to see how female directors position themselves to disrupt those norms and resist expectations in powerful ways. Authorship is one frame through which agency can be recognised, identifying how a director asserts her unique voice and perspective against a context that places expectations on what her gender will mean for her filmmaking.

## References

Berry, C. (1988). China's new 'women's cinema'. *Camera Obscura*, 6/3(18), 8–19.
Berry, C. (2014). The new gestural cinema: Yang Fudong and the gallery film. *Film Quarterly*, 67(3), 17–29.
Brady, A. (2008). *Marketing dictatorship: Propaganda and thought work in contemporary China*. Lanham: Rowman and Littlefield.
Braester, Y. (2005). Chinese cinema in the age of advertisement: The filmmaker as a cultural broker. *The China Quarterly*, 183, 549–64.
Braester, Y. (2010). *Painting the city red: Chinese cinema and the urban contract*. Durham: Duke University Press.
Chan, F. (2016). First, not only: Writing Chinese women's film authorship. In F. Chan and A. Willis (eds), *Chinese cinemas: International perspectives* (pp. 109–18). Oxford: Routledge.
Chow, R. (2007). 'Woman', fetish, particularism: Articulating Chinese cinema with a cross-cultural problematic. *Journal of Chinese Cinemas*, 1(3), 209–21.
Cui, S. (2003). *Women through the lens: Gender and nation in a century of Chinese cinema*. Honolulu: University of Hawai'i Press.
Cui, S. (2007). Ning Ying's Beijing Trilogy: Cinematic configurations of age, class, and sexuality. In Z. Zhang (ed.), *The urban generation: Chinese cinema and society at the turn of the twenty-first century* (pp. 241–63). Durham: Duke University Press.
Donald, S. H. (2012). Chinese women's cinema: Transnational contexts edited by Wang Lingzhen. *The China Quarterly*, 211, 882–84.

Lu, S. H. (2007). *Chinese modernity and global biopolitics: Studies in literature and visual culture*. Honolulu: University of Hawai'i Press.

Pang, L. (2017). *The art of cloning: Creative production during China's Cultural Revolution*. New York: Verso.

Pickowicz, P. (2012). *China on film: A century of exploration, confrontation, and controversy*. Lanham: Rowman and Littlefield.

Reynaud, B. M. (2019). Portraits de femmes dans la Chine de Réformes: Une analyse des films de Li Yu et Ning Ying. *Monde Chinois*, 1(57), 70–84.

Schaffer, K., and Song X. (2007). Unruly spaces: Gender, women's writing, and indigenous feminism in China. *Journal of Gender Studies*, 16(1), 17–30.

Silbergeld, J. (1999). *China into film: Frames of reference in contemporary Chinese cinema*. London: Reaktion.

Staiger, J. (2003). Authorship approaches. In D. A. Gerstner and J. Staiger (eds), *Authorship and film* (pp. 27–58). New York: Routledge.

Tasker, Y. (2010). Vision and visibility: Women filmmakers, contemporary authorship, and feminist film studies. In V. Callahan (ed.), *Reclaiming the archive: Feminism and film history* (pp. 213–30). Detroit: Wayne State University Press.

Veg, S. (2010). Opening public spaces. *China Perspectives*, 1, 4–10.

Volland, N. (2011). From control to management: The CCP's 'reforms of the cultural structure'. In A. Brady (ed.), *China's thought management* (pp. 107–21). Oxford: Routledge.

Wang, L. (2021). *Revisiting women's cinema: Feminism, socialism, and mainstream culture in modern China*. Durham: Duke University Press.

Wei, L. S. (2010). 'My motivation is to depict people I can identify with': An interview with Ning Ying. *China Perspectives*, 1, 66–70.

White, J. (1997). Films of Ning Ying: China unfolding in miniature. *CineAction*, 42, 2–9.

Wu, A. X., and Dong, Y. (2019). What is made-in-China feminism(s)? Gender discontent and class friction in post-socialist China. *Critical Asian Studies*, 51(4), 471–92.

Zhang, Z. (2007). Bearing witness: Chinese urban cinema in the era of 'transformation' (*zhuanxing*). In Z. Zhang (ed.), *The urban generation: Chinese cinema and society at the turn of the twenty-first century* (pp. 1–45). Durham: Duke University Press.

PART III

# GLOBAL HISTORIES

Chapter 12

# Figurations of the *Nyonya*: The Uses and Abuses of Peranakan Chinese Representation in Film

Felicia Chan

My chapter takes as its focus the figure of the *nyonya*, a term used to identify women of Peranakan descent in Southeast Asia, particularly in Singapore and Peninsular Malaysia. While Peranakan identity is generally considered to be made up of mixed ethnicities, and while within Southeast Asia there are other Peranakan communities – including Jawi Peranakans, Chetty Melaka Peranakans and the Peranakan Chinese residing in Central Java, Indonesia – the focus of my discussion remains on Peranakan Chinese representation as imagined to be from what was then known under the British colonial administration as the Straits Settlements, of Penang, Malacca and Singapore, within the context of an area that was once considered British Malaya (1826–1957). The origins of the Peranakan Chinese are predominantly understood to have been derived from the ocean crossings and eventual settlement and inter-marriages of sojourner-men from China and the local women in Malaya between the fifteenth and eighteenth centuries, although Peranakan culture and community have had to negotiate with prevailing historical and political structures of colonial empire-building and post-colonial nation-building, as will be discussed below. Karen Teoh (2016, p. 115) writes that Peranakan 'adaptability helped them survive the upheaval of imperialism, decolonization, and nation building, but it was also controversial for its suggestion of political flexibility'. These shifting negotiations underpin my use of the phrase 'figurations of the *nyonya*' in the title of this chapter, rather than 'representations' of the *nyonya*. I use the term 'figuration' in the spirit of Elizabeth St Pierre's call for the term 'figuration', to be employed as a way to 'think against [. . .] prescribed narratives' and to recover and account for 'other realities' beyond those shaped by dominant ontological and epistemological practice (St Pierre, 1997, pp. 279–80). Although the Peranakan culture is most often described as a 'hybrid' one, it is important to recognise that 'hybridity', as understood by the mixing of two apparent fixities (in this case, Chinese and Malay cultures), does not fully articulate an identity that is in a constant state of flux and negotiation with larger structural forces, such as nationhood, capitalism and cinema production.

Homi Bhabha writes of culture 'as a strategy of survival [that] is both transnational and translational'; on the one hand, it is 'transnational because contemporary postcolonial discourses are rooted in specific histories of cultural displacement', and on the other, it is 'translational because such spatial histories of displacement – now accompanied by the territorial ambitions of global media technologies – make the question of how culture signifies, or what is signified by culture, rather complex issues', where the 'transnational dimension of cultural transformation – migration, diaspora, displacement, relocations – turns the specifying or localising process of cultural translation into a complex process of signification' (Bhabha, 1997, p. 212). While he was not writing about Peranakan culture per se, his ideas are relevant; he argues for a naturalised people, the 'unifying discourse of "nation", "peoples", "folk" tradition – these embedded myths of culture's particularity – cannot be readily referenced'; yet these nonetheless '[make] one increasingly aware of the construction of culture, the invention of tradition, the retroactive nature of social affiliation and psychic identification' (Bhabha, 1997, p. 212). My argument takes as its basis that Peranakan identifications, particularly as represented in film and media cultures, tend to be shaped largely in the service of more dominant structures of identification, in general, and of ethno-nationalist structures, in particular. The female figure of the *nyonya* is almost exclusively employed in this regard. While for a time in the early twentieth century the *nyonya* woman was seen as a symbol of modernity, by virtue of being based in the emerging economies of colonial-era Southeast Asia, the representation of Peranakan women and culture is by and large constructed as *anachronistic* to modernity. Through a small number of case examples discussed below, I explore the figurations of the *nyonya* in two ways: (1) through the characters in the films who are identified or coded as Peranakan women, either through costuming, gestural mannerisms, or linguistic registers, and (2) through the feminisation of Peranakan representation as a whole, based on the *nyonya*'s mastery of the domestic space. The latter is important to consider, particularly as these feminine and matriarchal representations nonetheless operate firmly within the twin patriarchal structures of commerce and the nation-state and, thus, produces, as Teoh puts it, 'a gendered antiquarianism that belies the high anxiety surrounding race, history, and national belonging in these modern polities [of Malaysia and Singapore]' (2016, p. 117).

I discuss a small selection of films that bookend film history in Singapore from the colonial period to the present, particularly for how it stands in as a primer for a broader discussion of the cultural politics of a region known as 'Nanyang' ('Southern ocean' from the point of view of mainland China) and its relationship to the various structures of power and forces of influence. The pre-war film culture in Singapore and Malaya encompasses a broader history and politics shaping the Malay Archipelago, which exceed the confines of this chapter. My focus is on the figuration of the *nyonya* and her relationship to the construction of Chineseness within the amorphous geo-cultural boundaries of 'Nanyang' – a term which, while Sino-centric in nature, was nonetheless one employed by film producers and distributors of the time to refer to the markets constituted by the Chinese diaspora in Southeast Asia (Yap, 2021). I look at: (1) some early figurations of the *nyonya* in films produced locally and abroad in the pre-independence period, in which the *nyonya* is presented selectively as modern and local to Southeast Asia, and yet also apparently deracinated and culturally 'diluted' when compared to her sisters in China; and (2) contemporary figurations of the *nyonya* as represented through a visual vernacular employed in the Hollywood blockbuster *Crazy Rich Asians* (dir. Jon M. Chu, USA/Singapore, 2018), within the context of the global circulation of popular culture.

## 1. Early Figurations: Perceptions of Deracination and Cultural Dilution

The Straits Chinese, as the Peranakan Chinese from the Straits Settlements were sometimes referred to, served a number of symbolic functions in filmic representation in the pre-independence period. They served as popular cultural imaginaries of otherness, exoticism and sometimes dubious morals, such as in films from Hong Kong (as will be discussed), as well as popular imaginaries of self-representation for the Chinese diaspora in Southeast Asia, as self-made individuals overcoming hardships in a new land. As these representations operated along the customary binary lines of us/them and self/other, scholars and historians of the period remind us that such bilateral formulations fundamentally limit our understanding of how relations between imperial centres and colonies operated. Preferring the metaphor of a web, Frost challenges the dominant narratives of studies which have 'positioned Straits Chinese and groups like them as separate "hybrid" or "creolised" communities which mainly acted as intermediaries between the colonial state and transient Chinese populations'; instead, he argues that 'such groups freely interacted and mingled with newer arrivals across a whole range of public spaces and institutions' (Frost, 2005, p. 34), including in 'flexible kinship' patterns that 'cemented commercial and social relationships between established *Baba* Chinese and newcomers who sought to enlist their local status and knowledge' (p. 36). Frost goes so far as to attribute to these networks 'the making of Singapore' (p. 34). Frost argues that Baba merchants and traders, far from being marginalised, used these networks to assert economic and cultural influence in China (pp. 38–40). It is this influence, together with their proficiency in English, that also enabled the Straits Chinese to work for the colonial administration: 'British officials regularly used Baba Chinese as interpreters, informants and local political agents [ . . . ] and in 1867 conferred on *Baba* the status of British subjects by fact of birth within the Empire' (p. 40):

> As a settled, gentry-official class, co-opted by the colonial state as intermediaries between it and the wider Chinese population, Straits Chinese could present themselves as guardians of tradition and custom. [. . .] Processes of negotiation like this were fundamental to the successful operation of imperial authority in Singapore. Out of such repeated contact at both a commercial and a political level, multilingualism and a capacity to move from one public space to another while adopting the new codes and languages that were appropriate flourished among Straits Chinese families. Cultural adaptability became the hallmark of that particular elite for decades to come. (Frost, 2005, p. 41)

From this position as 'the King's Chinese', as they sometimes came to be called, Frost notes a process of re-sinicisation of Peranakan culture during the colonial period, in which there was an attempt to 'dilute' the Malay influence on its history. This was encouraged by the British, who 'saw the Straits Chinese as "naturally" belonging to China in a cultural sense while remaining British subjects (and intended them to continue this way)'; Frost argues that this move . . .

> . . . is crucial to our understanding of the formulation of ethnic Chinese identities during this period: literate, ethnic Chinese were fundamental agents in the Empire's eastward expansion [. . .] what might be described as a sanitised, opium-free, rationalised Chinese – a living justification for the entire imperial project. (Frost, 2005, p. 64)

While it was strategic for the Straits Chinese and the British colonial administration to foreground the Chineseness of the Peranakan community, Frost also notes a 'frequent omission' of the Peranakan Chinese 'from accounts of Chinese overseas', which 'reinforces an implicit assumption that the only "real" Chinese before this time were born in the Middle Kingdom, or [...] those bound to the homeland by diasporic institutions that related back directly to it' (p. 33). These multi-layered histories and identifications suggest that the ways in which the 'hybridity' of the Peranakan Chinese were performed, practised and understood were always subject to the prevailing political forces of the time; and the contest was often over their cultural 'Chineseness', which then bled into questions of ethno-nationalist identification. As Karen Teoh notes, the attempt to define 'Straits Chinese' or 'Peranakan' is a 'freighted task' and a 'political act in itself' (2016, p. 118), and any apparently straightforward description is 'complicated by the changing historical contexts in which the Straits Chinese lived, adapted, and identified themselves' (p. 119). It is from this position of a 'shifting political and cultural ground' (p. 119) that I address the films in this section, by examining how the figure of the *nyonya* was represented in Hong Kong cinema of the pre-war period, in contrast to how she was said to have been represented in films from Singapore in the same period.

In the colonial era, when travel within the empire constituted a form of intra-national movement, British territories such as Hong Kong and Singapore were closely connected, particularly after 1949, when 'Hong Kong's political, economic, social and intellectual spheres became intertwined with those of Southeast Asia when China became a communist republic' (Lai, 2015, p. 111). This had an impact on how the articulation of a Southeast Asian 'Nanyang' identity became a way of articulating an alternative Chinese identity outside of mainland China.[1] According to architectural historian Lai Chee Kien, ...

> Two significant consequences ensued: first, the outmigration of various groups from China to Hong Kong and sites in East and Southeast Asia, and second, the commencement for a mutual search for Nanyang identities and subject matter both for overseas Chinese in Hong Kong and for those in Southeast Asia, since prior connections to China were variously strained, withdrawn or severed. The discovery, articulation or invention of the Nanyang Chinese identity in Hong Kong became useful for the making of a relational self-identity of Hongkongers' [...] explorations of this Nanyang identity occurring in post-1950 art, literature, music and cinema. (Lai, 2015, p. 111)

Such a representation of the *nyonya* came up against campaigns to 'Malayanise' identities in the run-up to independence (see also Yap, 2021, p. 84).

Research into the historiography of film production in the territory is still relatively nascent, but according to E. K. Tan, there were at least four films from Hong Kong set in the Nanyang region in the 1950s and 1960s, and the films were 'attempts to secure and expand the Chinese overseas market for the Hong Kong film industry by showcasing the overseas Chinese and reflecting their values' (Tan, 2010, p. 156). The films were *Nyonyah* (dir. Yue Feng, 1952), *Rainstorm in Chinatown* (dir. Yan Jun, 1956), *Nonya and Baba* (dir. Yan Jun, 1956) and *Love with a Malaysian Girl* (dir. Liu Kei, 1969). Despite two of these titles naming a *nyonya* specifically, there was no ostensible Peranakan identity represented. Tan argues that, in these films, *nyonya* was code for 'an exoticization of a hybrid identity that [was] marked as otherness but taken for granted as inferior Chineseness' (p. 161), some of which take on a distinct racialised approach when the problematic *nyonya* figure is coded as Malay (p. 165). Made largely for the Hong Kong market at the time, these films traded on a culture that was 'at once foreign yet somewhat familiar to most Chinese communities' (p. 164).

In addition, the Peranakan proximity to Chineseness enabled these films to effectively sinicise its representation in two distinct ways: (1) through the construction of predominantly Mandarin- or Cantonese-speaking[2] characters (Peranakans in the pre-independence period would have spoken a creolised vernacular of Baba Malay and Hokkien phrases), and (2) through the narrative mode of the family melodrama that forms a distinct part of Chinese narrative filmmaking.[3]

Within Singapore and Malaya, Peranakan representation was a means by which diasporic 'Nanyang' communities could articulate their distinctiveness from the Chinese and European hegemons. Film historians have uncovered materials leading to an early film produced in Singapore, which is now lost, but whose script is available. The Asian Film Archive in Singapore has produced a volume gathering the research on the film *New Immigrant / Xinke* (dir. Guo Chao-wen, 1926–27). Hee Wai Siam writes of how *New Immigrant* 'accentuated its "Nanyang style" as a selling point [. . . by featuring] dances by various ethnic groups, including Western ballroom dances, fashionable dances, Chinese traditional costume dances and Malay dances' (Hee, 2014, p. 250). It is a film made ostensibly in the 'Nanyang style', a movement in literature and art emerging in the 1920s and lasting through the

1950s (Zeng, 2021). Crucially, even as the film is said to have 'reproduced the festive Peranakan culture and Malay dances' (Hee, 2014, p. 254), it did not shy away from articulating the cultural conflicts that arose between Peranakan communities that had been present in Singapore and Malaya long before and the 'new' Chinese immigrants who arrived following the development of trading infrastructure and routes by the British. These 'new' Chinese migrants were referred to by the Peranakans as *sinkeh* (Hokkien for the Mandarin *xinke*, as in the title of the film). Significantly, despite being a silent film, *New Immigrant* is said to have accommodated the linguistic plurality of Singapore at the time, where 'different linguistic registers', including the interspersal of Malay words within the Chinese (and its regional variants), are woven into the film (p. 253). Unlike the films originating from Hong Kong, which cast Nanyang as a sinicised region tainted by cultural others, *New Immigrant* is reported to have dramatised the tensions between the established Peranakan community and the new arrivals from China. Reading from the surviving script, Hee notes the following: (1) Shen (the eponymous 'new immigrant') struggles to adjust to the customs and practices of the Peranakan community: 'Shen experiences numerous difficulties with Nanyang customs, languages and food. For example, he is not proficient in English and Malay. He vomits after eating durian, dislikes curry and refuses to eat with his hands as the Peranakans often do. Shen's difficulties only provoke Hui's and Fu's [two Peranakan characters] ridicule' (p. 254); (2) the Peranakan culture is still nonetheless framed as one that has been 'contaminated by indigenous customs', and Shen sets out to 'civilise' Hui, a Peranakan woman, a *nyonya* (p. 255). At the end of the film, the two 'fall in love, marry and live happily ever after', which Hee posits as a 'cultural reconciliation' of the two communities (p. 255).

The availability of these early films is intermittent, and it is difficult to draw conclusions on larger narrative and thematic patterns. However, these select readings of early films from Singapore and Hong Kong reinforce perceptions of Peranakan culture as hybridised and creolised products of diasporic migration, both equally abhorrent and desirable. This ambivalence inflects uneasily on the unspoken discourses both of cultural purity based on mythic origins of an imaginary China and of cultural uniqueness based on geo-historical specificities of the Nanyang region. The ongoing tension between these two frames of reference carry well into Peranakan representation in contemporary cinema, as I will discuss below.

## 2. Global Figurations: Nyonya-Style Aesthetics

With the intensification of globalisation in the 2000s, Peranakan culture was framed as a way of articulating Singapore's uniqueness that set it apart from cultural groups elsewhere; Peranakan culture was seen as something that is 'uniquely Singapore', to quote the advertising slogan of the Singapore Tourism Board from 2004 to 2010. Karen Teoh notes that 'the untidy ambiguities of Peranakan history and culture are smoothed in this visual discourse into a rational and attractive form by nation-based nostalgia' (2016, p. 117), and '[for] Peranakan conservationists, this approach is a strategy for cultural survival and continued relevance that neutralizes the potential transgressiveness of their mixed-race origins and repeated reinventions of identity' (p. 117). A casual glance over any book catalogue on the region will uncover numerous titles devoted to cookbooks, coffee table books on artefacts, furniture, jewellery and architecture, a material culture exemplified by the figure of the *nyonya*. Writing of the 1970s, Teoh notes:

> Popular publications and social events such as Peranakan conventions displayed Nyonya cuisine, ceramics, and clothing, particularly the Malay-inflected *sarong kebaya*, a skirt of printed batik paired with an embroidered tunic. Nyonya adornments, such as jewelry, hair accessories, and shoes, became objects of desire and sought-after collectibles. Both Malaysian and Singaporean national airlines adopted a stylized *sarong kebaya* as the uniform for their female flight attendants, with the latter coining the now-notorious slogan 'Singapore Girl, You're a Great Way to Fly'. (Teoh, 2016, p. 123)

It is this *nyonya-style* that equally captures their representation in films, and one that operates precisely by being decoupled from its geo-political location and history.

In this section, I look at how this decoupling enables the global reach of the film *Crazy Rich Asians*, whose Peranakan-style was reported to be a conscious decision made by the film's American production designer, Nelson Coates (Teng, 2019). Hailed in some quarters as a triumph for Asian American cultural representation in mainstream cinema, the film has nonetheless garnered criticism for its monocultural representation of Singapore; Mark Gallagher offers an astute reading of its 'polarized reception' (Gallagher, 2020, p. 196). Chun-Lung Ma reads the film's mobile cosmopolitanism through the representation of a transnational Chineseness:

> *Crazy Rich Asians* presents Chineseness not as something that has a singularly defined essence shared by the ethnic Chinese characters but as

something specific and particular to their transnational heritage as well as the social and cultural environs of their places of residence. (Ma, 2021, p. 226)

What has hitherto been unaddressed, save for a footnote in Ma's account (p. 224), is how the film codes the wealth of the Young family of Singapore, headed by the formidable Eleanor (Michelle Yeoh), as stemming from a Peranakan heritage. Indeed, in the film, Peik Lin (Awkwafina) tells Rachel (Constance Wu) that the Youngs are 'old money' who travelled down the Straits of Malacca on a 'handbag'; the Straits Chinese link between Malacca and Singapore is unmistakeable. The Youngs' 'old money' is implied further through the architecture and the home furnishings, evoking the eclectic blend of eastern and western design tropes that constitute the traditional Peranakan 'Straits Eclectic' style (Henderson, 2003, p. 33). In the foyer of the main house, there is even a stuffed tiger in the background, which can be read as a gesture towards the Aw brothers, Chinese-Burmese tycoons who owned the Haw Par business empire in Southeast Asia, best-known for its Tiger Balm brand.

The Peranakan heritage in *Crazy Rich Asians* is represented mainly through the elaborately crafted *mise-en-scène*, while also gesturing to other signifiers of Chinese (read: PRC) soft power, such as in the dumpling-making scene. The type of dumplings (*jiaozi*) being made by the family in the film is more closely associated with the culinary traditions of northern China, rather than the predominantly southern Chinese that migrated to Singapore and Southeast Asia in the nineteenth century; nor is it part of Peranakan food heritage. While nothing restricts mobile cosmopolitans from consuming world cuisine (and indeed that is one of the markers of their cosmopolitanism), in the film this sequence is designed to underscore the traditions of the Young family, who are supposedly rooted in Malacca and Singapore, particularly when Nick (Henry Golding) recalls how he was taught lovingly as a child by his grandmother to make them. Narratively, the scene is designed to emphasise Rachel's exclusion, underscored by a crude reference to a bad American racist joke about Chinese eating babies. Meta-narratively, an anachronistic mix of cultural codes occurs here and throughout the film, in ways that weave in *nyonya*-style 'local' iconography together with the easy legibility of a global Chinese culture centred on modern Beijing.

The *mahjong* hall sequence where Rachel confronts Eleanor is another scene that reproduces a mix of cultural codes capable of multiple levels of address. Unable to best Eleanor in the spaces she controls, Rachel invites

Eleanor to a game of *mahjong* in what is supposed to be a public setting, evoking *mahjong* halls of old, where Chinese immigrants to Singapore gathered in the colonial era. Like poker in many Western films, *mahjong* is often employed in Chinese films as a visual metaphor for character strategy and plot intrigue. *Crazy Rich Asians* continues this practice. In a comparative analysis of *Crazy Rich Asians* and *The Joy Luck Club* (the only other Asian American film that became a mainstream hit in Anglophone markets), Xianggu Qi discusses how *mahjong* is used 'as a symbolic medium to organize diegetic narration, develop characters and negotiate Chinese identity' (Qi, 2021, p. 224). Qi offers this reading of the *mahjong* sequence in *Crazy Rich Asians*:

> In the film, the absence of China fittingly alludes to the Chinese diaspora's confluence into transnational traffic, free from the homeland's politico-historical restrictions. In this vein, the China-based, mono-determined, and stagnant Chineseness transforms into being global, polyvalent, fluid, salient and adaptive. The battle between Rachel and Eleanor cinematizes this transposition. Eleanor uses a Hokkien phrase, *kaki lang* (our own kind of people), to exclude Rachel from Chinese kind, which is visualized by her playing: she wants a match of the same exact tile of eight-bamboo to form a winning hand. Oppositely, Rachel needs an eight bamboo tile to comprise a running set (with difference) for winning. She, intentionally, is taking advantage of Mahjong strategy to counterattack Eleanor's narrow-mindedness. [. . .] Rachel not only proves her mastery of playing Mahjong, but also employs her seasoned strategy to convince Eleanor that she knows clearly what Chineseness means and what makes it last. (Qi, 2021, pp. 236–37)

I argue that what we have here is *more* than the assertion of an Asian American diasporic Chineseness against a static, 'culturalist' identification with historical China.

The scene is ostensibly set in Singapore but importantly shot in the Cheong Fatt Tze Mansion (also known locally as the 'Blue Mansion'), located in Georgetown, Penang, Malaysia, one of the three former Straits Settlements with sizeable Peranakan Chinese populations. The mansion has been architecturally restored and today operates as a luxury boutique hotel and occasional movie set. Meta-narratively, the scene reconnects Singapore and Penang as former Straits Settlements, and as Straits Chinese cities, while serving as a reminder that such heritage structures no longer really exist in Singapore. Multiple conservation efforts of old Peranakan houses in Singapore have nearly always capitulated to commercial development and to criticisms of inauthenticity (Henderson,

2003, pp. 40–41). Such community spaces (like a communal *mahjong* hall) in such lavish settings no longer exist in Singapore either, except as a fantasy recreation on the movie set. *Mahjong* is played in private homes or in games rooms of private clubs as social pastimes, but no longer in public settings; indeed unlicensed 'gaming houses' are now illegal in Singapore, and authorities can impose heavy fines. In colonial times, these communal halls were also usually clan-based,[4] and while these Chinese clans may exist in name, they no longer have a significant cultural presence in Singapore. As a set piece in the film, the *mahjong* sequence constitutes both a milestone in a character's (Rachel's) development and a turning point in the narrative (Eleanor is bested), as well as a palimpsest for a time and place that are already replete with, to borrow Teoh's phrase, 'anodyne nostalgia and commercialization' (2016, p. 115).

As the defender of tradition, the figure of Eleanor herself is coded as diasporic, as an archetypal *nyonya* matriarch who controls her household, her children, her servants and every dish before it leaves the kitchen. What she does not do is adopt the *nyonya*-matriarch's style of dress, except for a derivation during the wedding scene, or the linguistic inflections of Peranakan speech; partly because few in Singapore now speak Baba Malay apart from a smattering of phrases, and partly because, as Michelle Yeoh, she operates within the film's textual fabric as a transnational Chinese star who is widely recognised in international (American) markets. The figure who does dress with a passing semblance to a *nyonya* matriarch is the grandmother figure played by Lisa Lu. In the party scene, she is dressed in a flowing top and a short floral jacket held together by a large brooch, in passing resemblance to traditional *nyonya* dress of the *kebaya* and *kerosang* (large ornamental brooch used to pin the sides of a blouse together). Despite the costuming, Ah Ma (Grandma) here is also sinicised as a figure similar to the early films discussed in the first part of the chapter, in that she speaks in Mandarin rather than in Baba Malay, as would be typical of older *nyonya* women in her age group. In both the figures of Eleanor and Ah Ma, there are gestures towards a performative authenticity that operates only on the visual level, on the level of *mise-en-scène*, on the level of *nyonya*-style. This *nyonya*-style as a visual vernacular in Singapore is one that can be cultivated by various cultural players and tends to emerge at particular historical junctures that put pressure on national identity-formation.[5]

The film's assimilation to capitalism is evident from its very title, and its success at the box office complicates its representational politics.

Corrine Mitsuye Sugino outlines the problematics of its 'multicultural redemption narrative' (Sugino, 2019) in three ways:

> . . .first, by presenting capitalist ascendency as an antidote to racial violence; second, through assimilation to the values of whiteness as a form of redress for past exclusion; and third, by attempting to reconcile anti-Asian racism through anti-black rhetorical strategies and the devaluation of darker-skinned Asians. (Sugino, 2019)

Mark Tseng-Putterman (2018) goes so far as to argue that the film 'drips with an art-deco aesthetic, nodding to American cinema's black-and-white days with one party scene – which rivals Gatsby's finest – where women in flapper fashion swing and twirl to a Singaporean jazz band', to the extent of 'swapping Asian faces onto white bodies'. Mark Gallagher (2020) is more conciliatory to what he describes as the film's 'pan-Asian screen cosmopolitanism'. All these readings are made possible by the film's *nyonya*-style aesthetics and its attendant politics of Peranakan adaptation to history, colonial assimilation, post-independence marginalisation and return to global cultural commodification, as I have been arguing. The ornamentation of the *nyonya*-style adds power to the setting that already invokes a world in which global capital manufactures cultural authenticity for global cultural consumption.

## Concluding Remarks

While all modes of representation can be said to respond to their socio-political milieus in various ways, the figure of the *nyonya*, as a Southeast Asian woman operating within an East Asian (China) sphere of influence, presents specific challenges to the discourse on representation itself. Its politics lie not in the representation of the *nyonya* as an artefact, as an end-product, but in the *act of negotiating* as a mode of representation in its own right. As Karen Teoh puts it, . . .

> This enthusiastic embrace of the Nyonya is at once ironic and logical. As the personification of tradition, even backwardness, at the turn of the twentieth century, she was an object of embarrassment and a target of modernising reform efforts for Straits Chinese elites [. . .] By the turn of the twenty-first, she had become the most widely recognised and celebrated symbol of the modern Peranakan community – one that was presented to international tourists as well as domestic citizens for admiration and emulation. This about-face seems less abrupt when we consider that this figure of tradition was highly compatible with the postcolonial state's construction of a national historical narrative, acknowledging its complex multiethnic past

while keeping it safely contained within a diorama of domesticity. (Teoh, 2016, p. 124)

And so, the heritage projects and cookbook publications proliferate. This is not to repudiate genuine community efforts at cultural preservation, but to try and understand how these small acts of cultural rescue become proxies for larger ideological battles in which discourses of nationhood tied to cultural production and self-representation in global industries trade in superlative scales. For the Peranakan communities that remain, these acts of rescue continue to reach into a receding past, where grandmothers spoke Baba Malay and slaved away in kitchens to produce sumptuous feasts; the future has appropriated the *nyonya*-aesthetic for other cultural battles, without so much as a passing footnote to a rich and complex history.

## Acknowledgements

Many thanks to Dr MaoHui Deng for his comments on an earlier draft, suggestions for further reading and numerous invaluable conversations on Singapore's film history in general. This chapter is dedicated to the memory of Gladys Cheng.

## References

Berry, C. (2007). The Chinese side of the mountain. *Film Quarterly*, 60(3), 32–37.
Bhabha, H. K. (1997). Questions of cultural translation. In R. Krauss, A. Michelson, Y.-A. Bois, B. H. D. Buchloh, H. Foster, D. Hollier, and S. Kolbowski (eds), *October: The second decade, 1986–1996* (pp. 211–22). Cambridge: MIT Press.
Frost, M. R. (2005). *Emporium in imperio*: Nanyang networks and the Straits Chinese in Singapore, 1819–1914. *Journal of Southeast Asian Studies*, 36(1), 29–66.
Gallagher, M. (2020). *Crazy Rich Asians* and pan-Asian screen cosmopolitanism. *East Asian Journal of Popular Culture*, 6(2), 195–215.
Hee, W. S. (2014). *New immigrant*: On the first locally produced film in Singapore and Malaya. *Journal of Chinese Cinemas*, 8(3), 244–58.
Henderson, J. (2003). Ethnic heritage as a tourist attraction: The Peranakans of Singapore. *International Journal of Heritage Studies*, 9(1), 27–44.
Lai, C. K. (2015). Imagining Nanyang: Hong Kong and Southeast Asia in Wong Kar-wai movies. In L. Chee and E. Lim (eds), *Asian cinema and the use of space: Interdisciplinary perspectives* (pp. 109–25). New York: Routledge.
Ma, C. L. (2021). Negotiating Chineseness through English dialects in *Crazy Rich Asians*. In C. Y. Hoon and Y. Chan (eds), *Contesting Chineseness: Asia in transition*: Vol. 14 (pp. 223–37). Singapore: Springer.
Montsion, J. M., and Parasram, A. (2018). *The Little Nyonya* and Singapore's national self: Reflections on aesthetics, ethnicity and postcolonial state formation. *Postcolonial Studies*, 21(2), 154–71.

Qi, X. (2021). Mahjong, Chinese diaspora cinema and identity construction. *East Asian Journal of Popular Culture*, 7(2), 223–40.

Seet, K. K. (2014). 'Once again with feeling': *Emily of Emerald Hill* as floating signifier. In N. Holdsworth (ed.), *Theatre and national identity: Re-imagining conceptions of nation* (pp. 163–80). New York: Routledge.

St Pierre, E. A. (1997). An introduction to figurations: A poststructural practice of inquiry. *Qualitative Studies in Education*, 10(3), 279–84.

Sugino, C. M. (2019). Multicultural redemption: *Crazy Rich Asians* and the politics of representation. *Lateral* 8(2): [n. p.].

Tan, E. K. (2010). Hong Kong cinema and the portrayal of the Nanyang Chinese in the 1950s and 1960s. *Journal of Chinese Cinemas*, 4(2), 155–68.

Teng, Y. P. (2019, March 15). The Youngs of 'Crazy Rich Asians' became 'Peranakan' because of production designer Nelson Coates. *Yahoo! Life SEA*. Retrieved from https://sg.style.yahoo.com/youngs-crazy-rich-asians-became-peranakan-production-designer-nelson-coates-130201749.html

Teo, S. (2006). Singapore screen memories: Kong Ngee's *Nanyang Trilogy*. In W. Ain-ling (ed.), *The glorious modernity of Kong Ngee* (pp. 144–65). Hong Kong: Hong Kong Film Archive.

Teoh, K. M. (2016). Domesticating hybridity: Straits Chinese cultural heritage projects in Malaysia and Singapore. *Cross-Currents: East Asian History and Culture Review*, 5(1), 115–46.

Tseng-Putterman, M. (2018, 23 August). How *Crazy Rich Asians* is a step backward. *The Atlantic*. Retrieved from https://www.theatlantic.com/entertainment/archive/2018/08/asian-americas-great-gatsby-moment/568213/

Yap, S. E. (2021). Negotiating Chineseness in the post-WWII context of Singapore (1955–1965). In C. Y. Hoon and Y. Chan (eds), *Contesting Chineseness: Asia in transition: Vol. 14* (pp. 83–100). Singapore: Springer.

Yeh, E. Y. (2009). Pitfalls of cross-cultural analysis: Chinese *wenyi* film and melodrama. *Asian Journal of Communication*, 19(4), 438–52.

Yen, C.-H. (1981). Early Chinese clan organizations in Singapore and Malaya, 1819–1911. *Journal of Southeast Asian Studies (Singapore)*, 12(1), 62–91.

Zeng, Q. (2021). Becoming a Nanyang-style artist in postwar Singapore and Malaya: Georgette Chen's drawing and her construction of Asian themes. In C. Y. Hoon and Y. Chan (eds), *Contesting Chineseness. Asia in transition*: Vol. 14 (pp. 201–19). Singapore: Springer.

## Notes

1. There is also a series of films produced by the Hong Kong-based Kong Ngee Film Production Company that is collectively known as *The Nanyang Trilogy* (see Teo, 2006). The trilogy was shot in Singapore and Malaya and recently restored by the Asian Film Archive in Singapore. It comprises three Cantonese-language films: *Blood Stains the Valley of Love* (Chun Kim and Chor Yuen, 1957), *China Wife* (Chan Man, 1957) and *Moon Over Malaya* (Chun Kim and Chor Yuen, 1957). These do not make specific reference to Peranakan culture or communities, although in *Blood Stains* the figure of a young Malay woman from a local village is initially made out to be a practitioner of black magic (a persistent and racist stereotype).
2. *Nyonyah*, *Rainstorm in Chinatown* and *Nonya and Baba* are Mandarin-language films, and *Love with a Malaysian Girl* is in the Cantonese language.
3. Chris Berry (2007) referred to this mode as the 'family ethics' film in his analysis of *Brokeback Mountain* (Ang Lee, 2005). Emilie Yueh-yu Yeh (2009) writes

about the 'pitfalls of cross-cultural analysis' when conflating the Chinese *wenyi* mode with the Western term 'melodrama'; the granularity of these distinctions is beyond the scope of this chapter.
4. Early Chinese migrants to Singapore organised themselves around 'clans', often according to dialect or regional communities. See Yen (1981).
5. In a longer piece, the *nyonya*-style prevalent in Singapore's cultural context should be read within the contexts of two other major cultural texts that have been pivotal in inscribing and reinscribing the figure of the *nyonya* into the nation's cultural consciousness. The first is the English-language play *Emily from Emerald Hill* (Stella Kon, 1983) which has been performed in multiple iterations in the intervening decades, and the second is the Mandarin-language television series *The Little Nyonya* (2008), produced by the state-run MediaCorp TV. See Seet (2014); Montsion and Parasram (2018).

Chapter 13

# Temporally Performing a Region: A Feminist Analysis of Southeast Asian Women's Filmmaking

*MaoHui Deng*

Increasingly, scholars are turning their attention to the aesthetics of time in Southeast Asian cinemas. Bliss Cua Lim (2009), for instance, examines the ways in which fantasy cinema is used to highlight the unstable relationship between the region's past and present. May Adadol Ingawanij, in another study, argues that a certain strand of Southeast Asian moving-image practices draws from the region's animist praxis 'as a kind of historiographic work and a temporalizing form' (Ingawanij, 2021, p. 552). And, elsewhere, I draw on Marc Augé's concept of the 'non-place' to think through Singapore cinema's 'very loose – if at times seemingly unrelated – relationship to the past' (Deng, 2020, p. 39). Despite the very different temporal aesthetics identified and analysed, in this chapter I want to suggest that one common thread which ties many of these approaches together is a focus on the present tense while letting the region's longer (and messier) histories and futures steal their way into the mix. Such an idea, I argue, constitutes a relational feminist approach towards filmmaking that resists the patrilinearity and fixity of Southeast Asia as a region.

Within this chapter, Southeast Asian women's cinema becomes exemplary of such a relational feminist approach because, according to Jasmine Nadua Trice, 'for women filmmakers, taking a reflexive stance toward historical representation allows them to claim mastery over both the fictions of more mainstream historical narratives, as well as the *process* of representing history itself' (Trice, 2019, p. 35; emphasis in original). Films that might fall under such a category include *By the Time It Gets Dark* (Anocha Suwichakornpong, 2016); *Krabi, 2562* (Ben Rivers and Anocha Suwichakornpong, 2019); *Nervous Translation* (Shireen Seno, 2018); *Landscape Series #1* (Nguyễn Trinh Thi, 2013); *Letters to*

*Panduranga* (Nguyễn Trinh Thi, 2015); *Shirkers* (Sandi Tan, 2018); *In Time to Come* (Tan Pin Pin, 2017); and *Sepet* (Yasmin Ahmad, 2004). Many of these films by women filmmakers can be described as implying 'a nonlinear, gendered, historiographic mode of representation, thereby troubling teleological, objective models of history' (Trice, 2019, p. 12).[1] In unsettling the linearity of 'Southeast Asian-ness' through various formal strategies, I argue that these films adopt a temporal strategy that celebrates the present tense in a relational manner and, in turn, invite us to think of the concept of 'area' from a temporal viewpoint.

## Thick Time

Throughout, I will refer to Seno's *Nervous Translation* as an emblematic case-study for the chapter. To begin, I conduct a close analysis of the opening moments of *Nervous Translation* in order to highlight the ways in which the film's formal properties draw the audience's attention to the multiple temporalities in negotiation. *Nervous Translation* is set from around 1986 to 1988 in the Philippines and ends with the arrival of Typhoon Unsang (the first of the three tropical cyclones to hit the nation in the span of two weeks). This is a significant period in the Philippines, as Ferdinand Marcos, the dictator who ruled over the nation from 1965 to 1986, was deposed by the 1986 People Power Revolution. Corazon Aquino was then sworn in as the new president in the same year and ushered in a fresh period of democracy in the Philippines, which ultimately saw American military presence withdrawn from the nation in 1992. While the film is set in a significant moment in Philippine history, the temporality of the film is set – insistently – in the present tense and in the everyday; more specifically, it is set in the present tense and everyday of Yael, the child protagonist, where multiple temporalities, past and future, coalesce. From the start of the film, the audience is drawn into the world of Yael as she returns to an empty house after school. She sits down by the door, takes off her shoes and proceeds to methodically wipe them clean with tissue paper. Commenting on this particular moment in an interview, Seno says:

> I think shoes are important too – they are like material witnesses to the day-to-day of our lives, and I wanted to connect that to the infamous collection of shoes Imelda Marcos had to leave behind during the People Power Revolution, testifying to her greed. I used to clean the soles of my shoes when I was a child. It was a kind of therapeutic ritual for a shy kid obsessed with order. Opening the film with Yael arriving home and cleaning the soles of her shoes brings us straight into Yael's world. (Seno, in Northrop, 2018)

Put differently, *Nervous Translation* is a world that is largely filtered through a child, whose everyday materiality is then variously linked to the larger geopolitics of Southeast Asia (such as Imelda Marcos's shoes, for instance) and beyond. Indeed, while Yael tends to her shoes, there is a jump cut that interrupts the action, removing – for the audience – a few moments of the process, as we are brought into a different temporal world, one which is marked by a heightened coexistence of multiple temporalities.

As Yael focuses on cleaning her shoes, and as the audience is temporally invited into *her* world, the film cuts to the opening title sequence where the film's title, composed of broken bits of tissue paper, falls onto the floor. The music for the sequence, composed by Itos Ledesma, is upbeat and comprises various electronic instruments that project a hopeful and futuristic tone. After the opening title, the audience is shown Yael alone at home watching television. The phone rings, and she answers it – as that happens, the score fades out. The person on the other end of the phone greets Yael and asks whether she is ready for 'Mad Minute'. The film cuts to a shot of Yael writing her name on a mathematics practice sheet, then a shot of Yael starting a digital stopwatch. Next, as the consistent ticking of the stopwatch takes over the sonic sphere, the film cuts back to the shot of Yael on the phone, as her friend asks her a series of arithmetic questions. When she begins to answer them, the film cuts to a montage that variously shows Yael working on her homework, brushing her teeth, making herself a chocolate milkshake, choosing a station on the radio, trying to guess the password on a lock, watching television and returning home. Finally, the minute is up; her friend stops the questions, bids goodbye, and they both look forward to tomorrow's rendition of Mad Minute.

This is a complex sequence that positions the present-tense-ness of Yael's world as one that is marked by the coalescence of multiple temporalities, past and future. Aurally, time passes in a relentlessly linear fashion, as marked by the incessant beeping of the stopwatch. This temporal linearity is made all the more homogeneous by the seemingly recurring nature of Mad Minute – this could indeed be a question from any other day in Yael's life and could also easily replace another mathematics question. However, this moment of homogeneity is punctured by the arrhythmic editing of the montage, as the shots of Yael passing time in the house by herself variously irrupt into the sequence. For Gilles Deleuze, largely, a montage can be understood as something having changed – where the narrative has progressed from one point to another point – and 'this whole which changes, this time or duration, only seems to be capable of being apprehended indirectly, in relation to the movement-images which express it' (Deleuze, 2013a, p. 33). That is to say, in order to understand the change that occurs in and through a montage, the audience has to make sense of it all by placing the images in a linear manner and to tightly link the shots that precede with the shots that proceed; in doing so, time is tied linearly through movement. The opening montage of *Nervous Translation*, however, does not fit into this understanding of editing pattern. We do not necessarily know which set of action comes before and which comes after (it does not matter whether she makes the chocolate milk or tries to guess the lock's passcode first), nor is it necessary for the audience to impose such a linearity onto the montage. Indeed, *nothing* changes at the end of the montage, as Yael is still passing time, waiting for her mother to return home from work; I would suggest that the shots work to highlight the mundane and repetitive quality of Yael's everyday life. The shots temporally decontextualise her lived experiences and are not strictly tied to the shots that come before and after. In this sense, we can think of the events in the montage as audio-visual images of everyday banality that could be sometime in the past, sometime today, sometime in the future, or even all happening at once in a compressed manner. For Deleuze, everyday banality gives rise to a direct presentation of time: 'There is becoming, change, passage. But the form of what changes does not itself change, does not pass on. This is time, time itself, "a little time in its pure state": a direct time-image' (Deleuze, 2013b, p. 17). Because this understanding of time is no longer tied to and understood via movement through space, time, in this montage, is allowed to be time itself – in all its heterogeneity – and therefore is not necessarily locked into strict linearity.

The mundaneness of Yael's everyday life is further demonstrated after the Mad Minute montage. As she hangs up the phone, the amplified sound of the house's grandfather clock ticking enters the film's diegesis. Yael has now finished watching *Blue Bustamante* (Miko Livelo, 2013) – a film about a father migrating from the Philippines to Japan in 1990, where he finds work as a stunt double in the *Super Sentai* series – on the television, and as she turns off the television, she puts her hand onto the screen. This gesture produces a static sound that is also mixed into the soundscape. While that happens, Seno cuts to a series of still shots showing the everyday objects in the house: a sofa; a box of tissue papers under the couch; the frontpage of a newspaper where President Marcos is proclaiming calm in (for) the nation; and a wooden mural of Leonardo da Vinci's *The Last Supper*. The sequence ends with her walking slowly to the radio and listening to a message that her father (who is working in Saudi Arabia) had recorded for her mother. For one, these still shots recall Deleuze's analysis of the infamous shot of the vase in Yasujirō Ozu's *Late Spring* (1949), where the vase – sandwiched between shots of the protagonist staring into the ceiling and then crying – is understood as an example of still life where 'everything that changes is in time, but time does not itself change, it could itself change only in another time, indefinitely' (Deleuze, 2013b, p. 17). Expanding further, Siying Duan describes such pillow shots (or empty shots) as expressing or pointing 'at "the virtual" without fully actualising it' (Duan, 2021, p. 356). In this sense, then, in these still shots, we see time as pure duration, as a messy interplay of past, present and future. Beyond that, the audio-visual images that are shown in the opening sequence also pointedly gesture towards various aspects of history and futurity: the opening music, comprised of electronic instruments underscoring the magical appearance of the film's title through bits of torn tissue papers coming together, hints at a more hopeful and imaginative future (such electronic instrumentation and futuristic musical imagery pepper the film's score throughout); the wooden mural of *The Last Supper* is both an emblem of biblical times and a reminder of the Philippines as a colony of Spain for more than three centuries; *Blue Bustamante* is anachronistically from 2013, which gestures towards the Philippines' relationship with Japan in the 1980s and 1990s (and beyond); and the father is working in Saudi Arabia in the hopes that the family can have a better future.[2]

Altogether, the opening moments of *Nervous Translation* can be understood as highlighting the ways in which the past and the future can (and do) coexist in the present tense. Such a temporal aesthetic can also be seen in various other Southeast Asian women's cinema: in *In Time to Come*, a Singapore documentary that is primarily about the opening of a time capsule from 1990 and the preparation of a new time capsule for the future, objects from the past and for the future are confronted and observed by the present tense of the film's long takes; in *Krabi, 2562*, merely the title itself points to a coexistence of multiple ways of thinking about time: the year 2562 positions Thailand somewhere in the future if understood through the Gregorian calendar, and the year 2562 positions Thailand in the present day (2019, the year of the film's release) if understood through the Buddhist calendar; and, in *Landscape Series #1*, a short film that consists of a series of 35mm slides projected via a Kodak Carousel slide projector, the homogeneous and mechanical clicking of the projector is put in conversation with still photographs of people pointing at – indexing – empty landscapes, highlighting the present-day landscape as haunted by / witness to something that has since passed.[3] Such a temporal strategy evident in much Southeast Asian women's filmmaking, I suggest, is a feminist approach that draws our attention to the friction between multiple temporalities, where past and future coalesce thickly in the present tense – importantly, so I contend, this is an approach that *does not straightforwardly* reject the linearity of time in favour of the messiness of non-linear time.

To elaborate further, the ways in which our everyday lives are organised around and by the logic and rhythms of time have been a significant concern to many feminist scholars. Largely speaking, since around the fourteenth century, our everyday lives around the world have been structured by the linearity of clock time in an increasingly accelerated manner.[4] This clock time, where a minute in an hour could be neatly replaced with another minute in a different hour, is described by Walter Benjamin as 'empty, homogeneous time' (Benjamin, 1992, pp. 244–55), and by Henri Bergson as time that is understood through the 'juxtaposition in space' (Bergson, 1950, p. 85). According to feminist scholars such as Elizabeth Grosz (2004) and Sam McBean (2015), such a comprehension of time is deeply patriarchal and leads to a strict imposition of social hierarchies. Elizabeth Freeman calls this process of temporal ordering 'chrononormativity', 'or the use of time to organize individual human bodies toward maximum productivity' (Freeman, 2010, p. 3). She writes:

> In a chronological society, the state and other institutions, including representational apparatuses, link properly temporalized bodies to narratives of movement and change. These are teleological schemes of events or strategies for living such as marriage, accumulation of health and wealth for the future, reproduction, childrearing, and death and its attendant rituals. (Freeman, 2010, p. 4)

From Freeman's description of chrononormativity, it quickly becomes clear as to how a society organised by linear, clock time reinforces patriarchy. As an example, in chrononormative societies, women's bodies are disciplined by the 'biological clock', as they are pressured to get married by a certain age so that they can have children by a certain age, to take care of the children for at least eighteen years and so on and so forth. Men, conversely, are not necessarily confined to the repetitive temporalities of the domestic but are, instead, asked to be 'in time' with the linearity of the mechanical clock and to labour from – for instance – nine to five so as to further the aims of capitalism.

Furthermore, this linearity and homogeneity have also seeped into the ways in which 'history' is conceptualised – such a mode of history, as writers such as Reinhart Koselleck (1985) and Elizabeth Deeds Ermath (1991) argue, is one that is teleological and universal. In this modern understanding of history, the past and the future are linked in a causal manner, and this narrative of progress is one that can apply to / will reach all parts of the world. This approach to history was notoriously propagated by Hegel (1975), who argued that Europe is in the 'now' of history, whereas the other parts of the world are still in the 'past' needing to catch up with time. Consequently, one of the implications of linear world history is that places beyond Europe were (and still are) regularly characterised through gendered terms: feminine and 'out of time'.[5]

For Julia Kristeva, we can think through questions of feminism using a temporal framework in two ways. First, for her, the early feminists 'aspired to gain a place in linear time as the time of project and history' – this is primarily an attempt to make women 'universal' and to ask for the same 'universal rights' that men had (Kristeva, 1981, p. 18). Second, as Kristeva avers, the subsequent second-wave feminists sought to position themselves 'outside the linear time of identities', by rejoining both 'the archaic (mythical) memory' and 'the cyclical or monumental temporality of marginal movements' (Kristeva, 1981, pp. 19–20). Since Kristeva, there has been a gradual shift in more recent writings on feminism where neither the linearity of clock time is rejected, nor is the heterogeneity of non-clock time wholeheartedly embraced. Rather, linearity and non-linearity are put in conversation with each other.[6]

Characterising this feminist approach is a focus on the present tense as that of becoming rather than being. For Rachel Loewen Walker, we can understand such a feminist temporality as 'the living present'. She writes:

> The living present is heavy with lineages that mimic, critique and undo our assumed histories, and, rather than wiping away the past or seeking absolution for our actions, we can embrace this thick temporality, recognizing its ability to deepen our accountabilities to those pasts and their possible futures. In this way, such a focus becomes a necessary form of ethical engagement with the world which begins not from the point of subject/object relations (or human/inhuman, nature/culture or cause/effect, for that matter), but from the position of being always already entangled in a vital materiality. (Walker, 2014, p. 56)

Walker formulates her argument by building on scholars such as Karen Barad (2007) and Deleuze, who both propose that no one entity is separate from another, and that individual human and more-than-human phenomena 'only find meaning or expression through their co-creative connections and entanglements with other entities' (Walker, 2014, p. 49).

Walker's proposal constitutes a relational understanding of the universe, where everyone and everything is entangled with one another in a constant state of change – if we are all enmeshed with one another, then Othering will be made more difficult. From such an angle, as Stephanie Clare argues, contemporary feminist scholars can be understood as being interested in the ways in which power and agency emerge 'in the process of becomings' (Clare, 2009, p. 24). Consequently, if all entities are to be in a constant state of becoming, then the present tense becomes the most potent way to make sense of all the changes that are happening. In turn, this outlook is interested in the relationship between the homogeneous and heterogeneous aspects of time so as to understand how the interactions – the process of actualisation – allow for differences to occur.

Time, in such a worldview, is thick with temporalities in the present tense, and we can see such a feminist outlook in the Southeast Asian women filmmaking that I discussed above. Returning to *Nervous Translation* as an example, the audience is encouraged to hold this relational approach in view from the get-go, where we are brought into Yael's world and encouraged to experience the multiple temporalities that she negotiates on an everyday basis. This invitation continues through the rest of the film. In the house, where the majority of the film's narrative takes place, the soundscape is haunted by the incessant ticking of the clock, as the characters' discussions about their histories and futures are sonically juxtaposed with the homogeneity of clock time. When the film and Yael do step out of the house, one of the places to which we are brought is the shoe factory where Yael's mother works. In this sequence, the editing pattern is similar to that of the opening montage that I discussed – arrhythmic – and the audience is shown factory workers labouring on shoes in different stages of construction. The mechanical and machinal sounds of hammering, sawing and drilling, among other things, permeate the atmosphere. Through the editing and sound design, Yael's mother and the fellow co-workers' everyday lived experiences and labour are impressionistically related to the audience alongside the linearity of capitalist, clock time. In turn, in *Nervous Translation*, not only does Yael experience such a coalescence of temporalities, but her mother and the fellow co-workers in the factory do, too.

## Rethinking the Region Through Temporal Performances

Comprehended as such, this feminist approach towards time emblematic of Southeast Asian women's cinema is one that does not reject time's linearity, nor time's non-linearity. It is one that invites the audience to be attentive to the ways in which the friction of temporalities works in the living present, so as to work through the complexities of power relations. Here, I borrow the language of 'friction' from Anna Lowenhaupt Tsing. In her ethnography on the rainforests of Indonesia, Tsing proposes 'friction' as a frame to think through wider global connections. Friction, so Tsing writes, refers to 'the awkward, unequal, unstable and creative qualities of interconnection across difference' (Tsing, 2005, p. 4) and 'reminds us that heterogeneous and unequal encounters can lead to new arrangements of culture and power' (Tsing, 2005: 5). Understood in the context of this chapter, friction here allows us a way into thinking about Southeast Asia from a temporal viewpoint.

What is at stake in such a claim? Echoing Arnika Fuhrmann, this chapter argues that such an observation about the relational feminist strategies in Southeast Asian women's filmmaking offers us the opportunity to take up Harry Harootunian's challenge 'to rethink humanities approaches to the "area"' (Fuhrmann, 2017, p. 252).[7] For Harootunian, Area Studies as a discipline can be largely understood as a 'desire' to celebrate 'fixed spatial containers, such as geographic area, culture region or directional locality (East Asia, Southeast Asia, Northeast Asia)' and their 'capacity for modernising takeovers' (Harootunian, 2019, p. 48). He writes that Area Studies . . .

> . . . persists in privileging the spatial over the force and forms of time. This 'end of temporality' excludes time's agency (although not chronology) and spatializes certain world regions, transubstantiating multiple temporalities (with their different histories and modes of production) into a singular temporality that marks the distance between developed and undeveloped. This spatial privileging converts a purely quantitative measure of time – chronology – into a qualitative yardstick, whereby a different temporality becomes a symptom of backwardness. (Harootunian, 2019, p. 48)

In other words, Area Studies is largely developed and filtered through the frame of modernisation theory, which is a model that celebrates the progressive transition from premodern to modern.[8] Such an approach, as Prasenjit Duara observes, explains the nation and the region away through a mode of historicisation that is derived 'from the linear, teleological model of Enlightenment History' (Duara, 1995, p. 4). Modernisation theory, so Harootunian argues, poses a significant epistemological challenge for Area Studies, as it is unable to account for the plural modes of living in an area without consigning people to being 'out of time'. In doing so, in the homogenisation of narratives, there is a tendency in Area Studies to 'mask, if not eliminate, the regular cycles of existential time in everyday life' (Harootunian, 2019, p. 48). To move beyond the discipline's uncritical engagement with modernity (and thus also postmodernity) as a concept – or, as Harootunian provocatively suggests, 'to make the transition from area studies to cultural studies' (Harootunian, 2019, p. 46) – Harootunian calls for a shift from the spatial to the temporal, as well as to examine 'the differing temporal terms and cultural spaces and the coexistence of differing modes and forces of production' (Harootunian, 2019, p. 45).

Southeast Asian cinemas and Southeast Asian women's filmmaking provide an interesting opportunity to take up Harootunian's invitation, because there has been a burgeoning interest in the ways in which the national and regional are and have been relationally formed. Sang Joon Lee (2020), for instance, has very impressively examined how East and Southeast Asian cinemas might have been variously carved out separately, or lumped into a homogeneous whole, by globalised Cold War politics. Trice, in another example, proposes to think of Southeast Asia(n cinemas) through the scalar. She writes:

> How does region become a spatial logic for film production, distribution, and reception? Inspired by work in critical border studies, I would like to propose a shift from the concept of region as a fixed, geographic area to the idea of region as a historically contingent practice, a reterritorializing performance that emerges amid a confluence of specific cultural and economic circumstances. (Trice, 2021a, p. 188)

For Trice, the region is one that is performed; therefore, it is open to the constant process of re-performances. The lens of performance allows us to examine how film organisations and practitioners in Southeast Asia – 'a relic of the so-called Cold War' – have taken on the notion of the regional and 'reshaped it into a desired fiction', drawing 'regional boundaries through affective affinities and performative identities' (Trice, 2021a, p. 189). She argues that the region is one that 'is a contingent imaginary' and produced 'across multiple scales' – that is, institutionally, nationally, transnationally, regionally, globally and so on (Trice, 2019, p. 12). The concept of scales here, so Trice writes, is helpful 'because its emphasis on space can act as an alternative to teleological temporal models; scale suggests transnational or comparative spatial relations' (Trice, 2019, pp. 12–13).

I find Trice's ideas on the region as performance to be of interest here. However, I suggest that Trice's primary focus on the spatial as a way into the temporal opens herself up to Harootunian's charge that Area Studies 'persists in privileging the spatial over the force and forms of time' (Harootunian, 2019, p. 48). I think that there is a missed opportunity in reframing the performance(s) of the region and the regional from a temporal viewpoint. Performance, so Peggy Phelan writes, 'in a strict ontological sense is nonreproductive'; it 'occurs over a time which will not be repeated. It can be performed again, but this repetition itself marks it as "different"' (Phelan, 1993, pp. 146–47). Embedded in Phelan's claim is a temporal one that is not too dissimilar from the ideas on relational temporalities put forward by the feminist scholars whom I discussed above – performances happen in the present tense. This present tense is one that is thick with temporalities, and each 'repetition' will not be the same, for it will be temporally negotiated in different ways. Performances are becomings: in each performance, in other words, is a new negotiation of temporalities, a new performance of time.

Elsewhere, I have developed a theoretical scaffold which argued that 'everyone and everything, enmeshed in extended ecologies, is engaged in different performances of time, as they each negotiate with different temporalities in relation to their surrounding world' (Deng, 2023, p. 5). Such a framework, I propose, allows us to think about how an entity is performing time and performed by time, and 'to pause and to unfurl the negotiations of temporalities into its multiple intersecting units' (Deng, 2023, pp. 115–16). Put differently, the concept of temporal performances pays attention to the ways in which different temporalities come together to negotiate in the present tense to give rise to entangled differences. Building on this framework, I propose that there is merit to think of the area as temporally performed – indeed, such a claim echoes Rahul Rao's (2020) argument that place is temporal and relational – and Southeast Asian women's filmmaking, in drawing the audience's attention to the thick temporalities in negotiation, invites us to do just that.

Returning to *Nervous Translation*, we can see the ways in which the national, regional and global are temporally performed by the different temporalities in negotiation. Midway through the film, Yael's extended family comes to visit. She is watching a Philippine horror film – *Di ingon 'nato* (dir. Brandon Relucio and Ivan Zaldarriaga, 2011) – with her cousins. The lights are dimmed, and the zombies in the film are chasing the humans. Yael and her cousins are simultaneously engrossed and horrified by the film: one of them covers her mouth and squeals, and Yael puts her hands out to imitate the physicality of a zombie. Subsequently, they fall asleep. As they sleep, the television segues into a station broadcasting a news segment about the rumblings of the People Power Revolution in an American accent. Then, as time passes, a late-night advertisement –

selling a pen – starts playing on the television. Yael wakes up and is completely captivated by the advertisement, especially the slogan 'For a beautiful human life'. She then spends the remainder of the film trying to save up enough money to buy the pen.

In this sequence, many temporalities come together to put forward a version of the Philippines that is actualised through its relationship with the regional and the global. First, Marcos being confronted by the People Power Revolution is reported through the news, and a kind of the past is being brought – reported – into the present. This is news that is filtered through an American accent (we never see the footage of the reportage and so can never be sure whether this is an American station or a Philippine channel). It highlights the important role that the US played in the Philippines through the long history of colonisation, and in Southeast Asia in general (in Vietnam, and in the formation of the Southeast Asia Treaty Organisation, the organisation that preceded the Association of Southeast Asian Nations, for example). Second, the presence of the Japanese advertisement for the pen, which ultimately becomes Yael's *objet petit a*, highlights Japan's significant economic influence in the Philippines in the 1980s. Since the 1960s, the 'flying geese' economic model had been propagated by Japan. The model argued that Japan should be the leader for technological advancement in East and Southeast Asia – it positioned Japan at the front of the flying formation, while the Philippines were put at the back of the line – and, accordingly, Japan invested heavily and ambitiously in the Philippines. In this sense, Yael's response to the Japanese advertisement not only highlights the Philippines' journey to becoming more capitalist, but also gestures towards the region's rapid economic development since the 1970s, which is also a direct result of post-World War II geopolitics and American capitalism, as well as Japan's (failed) imperial ambitions.[9]

Third, the film that the children watch is from the future. Like *Nervous Translation*, *Di ingon 'nato* is a Cebuano film funded by Cinema One Originals. Cinema One Originals is an independent film festival run as a subsidiary of ABS-CBN, a major film and television production company. It was started in 2005 with the aim to fund, produce and discover new Filipino filmmakers (both independent and mainstream) and to make money for the network (filmmakers surrender their rights to the company after five years). The model adopted by Cinema One Originals stands in direct contrast to the Cinemalaya Philippine Independent Film Festival, which also started in 2005 and similarly aimed to promote Filipino filmmakers. Unlike Cinema One Originals, Cinemalaya is funded with public money, and the filmmakers get their rights back after a few years.[10] The inclusion of this film from the future, like the inclusion of *Blue Bustamante* discussed earlier, is of interest. It is anachronistic and gestures towards the 'future' (not the 1980s) of Philippine cinema. As Trice notes, since the inception of both Cinemalaya and Cinema One Originals in 2005, a new Philippine film culture marked by a speculative future started to take shape. She writes:

> The speculative routes of alternative cinemas helped create a vision of a national cinema, not just as texts or an industrial sector but as a prospective, national film culture that in its ideal form would overcome the impasse of alternative cinema. (Trice, 2021b, p. 231)

In being temporally oriented towards the speculative future, the Philippine film industry and culture reshaped itself physically – malls were redesigned, independent cinemas were structured and reprogrammed, and film piracy shaped the geography of cities, to name only a few examples.

Later in the film, as Yael goes on her quest to get enough money to buy the pen for which she longs, as her desire seems to reach a peak in the narrative, a fantasy sequence irrupts into *Nervous Translation*. It is in the middle of the night, on an empty street lit by a few streetlights. A human-sized pen-humanoid enters the scene as an electronic score enters the film. The pen-humanoid is red in colour and walks towards the children before leading them away. The children are made up to be zombies. Their faces are pale, and their eye sockets are sunken. A child has a giant wound painted on their face, while another has hair made from cassette tape. Slowly, with their arms outstretched, they follow the pen in a catatonic manner. All while that is happening, the slogan 'For a beautiful human life' is constantly repeated in the score.

This sequence, reminiscent of Michael Jackson's *Thriller* (which was released in 1983 and was the best-selling record in the world then), becomes the example of an identification, a desire, that is actualised through the friction of multiple temporalities. In this version of the Philippines that is performed, the temporalities of American culture (the reference to *Thriller*), Japanese socio-politics (the pen), Saudi Arabia's economic influences (the broken tape on the child's hair, encapsulating the recorded conversations between mother and father) and the Philippine film industry (the allusion to *Di ingon 'nato*) all come together to relationally perform a Philippines which is slightly absurd and fantastic, which is deeply complicit in sustaining a damaging global capitalist system and which is bountifully hopeful. But, beyond that, the hybridised-homage to *Thriller*, mediated and performed through the multiple temporalities of the film's Philippine present tense, also recalls the closing credits of Taika Waititi's *Boy* (2010), where a group of indigenous Maori people perform a hybridised rendition of *Thriller*, a haka and Pātea Māori Club's 'Poi E' (1984), opening the analysis to further temporalities from across a world of cinemas.[11]

This fantastic moment in *Nervous Translation*, then, is one that imagines a Philippines that can only but be understood through its temporal relationship with other entities in the region and in the world. The national, regional and global are informed by different temporalities, which are always in a constant state of conversation with one another. Such an approach recalls Lúcia Nagib's oft-cited suggestion that world cinema has 'no beginning and no end, but is a global process' (Nagib, 2006, p. 35). A world of cinemas, 'as the world itself, is circulation' (Nagib, 2006, p. 35). Put another way, thinking of the area as temporally performed, as *Nervous Translation*, emblematic of Southeast Asian women's filmmaking, invites us to do, we are thinking about the ways in which time is negotiated and circulated. In questioning the patrilineality of an area by pointing to a living present thick with time, Southeast Asian women's filmmaking challenges Eurocentric frameworks of national and cultural histories imposed on non-European countries by re-emphasising the interconnections of history, culture and politics in the world from a temporal framework.

## References

Anderson, B. (1998). *The spectre of comparisons: Nationalism, Southeast Asia and the world*. London: Verso.
Barad, K. (2007). *Meeting the universe halfway: Quantum physics and the entanglement of matter and meaning*. Durham: Duke University Press.
Benjamin, W. (1992). *Illuminations* (H. Arendt, ed., and H. Zohn, trans.). Oxon: Fontana Press.
Bergson, H. (1950). *Time and free will: An essay on the immediate data of consciousness* (F. L. Pogson, trans.). London: George Allen and Unwin.
Browne, V. (2014). *Feminism, time, and nonlinear history*. New York: Palgrave Macmillan.
Chamberlain, P. (2017). *The feminist fourth wave: Affect temporality*. Cham: Palgrave Macmillan.
Clare, S. (2009). Agency, signification, and temporality. *Hypatia*, 24(4), 50–62.
Corey, P. N. (2018). Siting the artist's voice. *Art Journal*, 77(4), 84–96.
Deleuze, G. (2013a). *Cinema I: The movement-image* (H. Tomlinson and B. Habberjam, trans.). London: Bloomsbury.
Deleuze, G. (2013b). *Cinema II: The time-image* (H. Tomlinson and R. Galeta, trans.). London: Bloomsbury.
Deng, M. (2020). Singapore as non-place: National cinema through the lens of temporal heterogeneity. *Asian Cinema*, 31(1), 37–53.
Deng, M. (2023). *Ageing, dementia and time in film: Temporal performances*. Edinburgh: Edinburgh University Press.

Doane, M. A. (2007). The indexical and the concept of medium specificity. *Differences: A Journal of Feminist Cultural Studies*, *18*(1), 128–52.

Duan, S. (2021). Thinking, feeling and experiencing the 'empty shot' in cinema. *Film-Philosophy*, *25*(3), 346–61.

Duara, P. (1995). *Rescuing history from the nation: Questioning narratives of modern China*. London: University of Chicago Press.

Emmerson, D. K. (1984). 'Southeast Asia': What's in a name? *Journal of Southeast Asian Studies*, *15*(1), 1–21.

Ermath, E. D. (1991). *Sequel to history: Postmodernism and the crisis of representational time*. Princeton: Princeton University Press.

Freeman, E. (2010). *Time binds: Queer temporalities, queer histories*. Durham: Duke University Press.

Fuhrmann, A. (2017). This area is [NOT] under quarantine: Rethinking Southeast/Asia through studies of the cinema. In K. Mielke and A. Hornidge (eds), *Area studies at the crossroads: Knowledge production after the mobility turn* (pp. 251–68). New York: Palgrave Macmillan.

Fukuyama, F. (1992). *The end of history and the last man*. New York: Avon Books.

Glennie, P., and Thrift, N. (2009). *Shaping the day: A history of timekeeping in England and Wales 1300–1800*. Oxford: Oxford University Press.

Grosz, E. (2004). *The nick of time: Politics, evolution, and the untimely*. Durham: Duke University Press.

Harootunian, H. (2019). *Uneven moments: Reflections on Japan's modern history*. New York: Columbia University Press.

Hegel, G. (1975). *Lectures on the philosophy of world history* (H. B. Nisbet, trans.). Cambridge: Cambridge University Press.

Hemmings, C. (2011). *Why stories matter: The political grammar of feminist theory*. Durham: Duke University Press.

Ingawanij, M. A. (2021). Cinematic animism and contemporary Southeast Asian artists' moving-image practices. *Screen*, *62*(4), 549–58.

Koselleck, R. (1985). *Futures past: On the semantics of historical time* (K. Tribe, trans.). Cambridge: MIT Press.

Kristeva, J. (1981). Women's time (A. Jardine and H. Blake, trans.). *Signs*, *7*(1), 13–35.

Lee, S. J. (2020). *Cinema and the cultural cold war: US diplomacy and the origins of the Asian cinema network*. London: Cornell University Press.

Lim, B. C. (2009). *Translating time: Cinema, the fantastic, and temporal critique*. Durham: Duke University Press.

Lim, M. K. (2019). *Philippine cinema and the cultural economy of distribution*. Cham: Palgrave Macmillan.

Lugones, M. (2007). Heterosexism and the coloniality of gender. *Hypatia*, *22*(1), 186–209.

Macdonald, R. (2019). Southeast Asia and the AEC, an introduction. In R. Macdonald (ed.), *Southeast Asia and the ASEAN economic* (pp. 1–37). Cham: Palgrave Macmillan.

McBean, S. (2015). *Feminism's queer temporalities*. Abingdon, Oxon: Routledge.

Mohanty, C. T. (2003). *Feminism without borders: Decolonizing theory, practicing solidarity*. Durham: Duke University Press.

Nagib, L. (2006). Towards a positive definition of world cinema. In S. Dennison and S. H. Lim (eds), *Remapping world cinema: Identity, culture and politics in film* (pp. 30–37). London: Wallflower Press.

Northrop, A. (2018). *The spaces that inhabit us: Shireen Seno on* Nervous translation. Retrieved from https://read.kinoscope.org/2018/12/07/the-spaces-that-inhabit-us-shireen-seno-on-nervous-translation/

Ogle, V. (2015). *The global transformation of time: 1870–1950*. Cambridge: Harvard University Press.
Phelan, P. (1993). *Unmarked: The politics of performance*. London: Routledge.
Rao, R. (2020). *Out of time: The queer politics of postcoloniality*. Oxford: Oxford University Press.
Rodriguez, R. M. (2010). *Migrants for export: How the Philippine state brokers labor to the world*. London: University of Minnesota Press.
Said, E. W. (2003). *Orientalism*. London: Penguin.
Sim, G. (2018). Postcolonial cacophonies: Yasmin Ahmad's sense of the world. *Positions: East Asia Cultures Critiques*, 26(3), 389–421.
Trice, J. N. (2019). Gendering national histories and regional imaginaries: Three Southeast Asian women filmmakers. *Feminist Media Histories*, 5(1), 11–38.
Trice, J. N. (2021a). Performing region in Southeast Asian film industries. *Journal of Cinema and Media Studies*, 60(3), 188–93.
Trice, J. N. (2021b). *City of screens: Imagining audiences in Manila's alternative film culture*. Durham: Duke University Press.
Trinidad, D. D. (2017). Domestic factors and strategic partnership: Redefining Philippines-Japan relations in the 21$^{st}$ century. *Asian Politics and Policy*, 9(4), 613–35.
Tsing, A. L. (2005). *Friction: An ethnography of global connection*. Oxford: Princeton University Press.
Walker, R. L. (2014). The living present as a materialist feminist temporality. *Women: A Cultural Review*, 25(1), 46–61.
Watson, J. K. (2016). Aspirational city: Desiring Singapore and the films of Tan Pin Pin. *Interventions: International Journal of Postcolonial Studies*, 18(4), 543–58.
Wilson, P., and Stewart, M. (2008). Indigeneity and indigenous media on the global stage. In P. Wilson and M. Stewart (eds), *Global indigenous media: Cultures, poetics, and politics* (pp. 1–35). Durham: Duke University Press.

# Notes

1. See also Corey (2018), Sim (2018) and Watson (2016).
2. See Rodriguez (2010) on how the Philippine state brokers labour to the world so as to make a profit for the nation.
3. The index, so Mary Ann Doane writes, gestures to a moment that could be temporally described as 'this was once the present' (Doane, 2007, p. 140).
4. See Glennie and Thrift (2009), and Ogle (2015) for the long history of clock time.
5. See Mohanty (2003), Said (2003) and Lugones (2007).
6. See, for example, Hemmings (2011), Browne (2014) and Chamberlain (2017).
7. See Anderson (1998), Emmerson (1984) and Macdonald (2019) as examples of the homogeneous spatial approach towards a regional history which Harootunian criticises.
8. See Fukuyama (1992) as an example of modernisation theory.
9. See Trinidad (2017) on Philippines-Japan relations. Japan had to focus on strengthening their economic position in the region, because their military power had been severely curtailed after World War II.
10. See Lim (2019) on the distribution and exhibition of independent Philippine cinema.
11. See Wilson and Stewart (2008) on the temporalities of global indigenous media.

Chapter 14

# Celebrating Women in Global Cinema: Disruptive Programming and East Asian Women on International Screens

*Fraser Elliott*

The turn of the twenty-first century saw a proliferation of film festivals around the world. Attempts to quantify the exact number by scholars in the early 2010s suggest that, in 2013, there were between 700 and 3,000 recurring events taking place on an annual basis (de Valck, 2013; Follows, 2013). Despite the challenges posed by the COVID-19 pandemic, the British Council (2022) website lists 181 ongoing film festivals in the United Kingdom alone. Across the UK this has meant good things for fans of East Asian cinema, and the contributions of women therein, as there are now a number of UK-based film festivals, curatorial initiatives and organisations which support and make available the work of East Asian filmmakers on an annual – or more regular – basis. Current operations include, but are by no means limited to: the Chinese Visual Festival and its spin-offs Focus Hong Kong and Vision Taiwan; Hong Kong Film Festival UK; UK-China Film Collab; Taiwan Film Festival Edinburgh; Queer East; London East Asia Film Festival; Japan Foundation Touring Film Programme; London Korean Film Festival; Scotland Loves Anime; Chinese Film Forum UK (CFFUK); as well as organisations such as MilkTea who also extend their focus to British East Asian audiences and creatives.[1]

This is a significant change from twenty years ago and has provided regional audiences a range of opportunities to see different kinds of films from East Asia (with many of those based in England's capital offering regional touring programmes in cities across the UK, despite the inclusion of 'London' in their names). Vitally, this is an *exhibition* trend, and it is one that bypasses many of the traditional routes through which films historically made it to British audiences. There is less need, for example, for these films to travel through the traditional film festival ecosystem, nor do they need to be acquired by national distributors. For films which are made by or about women in East Asian cinema, this is an important development, because their work is exactly the kind that was historically marginalised or elided by those structures of distribution and circulation that had previously been the gatekeepers of international film for UK audiences. These histories have been explored in scholarship – from the restrictive fascination with male auteurs in Japanese cinema (Stringer, 2011) to the masculine martial arts heroes of Hong Kong's popular cinema in the 1970s (Elliott and Willis, 2020, p. 22) – so I will not rehearse them here, but it is worth remembering just how rigid and influential these processes can be. They hold such power that, in the early 2000s, distributor Tartan effectively invented a 'genre' of film that they labelled 'Asia Extreme'; under this label, they collated a vast and diverse number of films from across East Asian regions and presented them to audiences as a unified cinematic movement from a homogenised foreign location (Shin, 2008).

It is against these rigid structures of film circulation that those curatorial initiatives listed above are working. The question, then, of whether or not this kind of curatorial work can effectively counter limiting representations of the contributions by women from the film industries of East Asia and elsewhere is a pertinent one. It exists in the collision between the utopian possibilities of Lobato's (2012) 'shadow economies' – the democratic potential of curation in the digital age – and the more rigid structures of the international film ecosystem whose histories have been commanded by patriarchal and colonial discourses. While the internet has opened up disruptive possibilities when it comes to the (often illegal) access to films from around the world, Patricia Caillé (2016) reminds us that these activities continue to intersect with traditional gatekeepers in film circulation. Rather than separate processes, the new contemporary exhibition initiatives discussed in this chapter must interact with established spaces as parts of a 'chain of intermediaries participating in the production and circulation of films on different media' (Caillé, 2016, p. 72). These processes remain particularly relevant when dealing with films whose locations of production are foreign to those of their consumption, as the complexities of identities and histories might be obscured by curation practice. Caillé's study focuses on Maghrebi films with French funding, and in her research she notes the cultivation of an ongoing disconnect between cultures of production and reception, noting that, when the films of her focus played in France, they were valorised in ways that did 'not coincide with the history of any of [their] national cinemas, nor with the history of films by women filmmakers in [those] countries' (p. 77).

These are challenges that curators must confront when working in a space of disruptive programming, and there are political risks involved regarding the efficacy that such work can effectively hold. Maria Vélez-Serna (2020, p. 16), for example, studies exhibition initiatives such as those listed above as examples of 'transient events' whose interactions with the established status quo are precarious. She calls this a 'contradiction of temporary action' whereby – just as Felicia Chan (2016) explores with regard to the repeated labelling of women's contributions to film as 'first' or 'only' – initiatives and categorisations designed as progressive and interventional can become tokenistic and paradoxically ghettoise their subjects within the patriarchal structures that they had hoped to disrupt.

In this chapter I explore these challenges through the case-study of Celebrating Women in Global Cinema (CWiGC), a curatorial initiative that took place at HOME, an independent cinema and cross-art-form venue in Manchester, England. For the duration of 2019, HOME curated their film programme under this banner, in a celebratory mode that channelled the organisation's 'clear and on-going commitment to the programming of work from women filmmakers from various socio-economic and geographical backgrounds' (Hayward and Willis, 2022). Co-curated by Rachel Hayward and Andy Willis,[2] CWiGC serves as example of a sustained, twelve-month-long curatorial initiative undertaken by a major venue that wanted to contribute to the destabilisation of the global film canon and the production of a more representatively heterogeneous understanding of cinema. As an example of a (relatively) well-funded, large independent cinema venue in the UK's fifth most populous city, HOME exists explicitly at that point on Caillé's 'chain' where independent programming and disruptive ambition meets institutionalised, nation-wide structures. As such, this chapter uses CWiGC as a case-study through which to contextualise and unpack a kind of curation practice that is becoming a vital way for UK audiences to access films by women from East Asia. I will detail the specific characteristics and determinants that enabled this kind of curatorial work to take place, both industrial (the availability of funding, institutional collaboration, programming independence) and social (developing conversations around sexism in the film industry, both locally and internationally through the #MeToo movement). Through this, I will discuss how CWiGC attempted to develop a model that navigates the risks of tokenism in this space. The aim of this chapter is to consider, from an exhibition studies perspective, the positioning of these programming initiatives within wider contexts of representation of women in East Asian cinema in international film cultures and to foreground the role of *circulation* as a process that upholds and maintains the possibilities explored throughout the rest of this edited collection.

HOME is one of the largest independently programmed arts venues in the UK. Its building houses five cinema screens, two theatres, three art gallery spaces, numerous bars and a restaurant. During 2019, the three art forms – then termed Visual Art, Film and Theatre – all had their own programming teams and personnel, although their operations often involved collaboration across departments. The Film team's cinema programme consists mainly of releases that fall under the British Film Institute's (BFI) understanding of 'specialised' film – what we might colloquially term 'arthouse' – which includes, for example, foreign-language film, documentary and archive screenings (BFI, 2016). Many of these films will be on general theatrical release, showing at similar venues nation-wide, but a significant portion of HOME's screenings are one-offs curated internally or through collaboration with external partners in the form of events, short seasons and festivals. Examples of this would include FilmFear, a horror season that takes place every October, in collaboration with the television channel FilmFour, and Not Just Bollywood, an annual season focusing on independent Indian cinema curated by Rachel Hayward and local academic Omar Ahmed.

There are many more like these two, and for the duration of 2019 the CWiGC focus fed into almost every aspect of this curation and programming. That year's iteration of Not Just Bollywood, for example, included only films directed by women and saw a 28 per cent increase in audience admissions from the previous year. The venue's largest annual festival – ¡VIVA!, a celebration of Spanish and Latin American cinema – contained mainly films with women creatives in central roles. Outside of these offerings, HOME curated screenings around figures such as Yasmin Ahmad, Ngozi Onwurah, Lina Wertmüller and Rebecca O'Brien, and themes such as 'Women, Organise!' which showcased films about women's activism and work in trade unions. A number of films from these initiatives toured exhibition venues across the UK, thanks to connections which had been established in earlier programming work, as will be explored below. Equally, many films programmed collaboratively with external parties screened at HOME: from short seasons on Margarethe von Trotta and Euzhan Palcy with the Independent Cinema Office (ICO) and Barbican, respectively, to HOME's venue-specific contribution to the BFI's 'Musicals' season which focused on the work of Betty Comden.

The work of women in East Asian cinema formed a key strand to CWICG, as part of both HOME's in-house curation and collaboration with external parties. This began with the annual Chinese New Year screening which that year was *Havana Divas* (2018), the S. Louisa Wei-directed documentary that traces histories of the Chinese diaspora in Cuba. In the summer, Hong Kong director Angie Chen visited HOME for a short retrospective of her work and two Q&A events. In the autumn, a short season of films highlighting the work of women action stars in the golden era of Hong Kong cinema titled 'The Original Ass Kickers' screened. Finally, director Jessey Tsang Tsui-shan joined a live table discussion and a Q&A for her most recent film, *The Lady Improper* (2019). As an example of the external collaborations that followed this theme, every film in the 2019 edition of the Japan Foundation Touring Film Programme which played at HOME fit the CWiGC criteria, and director Toda Hikaru joined for a Q&A at the venue.

In truth, the work of East Asian women filmmakers played a larger role in the development and delivery of CWiGC than simply those films included in the twelve-month programme itself. Ten years prior, in 2009, Hayward and Willis were part of the curation team behind Visible Secrets: Hong Kong's Women Filmmakers. This was a season of films shown at Cornerhouse, HOME's predecessor, which celebrated and highlighted the work of contemporary women directors in Hong Kong from the well-known films of Ann Hui to the lesser-known work of Jessey Tsang, Angie Chen, Ivy Ho and others. It was a season born out of the desire to challenge 'misguided assumptions' about films of the region: 'in particular, the notion that there were very few women directors within the Hong Kong film industry', an impression that curator Andy Willis thought had 'undoubtedly been encouraged over recent years by the limited number of their films that make it onto the international film festival circuit and the substantially smaller amount that gain cinema distribution in the UK' (Willis, 2010, p. 165). Here, Willis acknowledges clearly the desire (and need) to intervene directly at the point of exhibition in order to overcome the limiting practices of the film festival ecosystem. The curation team behind Visible Secrets formed into the Chinese Film Forum UK shortly thereafter with a grant from the Arts and Humanities Research Council. In the twelve years since Visible Secrets, the CFFUK has continued to collaborate with HOME and to develop their curatorial and research practice which, in part, aims to diversify the kinds of regional Chinese film productions that UK audiences get to see theatrically. To reflect on this history, HOME and CFFUK hosted the 'Women in East Asian Cinema' event in December 2019 to close the year of CWiGC. This was a crossover event of academic presentations, film screenings and guest Q&As with director Jessey Tsang, which laid the foundations for this edited collection. Both Hayward and Willis (2022) credit the Visible Secrets event as foundational – in terms of staff experience and collaborative networks – for the more ambitious twelve-month focus of CWiGC in 2019.

This collaborative network refers to the vast collection of programmers and exhibitors which have proliferated over the last ten to fifteen years, building on the 'expansion of the publicly funded cinema sector in the 1980s' that Willis (2010, p. 161) suggests laid the groundwork for work such as Visible Secrets. The ICO, an organisation which provides consultation and support services for otherwise independent exhibitors, currently lists close to 500 non-multiplex cinema sites existing across the UK, ranging in size from larger venues such as HOME, down to university film societies (ICO, 2022). There are multiple forms of support helping to develop venues in this sector. The ICO and similar organisation INDY Cinema Group, for example, offer assistance to new venues in terms of film booking, scheduling and marketing, through collaborations designed to equip new venues with the knowledge and experience needed to run themselves without assistance in the future. The 500 exhibitors supported by the ICO include an incomplete selection of chains which focus on similarly 'specialised' material, such as Picturehouse, Curzon and Everyman, whose boutique versions of non-multiplex theatres have found footing in lots of UK cities. In a programming sense, although their venues offer films more associated with the international film festival ecosystem, they are structured similarly to a multiplex model: programmed centrally from London, with the same film choices screening across venues nation-wide, with slight regional variations.

In addition to these formal and informal networks, a common form of support available to independent exhibitors has been the BFI's Film Audience Network (FAN) which, since 2012, has spearheaded the institution's efforts to democratise regional access to cinema in the UK. The BFI FAN is a collection of eight 'film hubs' located in different regions of the UK which 'aims to build more diverse audiences for UK and international film and support the exhibition sector' (BFI, n. d.). Together the hubs support over 1,500 members of a range of sizes with funding opportunities and communication across a network of like-minded and collaborative institutions. Although this network comes with its own idiosyncrasies, regional restrictions and funding preferences, it has, along with its tangential groups, been useful in supporting an array of conversations and opportunities for East Asian cinema in the UK: particularly those, such as the films of many women filmmakers, that have not made it to the country through the logic of the market alone. Examples of these initiatives are plentiful. Some are driven from inside the institution, such as the BFI's own Japanese cinema season which was the focus of their 2020/21 summer programming and offered funding for venues across its vast regional networks to curate screenings around this national focus.[3] Others come from outside, and of those initiatives mentioned in the opening of this chapter, the London Korean Film Festival, Chinese Visual Festival, Japan Touring Film Programme, Scotland Loves Anime and Queer East all receive(d) funding from the BFI FAN. The formal and informal networks encouraged by these structures allow venues and initiatives to pool resources in their collaborative curation. In 2016, for example, HOME curated the twenty-one-film season 'Crime: Hong Kong Style' with partial financial support from the BFI, and this gave them the funds to bring director Felix Chong to Manchester, which was then used as a base from which he could visit other cities and attend screenings at a much lower cost for those regional venues.

Even solely through this consideration of events with funding support from the BFI, we can see how substantial the role of *exhibition* and this exhibitor network has become in presenting East Asian cinema to those British audiences who might not have access elsewhere. This is significant because, over the same period of time, the UK's traditional *distribution* network became quite a hostile place for distributors of East Asian film – and 'foreign-language' productions more generally – as documented by Huw D. Jones (2014). Of the many challenges faced by these distributors, Stephen Follows notes that most are small companies which 'lack the resources to launch nationwide marketing campaigns and have far less leverage with exhibitors' (Jones, 2014, p. 7). In the early 2010s, Adam Torel, the founder of Third Window Films, a distribution label specialising in contemporary Japanese films, left the UK due to prohibitive costs and relocated to Japan (Wroot, 2018). This was at a time, at the beginning of the decade, when even critical darling Wong Kar-wai saw his 2013 film *The Grandmaster* undergo a two-year delay before reaching British audiences on the cusp of 2015. In general, this is a distribution environment at one end of the international film festival ecosystem whose limiting practices, as noted by Willis above, had a restrictive effect on the kinds of East Asian films made available to UK audiences. If we add the intersectional marker of womanhood into these cultural trends, we can see that the work of women was marginalised yet further by those cultural intermediaries that form the 'chain' of international film circulation.

As the 2010s came to a close, much of the discussion around the global film industry turned to its sexism, sexual harassment and marginalisation of women both on- and off-screen, driven by the #MeToo movement. Film circulation received rightful reassessment at this moment, with a newly intensified spotlight shone on the machinations by which films travel the world. The international film festival, as the bottleneck through which many East Asian films must pass to reach global audiences, was highlighted for its curatorial biases of race and gender. Criticisms of, for example, the Cannes Film Festival's 'whiteness' and its preference for the work of male directors – its 'boys club' mentality (Kemp and Roxborough, 2013) – are well-documented and shown clearly in the statistical discrepancy between the festival's lifetime screening history of eighty-two films directed by women, compared to its 1,645 directed by men (Wilkinson, 2018). For analysts Stephen Follows et al. (2016), this disparity between what is available on screen and the actual labour contributions of women to the industry is at the core of the problem: 'The lack of any trend towards an improvement in female representation, despite the frequent churn of individuals within the film industry, suggests that there are systemic issues which are sustaining and perhaps creating these biases'.

Representation is a knotty topic, however, and in addition to the simple availability of films in which women play visible on- and off-screen roles, it is vital to consider how those tastemakers within the 'chain' discussed above either consecrate or deconstruct gendered and sexist frameworks in these spaces. In notable moments when films from East Asian regions with prominent women creatives *have* made it into the UK's reception contexts, for example, they have often done so through the hands of gatekeepers and tastemakers who have supported them through gendered, essentialist frameworks embedded in colonial histories. There are many examples of this, such as the uncomfortable but not uncommon moments of British film critics fetishising East Asian actors in their writing: see the various lascivious readings of Maggie Cheung in reviews of *In the Mood for Love* (Elliott, 2017). At times, these connections to wider conversations about sexism and misogyny in the international film industry are alarming. Bey Logan, for example, once was one of the men responsible for framing Hong Kong's genre cinema to British (and international, English-speaking) audiences across the 1990s and early 2000s. He wrote prolifically in fan magazines such as *Eastern Heroes* and *Impact*; worked collaboratively with distribution operations in their film selections, special features and DVD commentaries; and, although he kept a performed distance from them, mingled with the BFI teams responsible for East Asian programming at their London venue (Logan, 1995a, p. 27).

Much of Logan's journalistic work at this time conformed to the 'lad' culture of British publishing during this era: typified by magazines including *FHM* and *Loaded* whose articles were 'highly heteronormative, frequently accompanied by sexualized images of women, [and] typically masculine sexual norms' (Coy and Horvath, 2011, pp. 146–47). A clear example of this approach – which framed these East Asian films as primarily for straight, non-Chinese, male consumers – is Logan's review of the Hong Kong film *Black Cat* (1991). For this, the by-line reads: 'Bey Logan goes on a pussy hunt, and tracks down the Black Cat herself, that sensuous, sexy, and ever-so-slightly psychopathic Jade Leung'; the article itself begins with his desire to exchange phone numbers with the star (Logan, 1995b, p. 60). Logan left these British spaces in the 1990s, when he moved to Hong Kong to work in film production there, taking up a role at The Weinstein Company. In late 2017, during the early stages of the #MeToo movement, numerous Hong Kong women accused Logan of sexual misconduct and harassment (THR Staff, 2017), raising challenging questions about his influence on these films and their circulation prior. Although this is one (extreme) example, it shows how some of those who have contributed to both the availability of and discourse around East Asian cinema in the UK have worked to embed those processes with problematic, sexist and often regressive views.

Exhibition initiatives afford curators a route around these prohibitive sexist practices embedded in the UK's gatekeeping and taste-making cultures, just as they allow programmers to bypass those restrictive hurdles of traditional distribution discussed above. The gears grind slowly inside the stalwarts of Britain's film culture, and the democratisation of funding for exhibition events is an acknowledgement of that. It is difficult for an organisation such as the BFI to facilitate this change without the help of curators working on the cutting edge of this progressive political work. We can see this through the way in which the institution talks about gender in global cinema in their flagship publication, *Sight and Sound*. In 2020, following these conversations around sexism in the film industry, the influential magazine released a list of 100 overlooked films directed by women (BFI, 2020). East Asian cinema receives a reasonable (albeit lacking, given the size of their respective industries) representation in this list, with eight films from Hong Kong, Japan, China and the East Asian diaspora included. Yet, the choice of the term 'overlooked' is curious for a magazine with such a commanding influence in the UK on which of the world's films are themselves *looked at*. There is an irony that, eight years prior, the same magazine's list of the '100 Greatest Films of All Time' contained only two entries directed by women (none from East Asia).

The 2020 list emerged after years of independent curatorial work from across the UK, which had been using exhibition sites (and often BFI money) to bring these conversations and contributions to the fore. There are too many to name here, and all vary in their feminist praxis and focus, but two prominent examples include: Birds Eye View, a collective working with cinemas across the UK whose 'Reclaim the Frame' initiative has, since 2018, brought nineteen cinemas and many more individuals together to support films about and by women; and Club Des Femmes, a 'queer feminist film curatorial collective' whose work aims to 'look beyond the mainstream' through radical exhibition work (Club Des Femmes, n. d.). These are two collectives of the many which collaborated with HOME during their year of celebrating women in global cinema. A vital characteristic of the disruptive curation of these two organisations – the former founded in 2003, the latter in 2007 – is that it is ongoing and sustained. Dismantling the canon is difficult work, but it is much harder for such work to be effective if it is based entirely on one-off, transient events.

This is a challenge addressed by Maria Vélez-Serna in her work on 'minor practices' within Scotland's contemporary exhibition scene, particularly those that create short, transient events with the intention of disrupting hierarchies or forming new collectives through communal film-watching. In her discussion, Vélez-Serna notes the precarity of this kind of work after decades of policies by the UK's Conservative governments to hollow out public spaces and to neo-liberalise creative pursuits. She asks 'whether a temporary configuration, a transient event, can have a reparative role', or whether such events actually maintain the status quo: they 'may offer glimpses of new solutions to the crisis [. . .] but they may also normalize the loss and the harm' (Vélez-Serna, 2020, pp. 15–16). She terms this the 'contradiction of temporary action' and, although these are not words ever used by HOME's curation team, it is clear that the design of CWiGC understood this risk and tried to overcome it. The sustained duration of CWiGC was central to the curatorial ambitions of the programme.

In its spread across the calendar year, it was intended in the first instance to be more meaningful in impact than a shorter, more conventional approach:

> The concept of a rolling, year-long programme committed to highlighting the women's contribution to the richness of global cinema [. . .] has the potential to provide a model for large-scale, extensive, and cross-connective programming initiatives that could be taken up across the UK specialised exhibition sector. (Hayward and Willis, 2022)

For this to be an achievable goal, curators Hayward and Willis placed importance on the internal composition of the HOME programming team and its already well-established relationships with external partners. The in-house programming afforded the project a clear curatorial vision which, in turn, provided a certainty and lucidity to its messaging that made it easier for external collaborators to come on board (Hayward and Willis, 2022). The plan was also for the CWiGC theme to continue after the specific twelve-month focus of 2019. Early offerings in 2020 fell under the umbrella including the 'In Her View: Women Documentary Filmmakers' season in January; however, these plans were complicated by the forced closure of all cinemas in the UK during the COVID-19 pandemic.

The hope for Hayward and Willis (2022) was that CWiGC could be seen as a model to be utilised across the sector in the future 'to address other gaps and omissions within the UK exhibition landscape'. Through this durational approach, in particular, opportunities arose with much more interventional potential than is commonplace for continually operating cinema venues such as HOME. This is a tension identified by Stephanie Strathaus in her reflections on programming at the Deutsche Kinemathek. Strathaus (2004) notes how transient events such as film festivals can communicate much more clearly and persuasively a politically motivated curatorial theme. Short events can be more readily packaged and their curatorial ethos more strongly communicated than day-to-day programming at a general exhibition venue. A festival such as Queer East – a London-based event that showcases queer filmmaking from across East Asia – provides audiences with clear messaging and a concise opportunity to view films from a variety of East Asian regions covering diverse aspects of the LGBTQIA+ experience. Its website succinctly defines itself as a 'LGBTQ+ festival that showcases rarely-seen queer cinema from East and Southeast Asia and seeks to amplify the voices of Asian communities in the UK'. The 2021 edition of the festival took place over eleven days, during which audiences could plan to see many, make connections and hold discussions across each one, either alone or with fellow festival attendees.

Curators at festivals such as these intentionally include 'discursive aspects' – moments of dialogue and contrast between film choices – to facilitate communication across the various screenings and events that constitute the festival. Although not about dictating *how* these films are read, it does guarantee a clear curatorial communication. The same cannot be said for ongoing programming at a cinema venue; for Strathaus

(2004, p. 6), it is 'much more difficult to communicate principles of curating film series, or retrospectives, outside the context of film festivals, namely, through monthly programming'. When the curatorial work of a venue is spread indefinitely over months and years, Strathaus contends that audience attention drifts away from any connective tissue between selections and towards a scenario where films are judged instead by their rarity or the quality of the prints from which they are screened. While transient events may court the risks of unintentionally maintaining a problematic status quo as understood by Vélez-Serna's analysis of 'temporary configurations', they nevertheless have much more of an opportunity to make an overt and consistently engaged-with political statement than monthly programming.

In sustaining the programming focus across a twelve-month period *and* in working to strengthen collaborative networks across the UK, HOME hoped to leverage the advantages of programming for *both* festivals and venues with CWiGC. It compelled HOME's audiences to confront these processes for an entire year, as a continued interruption or alteration of their general experience of, and temporal relationship with, filmgoing at their local venue. The dilution of the theme 'women in global cinema' is hopefully, then, a productive one in which signifiers such as 'woman' and 'East Asia' come to be seen as contributing elements to the intersectional composition of these films with various points of overlap and communication with all the other films released across the year. The films of, say, Jessey Tsang or Angie Chen are thus positioned alongside those by Lina Wertmüller or Rebecca O'Brien and the themes of 'Women, Organise!', for example. Rather than pacifying the political project, this work reflects a form of feminist praxis discussed by Imani Perry (2018, p. 229) as the 'living curatorial project', whereby life and resistance are enriched by the ongoing encounters with new collaborations 'and the possibilities therein'. For Perry, . . .

> . . . part of the benefit of thinking in terms of a living curatorial project is that one is focused less on the immediacy of a reaction to a thing (usually some form of product or commodified self) than on building up a series of artifacts and ideas and experiences to develop a sense of the world and self and we. (Perry, 2018, p. 245)

The year-long experience for HOME's audiences of repeatedly encountering a foregrounded acknowledgement of women's contributions to the films that they were attending to see worked to puncture and overcome the reactionary potential of other curatorial practices.

In this chapter, I have presented HOME's Celebrating Women in Global Cinema initiative as an emblematic example of the disruptive possibilities of contemporary curation in film exhibition. It represents well the potential embedded within collaborative, ongoing curatorial work that can rupture previously unwieldly and impenetrable cultural processes. This programming strategy was born quite directly out of the collaborative work that HOME's curators had done in the years prior with women working in the Hong Kong film industry, but that emerged from wider developments in Britain's film cultures. It also followed trends in both those industrial and social currents which have opened up a space for collaborative and disruptive exhibition work that bypasses the traditional 'chain' of the film festival ecosystem and houses potential for much messier and more diverse representations of women's contributions therein. CWiGC worked to resist essentialised representations or understandings of the films included in its selection, hoping instead to acknowledge their heterogeneity and to avoid presenting a static understanding of where they might fit in a global film canon. The curators hoped to achieve this through the year-long focus of the programme, and through their stress on using the curatorial theme as a means of developing and strengthening connections and ruptures.

Not all venues are as privileged as HOME in their programming freedom and institutional structure. However, thanks to the depth of the collaborative network that supports contemporary exhibition initiatives across the UK's regions, when thinking in terms as broad as 'women in East Asian cinema', audiences are, to a degree, set. The risks of transient events detailed by Vélez-Serna are in many ways overcome by the sheer quantity of curatorial initiatives whose programming (whether focused on national categorisation or intersectional feminism) provides audiences with a plethora of films to see. The collaborative network at the heart of Britain's contemporary 'arthouse' exhibition scene ensures a wide and sustained regional spread of screenings which, while certainly not spread equally with parity across the UK, can continue to puncture those limiting representations that reception contexts such as these have historically maintained. As is identified elsewhere in this collection (see Kukolova's chapter on South Korean filmmakers), this reception context is not divorced from the production bases of East Asia but, rather, plays a mutually constitutive role. While the effects of this curation will be felt most immediately within the UK, the hope is that it creates a newly productive contributor to a global film 'chain' and an international cycle of production and circulation that is more sustainable in its support of the work of women.

## References

BFI. (n.d.). *BFI Film Audience Network*. Retrieved from https://www.bfi.org.uk/get-funding-support/bring-film-wider-audience/bfi-film-audience-network
BFI. (2016). *Specialised films*. Retrieved from https://www2.bfi.org.uk/sites/bfi.org.uk/files/downloads/bfi-specialised-films-2016-06-30.pdf
BFI. (2020). *The female gaze: 100 overlooked films directed by women*. Retrieved from https://www.bfi.org.uk/sight-and-sound/female-gaze-100-overlooked-films-directed-by-women
BFI. (2021). *BFI Japan comes to big screens UK-wide this autumn*. Retrieved from https://www.bfi.org.uk/news/bfi-japan-autumn-programme
British Council. (2022). *Festivals directory*. Retrieved from http://film-directory.britishcouncil.org/festivals-directory
Caillé, P. (2016). Mapping the circulation of films by women filmmakers with Maghrebi funding in the digital age. In M. Hagener, V. Hediger, and A. Strohmaier (eds), *The state of post-cinema: Tracing the moving image in the age of digital dissemination* (pp. 71–86). London: Palgrave Macmillan.
Chan, F. (2016). First, not only: Writing Chinese women's film authorship. In F. Chan and A. Willis (eds), *Chinese cinemas: International perspectives* (pp. 109–18). Oxford: Routledge.
Club Des Femmes. [n. d.]. *Manifesto*. Retrieved from https://www.clubdesfemmes.com/manifesto/
Coy, M., and Horvath, M. A. H. (2011). Lad's mags, young men's attitudes towards women and acceptance of myths about sexual aggression. *Feminism and Psychology*, 21(1), 144–50.
De Valck, M. (2013). Film festivals and migration. In *The encyclopedia of global human migration: Vol. 3* (pp. 373–88). Chichester: Wiley-Blackwell.
Elliott, F. (2017). The sustained popularity of *In the mood for love*: Cultural consumption in Britain's reception context. In J. Wroot and A. Willis (eds), *Cult media: Re-packaged, re-released and restored* (pp. 201–20). London: Palgrave Macmillan.
Elliott, F., and Willis, A. (2020). Rapidly shifting landscapes: Two case studies in the UK distribution and exhibition of Chinese language films in the twenty-first century. In *Renegotiating film genres in East Asian cinemas and beyond* (pp. 17–40). London: Palgrave Macmillan.
Follows, S. (2013). *How many film festivals are there in the world?* Retrieved from https://stephenfollows.com/many-film-festivals-are-in-the-world/
Follows, S., Kreager, A., and Gomes, E. (2016). *Cut out of the picture: A study of gender inequality amongst film directors in the UK film industry*. Retrieved from https://stephenfollows.com/gender-inequality-in-the-uk-film-industry/
Hayward, R., and Willis, A. (2022). Celebrating Women in Global Cinema: Curating a year-long programming initiative at HOME, Manchester. In L. Tsitsou, H. Rana, and B. Wessels (eds), *The formation of film audiences: Conference proceedings*. Retrieved from https://www.dhi.ac.uk/books/film-audiences/celebrating-women-in-global-cinema/
Independent Cinema Office (ICO). (2022). *Cinemas in the UK and Ireland*. Retrieved from http://www.independentcinemaoffice.org.uk/advice-support/cinemas/
Jones, H. D. (2014, October 31). *The market for foreign language films in the UK*. Paper presented at the Migrating Texts colloquium. University College London.

Kemp, S., and Roxborough, S. (2013). Cannes: Competition remains a boys club with only one female contender. *The Hollywood Reporter*. Retrieved from https://www.hollywoodreporter.com/movies/movie-news/cannes-competition-remains-a-boys-442145/

Lobato, R. (2012). *Shadow economies of cinema: Mapping informal film distribution*. London: British Film Institute.

Logan, B. (1995a). She's got the power: Michiko Nishiwaki. In R. Baker and T. Russell (eds), *The essential guide to the best of Eastern Heroes*. London: Eastern Heroes Publications.

Logan, B. (1995b). Rap on a hot tin roof. In R. Baker and T. Russell (eds), *The essential guide to the best of Eastern Heroes*. London: Eastern Heroes Publications.

Perry, I. (2018). *Vexy thing: On gender and liberation*. North Carolina: Duke University Press.

Shin, C. Y. (2008). Art of branding: Tartan 'Asia Extreme' films. *Jump Cut*. Retrieved from https://www.ejumpcut.org/archive/jc50.2008/TartanDist/

Strathaus, S. S. (2004). SHOWING DIFFERENT FILMS DIFFERENTLY: Cinema as a result of cinematic thinking. *The Moving Image: The Journal of the Association of Moving Image Archivists*, 4(1), 1–16.

Stringer, J. (2011). Japan 1951–1970: National cinema as cultural currency. In D. Iordanova and R. Rhyne (eds), *Film festival yearbook 3: Film festivals and East Asia* (pp. 34–48). St Andrews: St Andrews Film Studies.

THR Staff. (2017). Harvey Weinstein's Hong Kong associate accused of sexual misconduct by multiple women. *The Hollywood Reporter*. Retrieved from https://www.hollywoodreporter.com/movies/movie-news/harvey-weinstein-s-hong-kong-associate-accused-sexual-misconduct-by-multiple-women-report-1066921/

Vélez-Serna, M. (2020). *Ephemeral cinema spaces: Stories of reinvention, resistance and community*. Amsterdam: Amsterdam University Press.

Wilkinson, A. (2018). 82 women protested gender inequity in the film industry on the red carpet at Cannes. *Vox*. Retrieved from https://www.vox.com/culture/2018/5/13/17347738/cannes-womens-protest-march-film-festival-cate-blanchett-agnes-varda-timesup-red-carpet

Willis, A. (2010). Cinema curation as practice and research: The Visible Secrets project as a model for collaboration between art cinemas and academics. *Screen*, 51(2), 161–67.

Wroot, J. (2018.) Moving from Japanese film distribution to production: An interview with Third Window Films' Adam Torel. *Bright Lights*. Retrieved from https://brightlightsfilm.com/moving-from-japanese-film-distribution-to-production-an-interview-with-third-window-films-adam-torel/

# Notes

1. See Appendix 1 for further information about each curatorial collective and organisation mentioned here.
2. During the season and at the time of writing, Rachel Hayward was Head of Film at HOME, and Andy Willis their Senior Visiting Curator and Professor of Film Studies at the University of Salford. I was employed as a member of the HOME film team between 2017 and 2020, responsible for delivering all cinema-related events (including Q&As and introduced screenings, for example), which gave me first-hand access to the information discussed here. The only curation work I did during CWiGC across 2019 was in my role as a member of the CFFUK, as detailed above.
3. See BFI (2021) for a list of examples.

# Appendix 1

**Birds Eye View.** Founded in 2003. Established 'Reclaim the Frame' in 2018: 'a mission to bring audiences together and build a community for films by women and non-binary filmmakers in cinemas across the UK'. Available at: https://www.birds-eye-view.co.uk/

**Club Des Femmes.** Founded in 2007. 'We are a queer feminist collective. We curate film screenings and events. Our mission is to offer a freed up space for the re-examination of ideas through art'. Available at: https://www.clubdesfemmes.com/manifesto/

**Chinese Film Forum UK.** Formed following the *Visible Secrets* season as discussed in this chapter. 'The Chinese Film Forum UK is a network based in Manchester that exists for the research and promotion of transnational Chinese film. The network includes Manchester Metropolitan University, University of Salford, The University of Manchester, Confucius Institute, Centre for Chinese Contemporary Art and HOME'. Information about past events available at: https://homemcr.org/event/chinese-film-forum-uk/

**Chinese Visual Festival.** Founded in 2011 by James Mudge together with programmer Jingjing Xie, the Chinese Visual Festival may have seen its last iteration in 2021 but still maintains a social media presence: https://twitter.com/cvf_london. Their spin-off **Focus Hong Kong** – organised by Mudge and Andrew Heskins – remained active into 2022 and is available at: https://focushongkong.uk/

**Hong Kong Film Festival UK.** Founded in 2021 by Hong Kong filmmakers in the UK, the festival 'aims to shine an international spotlight on Hong Kong's creativity and humanity through film [and] also strives to promote cultural interactions and exchanges between Hong Kong communities and UK citizens'. Available at: https://www.hkff.uk/about

**Japan Foundation Touring Film Programme.** An annual tour ran by the Japan Foundation since 2004: 'Each year, from recently released contemporary films to classics and anime, the Japanese films which we believe are worth showing but do not necessarily have an opportunity to be screened in this country are curated under a carefully chosen theme to highlight trends in Japanese cinema and showcase the versatility and uniqueness displayed by its filmmakers'. Available at: https://www.jpf-film.org.uk/about

**London East Asia Film Festival.** Founded in 2015. The 'LEAFF aims to champion the growing collaboration in East Asian filmmaking with a philosophy that marks a shift in the cinematic landscape of East Asia, and moves away from cultural and cinematic borders'. Available at: https://www.leaff.org.uk/about-leaff

**London Korean Film Festival.** Founded in 2003. Organised by the Korean Cultural Centre UK. Available at: https://www.koreanfilm.co.uk/

**MilkTea.** Founded in 2020/21. 'MilkTea shows the best of East & South East Asian cinema in the UK. Our work begins with screenings, but our goal is to build inclusion, communities & audiences'. Available at: https://www.milkteafilms.com/

**Queer East.** Founded in 2020. 'An LGBTQ+ film festival that showcases queer cinema from East and Southeast Asia'. Available at: https://queereast.org.uk/

**Scotland Loves Anime.** Founded in 2010. The 'UK's only film festival celebrating Japanese animation': https://twitter.com/lovesanimation. Also available at: https://www.lovesanimation.com/

**Taiwan Film Festival Edinburgh.** Founded in 2020. Taiwan Film Festival Edinburgh 'was a response to the global surge in interest in Taiwanese cinematography over the last decade and introducing some of the lesser-known Taiwanese cinematography to wider audiences'. Available at: https://taiwanfilmfestival.org.uk/. (Note: I was a co-curator in 2020 and Programme Consultant for the 2021 edition of this festival.)

**UK-China Film Collab.** Founded in 2019 with an AHRC Creative Partnership Development Grant. The organisation aims 'to inspire and encourage film related collaboration and debate between the UK and Greater China'. Available at: https://www.ukchinafilm.com/

# Index

NOTE: Name order follows the convention used in each chapter. Page numbers in *italic* indicate figures. Page numbers with n indicate endnotes.

action heroines, 61, 220
advertising, 160–1
agency
 defining, 94–5
 Hong Kong cinema, 40, 47
 Ning Ying, 178, 180
 Qiong Yao films, 94–5, 98, 101
 Takamine Hideko, 141, 143–5, 151
 Xu Jinglei, 76, 77
*Ah Fei* (1984), 102
Ahmad, Yasmin, 201, 219
Ahmed, Omar, 219
Aichi International Women's Film Festival, 119
AIDS *see* HIV/AIDS
*Akumyo* (*Tough Guy*) *yakuza* films, 86
*amah* maidservant, 38–9
Anderson, Aaron D., 85
Anderson, J. L., 139–40
*anime*, 83; *see also* Scotland Loves Anime
Area Studies, 201, 208–10
Armendáriz-Hernández, A., 118
Arnett, J., 62
'arthouse' film, 169, 219, 228
Arts and Humanities Research Council, 220
Arzner, Dorothy, 2
Asano, Taeko, 83, 84
'Asia Extreme' label, 130, 217
Asian Film Archive, 190, 198n
Association of Southeast Asian Nations, 211
Augé, Marc, 200
*auteurs*
 *auteur* theory, xv, 2, 140
 and female Korean screenwriter-directors, 124, 125, 126, 136
 Japanese cinema, 113, 217

Xu Jinglei, 77
authorship
 creative labour, 7
 female screenwriters, 135
 Haneda Sumiko and subjectivity, 113–18
 Ning Ying and editing, 166, 167, 172, 173, 180
*Awakening* magazine, 96
Ayase, Haruka, 79, 81, 82, 83, 84, 89, 90–1
*Azumi* (2003), 79

Bang Eun-jin, 126, 131
Bao Zhifang, xiv
Barad, Karen, 206
Bauman, Zygmunt, 34
beauty, 101
beauty queens, 42
Beckett, Samuel, *Waiting for Godot*, 132–3
Beijing, xvi, 17–18, 193
Beijing Film Academy (BFA), 166, 167
Benjamin, Walter, 205
Bergson, Henri, 205
Berlinale (film festival), 168
Berry, Chris, 164, 168, 174, 198n
Bertolucci, Bernardo, *The Last Emperor of China*, 166
BFI *see* British Film Institute
BFI London Film Festival, 124, 135
Bhabha, Homi, 186
Bi Hu, *Long Live the Wife*, 49n
Birds Eye View, 225, 231
 'Reclaim the Frame', 225, 231
*Black Cat* (1991), 224
*Blade of the Immortal* (2017), 79, 91

*Blonde Venus* (1932), 2
*Blood Stains the Valley of Love* (1957), 198n
*Blooming Under a Cool Moon* (1960), 40–1
*The Blossoming Rose* (1968), 41–3, *43*
*Blue Bustamente* (2013), 203, 212
Bollywood, xv, 219
Bong Joon-ho, 124, 126
   *The Host*, 137n
   *Memories of a Murder*, 137n
   *Mother*, 126
   *Parasite*, 126
Boo Ji-young, *Cart* (*Ka-teu*), 58
Bordwell, David, 154
Brey, Iris, 67, 72
Brinton, M. C., 128
British Film Institute (BFI), 2, 140, 219, 222–5
   BFI FAN (Film Audience Network), 221, 222
   BFI London Film Festival, 124, 135
Broomfield, Nick, 155
Brown, David, 85
*Burn, Burn, Burn* (2015), 58
Butler, Alison, 16, 114
Butler, Judith, 85
B-wave Korea, 52
*By the Time It Gets Dark* (2016), 200

Caillé, Patricia, 217, 218
Cai Shenshen, 74, 75, 77
Cannes Film Festival, 129, 168, 223
Cantonese cinema, 30, 31, 36, 40, 44, 45, 47–8, 154, 198n
career-woman figure (*nü qianren*), 32, 33
Cazdyn, Eric, 115
Celebrating Women in Global Cinema (CWiGC), 8–9, 153, 218–21, 225–6, 227–8
censorship, 74, 129
Central Motion Pictures Cooperation (CMPC), 95
C-Fem ('made-in-China feminism'), 172
CFFUK *see* Chinese Film Forum UK
*chaebols* (Korean conglomerates), 127
*chanbara* (sword action) films, 79, 80, 82, 83, 84, 86, 88, 91
Chan, Connie, 40, 41, 42
Chan, Felicia, 14, 172, 218
Chan, Jackie, *Dragon Lord*, 155
Chan, Willie, 155
Chang, Eileen, 44–5
   'Flower Withered', 45
Chang, J. J., 40
Chen, Angie, 153–65
   overview, 153, 164
   commercials, 160–1
   documentaries, 161–3
   Golden Harvest, 153, 158–9
   HOME retrospective, 164, 220, 227
   outside in, 154–6
   Scorpio Films, 153, 160–1, 163
   Shaw Brothers, 153, 156–8
   *Chaos by Design*, 153, 158–9, 160
   *Dragon Lord*, 155
   *He Lives by Night*, 155
   *I've Got the Blues*, 153, 161, 163, 164
   *Maybe It's Love*, 153, 156, 164
   *My Name Ain't Suzie*, 153, 156–8, 160, 164
   *One Tree, Three Lives*, 153, 154, 161, 162–3
   *This Darling Life*, 153, 161, 162
   *The Visit*, 154–5, 162
Chen Che *see* Qiong Yao
Cheng, Sammi, 33
Cheng, Y., 31
Chen Kaige, 166, 167
*Cherish Our Love Forever* (1998), 75
Cheung, Cherie, 156, 158
Cheung, Mabel, 3, 153, 154, 164
   *The Illegal Immigrant*, 156
Cheung, Maggie, 223
Chhachhi, Amrita, xiv
China
   Angie Chen commercials, 160
   defining East Asia, 5
   female gaze in Xu Jinglei's *Letter from an Unknown Woman*, 66–8, 73, 74, 77
   He Xiaopei, 14, 24
   LGBTQ+ communities, 15, 17
   'new wave', 167
   Ning Ying, authorship and editing, 8, 166–81
   *nyonya* figure and Peranakan Chinese representation, 187–9, 191, 193, 194
   queer feminism in post-Mao China, 17–20
   women's cinema and politics of pleasure, 16
   Young Feminist Activism, xvi
China Film Art Research Centre, 168
*China Wife* (1957), 198n1
Chinese Film Forum UK (CFFUK), 4, 216, 220, 231
Chinese Visual Festival, 216, 222, 231
Chin Han, 100
Chin Hsiang-lin, 100
Chiung Yao *see* Qiong Yao
Choe, Minja Kim, 128

Choi Jinhee, 57, 130
Choi, M., 128
Cho Junhyoung, 129
Cho Nam-joo, *Kim Ji-young: Born 1982 (82 Nyeonsaeng Gim Jiyeong)*, 61
Chong, Felix, 222
Chow, Rey, 178
Chow, Stephen, 38
Chow Yun Fat, 85
chrononormativity, 205
Chu, Donna, 32
Chung Po-yin, 29
cine-feminism, 58, 59
Cinema City, 155, 160
cinemagoing, 29–30, 34, 129–30
Cinemalaya Philippine Independent Film Festival, 211–12
*Cinema Library* (journal), 119
'cinema of pleasure', 15–16, 20–3, 26
Cinema One Originals, 211–12
cinematography, 59, 130, 135
circulation, 8, 219, 222, 223
Clare, Stephanie, 207
class, as motif, 51
clock time, 205, 206, 207, 215n
Club Des Femmes, 225, 231
Coates, Jennifer, 3
Coates, Nelson, 192
collectives, 52, 59
colonialism, 189, 195, 223
comedy, 44–5
commercials, 153, 160–1
Confucianism, 52, 55, 56, 59, 61, 95, 96
Cook, Pam, 2
'cooperative marriage', 25
Cornerhouse, Manchester, 220
'cosmopolitan cinema', 14
courtesans, 68, 70, 73, 74
COVID-19 pandemic, 216, 226
Cox, Alex, 153, 154
*Crazy Rich Asians* (2018), 8, 187, 192–6
creative labour
  overview, xv, 1, 4, 7
  Angie Chen and Hong Kong film, 153–65
  female screenwriter-directors in the South Korean film industry, 124–37
  Haneda Sumiko, authorship and gender perspective, 107–23
  Ning Ying, authorship and editing, 166–81
  Takamine Hideko and Matsuyama Zenzō collaboration, 138–52
*Crying Out Love, in the Center of the World* (2004), 83, 84

Cuba, 220
Cui Shuqin, 69, 170
culture, defining, 186
curatorial work, 8–9, 216–20, 222–8
Curzon cinemas, 221
CWiGC *see* Celebrating Women in Global Cinema
cyberspaces, 52

*Dangdai Dianying* (journal), 168, 169
*Deep in the Mountain* (1967), 95
Deleuze, Gilles, 202–3, 204, 206
Deng, M., 210
Deren, Maya, 70
  *Meshes of the Afternoon*, 99
Deutsche Kinemathek, 226
digital activism, 51–2
*Di ingon 'nato* (2011), 210, 211, 212
directors *see auteurs*; female directors
*Directors' Cuts* series, xiii
disabilities, 22
distribution, 127, 135, 222
Doane, Mary Ann, 29, 30, 215n
documentary
  Angie Chen, 153, 154–5, 161–3
  Haneda Sumiko, 107–13, 116, 120–1
  He Xiaopei, 13, 14, 20
  participatory or performative, 155
  women's cinema and politics of pleasure, 16
domestic labour, 45, 55
Donald, Stephanie, 172
Dong Kena, 68
Dong, Y., 172
Doyle, Christopher, 161
*The Dream of the Red Chamber* (1977), 100
DSO (collective), 52
Duan, Siying, 204
Duara, Prasenjit, 208
Dyer, Richard, *Stars*, 80, 85, 140–1

East Asia, defining, 1, 3, 4–5
editing and editors, 7, 166, 167, 171, 172, 180
education, 108, 109, 128
elder care, 117, 119
*Emily from Emerald Hill* (Kon play), 199n
Eng, Esther (Ng Kam-ha), 2–3
Engle, Paul, 154, 163
entertainment cinema, 15
Ermath, Elizabeth Deeds, 206
Evans, Harriet, 18
Everyman cinemas, 221
exhibitions, 216–20, 221–6, 228

factory girl figure, 30, 35, 36, 39–44, 47
fantasy cinema, 200
Fei Mu, *Spring in a Small Town*, 69
Fellini, Federico, 166
female agency
   defining, 94–5
   Hong Kong cinema, 40, 47
   Ning Ying, 178, 180
   Qiong Yao films, 94–5, 98, 101
   Takamine Hideko, 141, 143–5, 151
female directors
   Chinese film, 168–9
   and creative labour, xv
   and female gaze, 66, 67
   and female screenwriters, 125–7, 130–1
   Haneda Sumiko and authorship, 109, 118, 120–1
   recognition of, 3
   South Korea and *Microhabitat*, 59
female gaze, 1, 6, 66–8, 70, 72–3, 77, 101
female labourers, 33, 35, 36, 47
female rent collector figure, 37
female screenwriter-directors in the South Korean film industry, 7, 124–37
female spectatorship, 29–30, 31, 34–5, 48
female stars *see* stars
female voice-over, 68, 115, 116, 117
femininity, 22, 33, 34, 101, 120
feminism
   female gaze, 67
   feminist film criticism, 2, 15–16, 114
   global histories, xvi
   Haneda Sumiko and authorship, 114, 120
   'herstory' film narratives, 58
   Hong Kong cinema, 31, 45
   'housewife feminism', 45
   Ning Ying and Chinese filmmaking, 171–3, 179
   Qiong Yao films and Taiwan, 93, 96
   queer feminism in post-Mao China, 17–20
   second-wave feminism, 206
   South Korean womanhood and *Microhabitat*, 50–3, 56, 58, 59, 61
   temporal aesthetics, 206
   women's cinema and politics of pleasure, 15–16
feminist analysis of Southeast Asian women's filmmaking, 200–15
Feng Xiaogang, 168
figurations, 185
film circulation, 8, 219, 222, 223
film distribution, 127, 135, 222
film exhibition, 216–20, 221–6, 228

FilmFear, 219
film festivals, 3, 119, 124–5, 135, 168, 216, 221–3, 226, 228
film stars *see* stars
film studies, 1, 2, 4, 58, 113, 135, 140
Firebird Picture Company, 94
Focus Hong Kong, 216
Follows, Stephen, 222, 223
Fong, Eddie, 156
Fong, Mona, 156, 157–8
*Four Loves* (1965), 95
four virtues, 95, 103–4n
France, 217
franchising, 80
Freeman, Elizabeth, 205
French, Lisa, 67
friction, 208
Frost, M. R., 187–8, 189
Fu, P., 40
Fuhrmann, Arnika, 208
*Funny Face* (1957), 99

Gaines, Jane, 3
Gallagher, Mark, 192, 196
Gao Shanlan, 103n
gay communities, 19, 25, 159; *see also* LGBTQ+ movement
gaze *see* female gaze; male gaze
gender activism, 51–2, 59
gender equality, 21, 57, 62, 96
gender gap, 128
gender representations
   overview, xiv–xv, 1, 4, 5–7
   female agency and subjectivity in Qiong Yao films, 93–104
   female gaze in Xu Jinglei's *Letter from an Unknown Woman*, 66–78
   female labour in Hong Kong cinema, 29–49
   female stars and gender representations in *Zatoichi* franchise, 79–92
   He Xiaopei's home video aesthetics and queer feminist politics, 13–28
   South Korean womanhood in *Microhabitat*, 50–65
gender studies, 17, 18, 118
gestural cinema, 174
girl figures, 115–16
Gledhill, Christine, 3
global histories
   overview, xv–xvi, 8
   Celebrating Women in Global Cinema and disruptive programming, 216–30
   feminist analysis of Southeast Asian women's filmmaking, 200–15

*nyonya* figure and Peranakan Chinese representation, 185–99
*The Goddess* (*Shennü*, 1934), 169
*Godzilla: Final Wars* (2004), 89
Gohar, Miss (aka Gohar Khayyam Mamajiwala), xv
Golden Harvest, 153, 158–9
González-López, Irene, 3–4, 118
Grand Motion Picture Company (GMP), 95
Grgić, Anna, 16
Grosz, Elizabeth, 205
Gui Yalei, 100
*Gull* (2020), 59
Guo Shaohua, 66, 75
Gwanghwamoon, 59

*Ha* (*Tooth*, 1953), 108
Hamano Sachi, 119
Haneda Sumiko, 107–23
  overview, 7, 107, 120–1
  early inspirations, 107–8
  female authorship and subjectivity, 113–18
  labelling Haneda, 118–20
  *Akiko – Portrait of a Dancer*, 114, 117, 119
  *And Then Akiko is . . . A Portrait of a Dancer*, 113
  *The Cherry Tree with Gray Blossoms*, 113, 115–16, *116*, 119
  *Children in the Classroom*, 108
  *Dedicated Treasures of Horyuji-Temple*, 115, 116
  *Far-Away Home: Lushun and Dalian*, 117–18
  *In the Beginning, Woman was the Sun: The Life of Hiratsuka Raicho*, 114
  *Into the Picture Scroll – The Tale of Yamanaka Tokiwa*, 113
  *Kabuki yakusha Kataoka Nizaemon*, 118
  *The Life of Hiratsuka Raicho*, 117, *117*, 119
  *Ode to Mt Hayachine*, 113
  *Welfare System Chosen by Residents in a Township*, 117
  *Women's College in the Village*, 109–13, *111*, 112, 114, 120
  *Women's Testimony: Pioneer Women in Labour Movement*, 114, 115, 117, *117*
Hani Etsuko, 108
Hani Susumu, 110, 118, 120
*Happiness of Us Alone* (1961), 143, 147, 148
Hara, Setsuko, 85

Haraway, Donna, 24
Hark, Tsui, 154
Harootunian, Harry, 208–10
Haskell, Molly, 1
*Havana Divas* (2018), 220
Hayward, Rachel, 218, 219, 220, 221, 225–6, 230n
Hee Wai Siam, 190, 191
Hegel, G. W. F., 206
'herstory' film narratives, 31, 58
He Xiaopei
  overview, 6, 13–15, 26–7
  cinema of pleasure, 20–3
  home video aesthetics and queer feminist politics, 13–28
  images, *14*, *21*, *26*
  queer feminism in post-Mao China, 17–20
  queering the 'home video' genre, 23–6
  women's cinema and the politics of pleasure, 15–16
  *The Bad Women of China*, 14, 25
  *Gay Cats*, 25
  *Happily Ever After*, 25
  *Love You Too*, 22
  *The Lucky One*, 14, 19, 21–2, *21*
  *Our Marriages: When Lesbians Marry Gay Men*, 14, 25–6, *26*
  *Playmates*, 14, 25
  *Polyamorous Family*, 13–14, 25
  *Yvo and Chrissy*, *14*, 18, 22–3
Hibari, Misora, 85
Hieu Chau, 59
Hiratsuka Raicho, 114, 117, 119
historicisation, 208
history, 200, 205–6
Hitchcock, Alfred, *Rear Window*, 156
HIV/AIDS, 19, 20, 21, 22
HKIFF *see* Hong Kong International Film Festival
HKMDB *see* Hong Kong Movie Database
HKWF *see* Hong Kong Women Filmmakers
Ho, Ivy, 220
Hollywood, xv, 2, 15, 29, 48, 127
HOME, Manchester, 9, 218–22, 225–8
  Angie Chen retrospective, 153, 164, 220
  'Crime: Hong Kong Style', 222
  'In Her View: Women Documentary Filmmakers', 226
  'The Original Ass Kickers', 220
  'Women in East Asian Cinema' event, 220
  'Women, Organise!' 219, 227
'home video' genre, 6, 13, 14, 15, 23–6
homosexuality, 15, 19, 25, 159; *see also* LGBTQ+ movement

Hong Eun-won, *A Woman Judge*, 137n
Hong Ji-young, 131
Hong Kong cinema
  action heroines, 217, 220
  Angie Chen and Hong Kong film, 7, 153–65
  curatorial work, 228
  factory girl figure, 39–44
  female figures before career woman and Kong girl, 31–4
  female labour in Hong Kong cinema, 29–49
  female labour overview, 6, 29–31, 47–8
  HKWF, 3
  landlady and housemaid figures, 36–9
  and Logan, 223, 224
  middle-class housewife figure, 44–7
  'new wave', 153, 156, 157
  *nyonya* figure and Peranakan Chinese representation, 187, 189, 190
  on-screen representations and beyond, 34–47
  Visible Secrets: Hong Kong's Women Filmmakers project, 220–1
  women's cinema and politics of pleasure, 16
Hong Kong Film Festival UK, 216, 231–2
Hong Kong International Film Festival (HKIFF), 100, 163
Hong Kong Movie Database (HKMDB), 156
Hong Kong Women Filmmakers (HKWF), 3, 4
Hong Sang-soo, 124, 126, 137n
Hong Sung-eun, *Aloners (Honja saneun saramdeul)*, 58
Hori Hikari, 119
*A House Is Not a Home* (TV drama, 1977), 32
*The Housemaid (Hanyeo*, 1960), 55–6, 57, 129
*The Housemaid* (2010), 55
housemaid figure, 35, 36, 55
*The House of 72 Tenants* (1973), 38
'housewife feminism', 45
housewife figure, 29, 30, 36, 44–7, 49n
Howard, Christopher, 90
Howson, R., 52
Huang Shuqin, 167
Hui, Ann, 3, 153, 154, 164, 220
  *Love in a Fallen City*, 156
  *A Simple Life*, 38–9
Hu Mei, 167
  *Army Nurse*, 68
hybridity, 186

*Ichi* (2008), 79–92
  overview, 6, 79–81, 90–1
  star power and gender stereotypes, 84–90
  in the *Zatoichi* franchise, 81–4
ICO *see* Independent Cinema Office
image-maker of film, 69, 70
Im Kwon-taek
  *Beyond the Years*, 126
  *Revivre*, 126
  *Salut d'Amour*, 126
Im Sang-soo, 126, 129
  *The Old Garden*, 135
Independent Cinema Office (ICO), 219, 221
indexes, 204, 215n
Indian cinema, 219
INDY Cinema Group, 221
Ingawanij, May Adadol, 200
Institute of Development Studies (IDS), 18, 20
international film festivals *see* film festivals
internet, 217
*In the Face of Demolition* (1953), 37
*In the Mood for Love* (2017), 223
*In Time to Come* (2017), 201, 204
Ip, Deannie, 158
'iron lady' figure (*nü qianren*), 32, 33
Iwanami Hall, 119
Iwanami Productions, 108, 109, 111, 112, 113, 115

Jackson, Michael, *Thriller*, 212, 213
Japan
  BFI Japanese cinema season, 222
  defining East Asia, 5
  female stars and gender representations in *Zatoichi* franchise, 79–92
  Haneda Sumiko, authorship and gender perspective, 7, 107–23
  'housewife feminism', 45
  male *auteurs*, 217
  and Philippines, 204, 211, 212, 215n
  Shochiku Studio woman's films, 48
  Takamine Hideko and Matsuyama Zenzō collaboration, 7, 138–52
Japan Foundation Touring Film Programme, 216, 220, 222, 232
Jeon Go-woon, 52, 58, 60, 61, 62, 63, 131, 134
Jeong, E., 52
Jeong So-yeong, *Pilnyeo*, 128
*Jeune Femme* (2017), 58
Jinyan Zeng, 16
Jiyū Kōbō ('Freedom Studio'), 113

Johnson, Derek, 80
Johnston, Claire, xiii, 2, 15, 16
Jolly, Susie (Sue), 18
Jones, Huw D., 222
Jørholt, Eva, 16
*The Joy Luck Club* (1993), 194
Jung Seo-kyoung, 126, 131, 134
   *Little Women*, 137n
Jung So-Young
   *The Man I Betrayed*, 130
   *The Woman I Betrayed*, 130

*kabuki* theatre, 88
Kanda, Akiko, 113, 114, 117, 119
Kang Je-gyu, 126
Kaplan, Ann E., 2, 66, 97
Karlsson, Mats, 85
Katayama, Kyoichi, *Socrates in Love*, 83
Katori, Shingo, 79, 89, 90
Katsu, Shintaro, 79–83, 85–90
Kei, Sek, 29, 156
Khoo, Olivia, 16
Kida Shō, 140
Kim Do-young, 61
Kim Eun-hee
   *Kingdom: Ashin of the North* (film), 135
   *Kingdom* (series), 135
Kim, H. K., 60
Kim, J., 59
*Kim Ji-young: Born 1982 (82 Nyeonsaeng Gim Jiyeong*, 2019), 61
Kim Ki-duk, 126
Kim Ki-young, 129
Kim Mee-hyun, 125, 126
Kim Mi-hee, 126
Kim Mi-yeong, 126
Kim Sang-jin
   *Attack the Gas Station*, 126
   *Kick the Moon*, 126
Kim So-Jung, *A Blue Mouthed Face*, 58
Kim Soo-hyun, 128–9, 130, 137n
   *The Housemaid*, 129
   *The Man I Betrayed*, 130
   *Pilnyeo*, 128
   *Rainbow*, 128
   *The Woman I Betrayed*, 130
Kim Sun-min, 137n
*Kingdom* (series), 135, 137n
Kinoshita Keisuke, 141, 142
   *Carmen Comes Home*, 142
   *Twenty-Four Eyes*, 138, 142, 143, 149
Kitano, Takeshi, 83, 87–8, 90
   *Zatoichi* (2003), 79, 81, 84, 87–9, 90
Knight, Julia, 3

Kobayashi Masaki, *The Human Condition*, 142
Kodansha, 83
Kon, Stella, *Emily from Emerald Hill*, 199n
Kong, Patrick
   *Love is Not All Around*, 33
   *Marriage with a Fool*, 33
'Kong Girl' (*gang nü*), 32–3
Kong Ngee Film Production Company, *The Nanyang Trilogy*, 198n
Korean cinema
   female screenwriter-directors in the South Korean film industry, 124–37
   Korea and South Korea terminology, 137n
   'Korean Wave', 5
   South Korean womanhood and millennial trauma in *Microhabitat*, 50–65
Koselleck, Reinhart, 206
Kozloff, Sarah, 69
*Krabi, 2562* (2019), 200, 204
Kristeva, Julia, 206
Kudō Mitsuru, 109, 113, 117
*Kuei Mei* (1985), 102
Kuhn, Annette, 29
*Kungfu Hustle* (2004), 38
Kurosawa Akira, 140
Ku Yenlin, 96
Kwak Sin-ae, 126

*Lady from Shanghai* (1946), 2
Lai Chee Kien, 189
landlady figure, 30, 35, 36, 37–8, 39
*Landscape Series #1* (2013), 200, 204
*Last Night Light* (1983), 102
Latin American cinema, 219
Law, Alex, 156
Law, Clara, 3
LEAFF *see* London East Asia Film Festival
Ledesma, Itos, 202
Le Di, 42
Lee Chang Dong, *Peppermint Candy* (*Bakha Satang*, 1999), 60
Lee, J., 52
Lee Jeong-hyang, 131
Lee Kyoung-mi, 125, 131
   *Crush and Blush*, 131–2
   *Lady Vengeance*, 131
   *The School Nurse Files*, 131, 133
   *The Truth Beneath*, 131, 133–4
Lee, Maggie, 162
Lee, Sangjoon, 5
Lei Feng, 174

lesbian characters, 159; *see also* LGBTQ+ movement
*Letter from an Unknown Woman* (2004), 66–78
  overview, 6, 66–8
  empowering death, 75–7
  female gaze and visual pleasure, 72–3
  feminist character, 73–5
  gazing and feeling(s), 69–71
  voice-over and image maker, 68–9
*Letters to Panduranga* (2015), 200–1
Leung, Jade, 224
Leung, P. K., 36
LGBTQ+ movement (lesbian, gay, bi, trans, queer +), 15, 17–18, 19, 25, 158, 159, 226
Lim, Bliss Cua, 200
Lim, S. H., 58–9
Lin, Brigitte (Brigitte Lin Ching Hsia), 85, 100–1
Lin Fengjiao, 100
Ling Bo, 42
liquid modernity, 34
*The Little Nyonya* (TV series), 199n
Liu Chia-chang, 155
Liu Lili, 94, 96, 101, 102
living present, 206
Li Xiaomeng, 66
Li Yüen-chen, 96
Lobato, R., 217
Logan, Bey, 223–4
London East Asia Film Festival (LEAFF), 216, 232
London Korean Film Festival, 124, 135, 216, 222, 232
*Long Live the Missus!* (1947), 44
*Looking for Mr Goodbar* (1977), 2
Lorde, Audre, 24
Lorente, Jose Abad, 22
Lou Ye, *Suzhou River*, 170
*Love Affair of Rainbow* (1977), 103n
*Love Eternal* (1968), 95
*Love in Spring* (1966), 93–4
*Love with a Malaysian Girl* (1969), 190, 198n
Lü Hsiu-lien (Annette Lü), 96
Lu, Lisa, 195
Lupino, Ida, 2
luxury consumption, 54, 55, 56

Ma, Chun-Lung, 192–3
McBean, Sam, 205
McCracken, Grant, 55
*McDull Prince de la Bun* (2004), 39
Machiko, Kyo, 85
McHugh, Kathleen, 137n

Mackie, Vera, 45
*Madame Freedom* (*Jayu Buin*, 1956), 57
*Madam Yu Ching* (1984), 102
Maghrebi films, 217
*mahjong*, 45, 46, 47, 193–4, 195
maidservant figure, 38–9, 45
Mak, Angela, 164
Makoveeva, Irina, 101
Malacca, 185, 193
Malaya, 186, 187, 190, 191
Malaysia, 8, 185, 187
male gaze
  feminist film theory, 1, 2, 61
  Ning Ying's *I Love Beijing*, 178
  Qiong Yao films, 94, 101, 103n
  Xu Jinglei's *Letter from an Unknown Woman*, 6, 66, 67, 70
male stars, 80, 90; *see also* stars
Mandarin, 195, 198n
*manga*, 83
Maori people, 213
Marchetti, Gina, 3, 16
Marcos, Ferdinand, 201, 203, 211
Marcos, Imelda, 201, 202
*The Marigolds* (1980), 94, 97–8
marriage, 47, 54, 102, 128, 151
*Marriage Story* (1992), 127–8
martial arts films, 85, 96, 217
Martinez, Dolores, 81, 91
masculinity, 52
Mason, Richard, *The World of Suzie Wong*, 156–7
Masuzawa Toshio, 108
Matsuyama Zenzō
  and Takamine Hideko, 139, 141, 142–51, 147
  *The Bridge Between*, 147, 148–9
  *Burari Bura-bura Monogatari*, 147, 149
  *Dark the Mountain Snow*, 147, 149–50
  *Happiness of Us Alone*, 143, 147, 148
Mayer, Sophie (So), 16, 28n
MBC TV, 128, 137n
Megalia, 51
melodrama, 60, 97, 129–30, 133, 137n, 190, 199n
#MeToo movement, xvi, 58, 218, 223, 224
Metrograph cinema, New York, 164
Metro Tartan, 130
Metz, Christian, 100
*Microhabitat* (*Sogongnyeo* 2017), 6, 50–65
middle classes, 50, 56
middle-class housewife, 44–7
MilkTea, 216, 232

millennials, 50, 52–6, 58, 60–3
misogyny, 50–3, 58, 63, 223
Mitsuhiro Yoshimoto, 140
modernisation theory, 208, 215n
*Molka* (hidden camera) rallies, 51
monstrous-feminine, 61
montage, 202–3, 207
Montpelier, R., 59
Moon, G., 55
*Moon Over Malaya* (1957), 198n
Morgan, Robin, 58
motherhood, 38
Motion Picture Law (Korea), 127, 129
*Movie Fans* (1966), 43
Mo Yin, 163
Mulvey, Laura, 2, 15–16, 26, 67
*My Favourite Season* (1985), 102

Nagib, Lúcia, 213
Nakadai Tatsuya, 142
Nakamura, Shido, 82
Nakao, Mie, 87
'Nanyang' identity, 187, 189, 190, 191
narration *see* voice-over narration
Naruse Mikio, 138, 141, 142
   *A Wanderer's Notebook*, 142
national cinemas, xv–xvi
*Nervous Translation* (2018), 8, 200, 201–4, 207, 210–13
Netflix, 127, 131, 133, 135, 136, 137n
*New Immigrant* (*Xinke*, 1926–27), 190–1
'New Men in Solidarity', 56
'new wave'
   China, 167
   Hong Kong, 153, 156, 157
   Taiwan, 102
'new women', 102
Ng Kam-ha (Esther Eng), 2–3
Nichols, Bill, 155
Nieh Engle, Hualing, 154, 161, 162–3
Ning Ying, 166–81
   overview, xv, 7–8, 166–7
   disruptive filmmaking, 173–80
   filmmaking approach, 170–3
   institutional context, 167–70
   *For Fun*, 166, 170
   *I Love Beijing*, 8, 166, 167, 170, 171, 173–9, 175–9
   *On the Beat*, 166
   *Perpetual Motion*, 167, 170
   *Railroad of Hope*, 167
Nizaemon Kataoka, 118
non-fiction filmmaking, 107, 111; *see also* documentary
*Nonya and Baba* (1956), 190, 198n
Not Just Bollywood, 219

*nyonya* figurations
   overview, 8, 185–7, 196–7
   early figurations, deracination and cultural dilution, 187–91
   global figurations and *nyonya*-style aesthetics, 192–6
*nyonya* figure and Peranakan Chinese representation, 185–99
*Nyonyah* (1952), 190, 198n

O'Brien, Rebecca, 201, 227
*Oldboy* (2003), 60, 125
*An Old Lady* (2020), 59
Omura Shizuo, 109, 112
Onwurah, Ngozi, 201
Ophüls, Max, 6, 68, 74
   *Letter from an Unknown Woman*, 75, 76
Ortner, Sherry, 94
Osawa, Takao, 81, 83
Ōtake Yōko, 119
Ozu Yasujirō, 140
   *Late Spring*, 204

Pai Hsien-yung, 163
Pang, Edmund, *Love in a Puff*, 33
Paquet, Darcy, 59, 126–7, 130
Park Chan-wook, 60, 124, 125, 126, 131
   *Lady Vengeance*, 125, 126, 131
   *Oldboy*, 60, 125
   *Sympathy for Mr Vengeance*, 125
Park Chung-hee, 129
Park Eun-kyo, 126, 131, 134
Park Hyun-jin, 134, 135
   *Love and Leashes*, 135
   *Lovers of Six Years*, 135
Park, S. H., 59
Pātea Māori Club, 'Poi E', 213
patriarchy, 52, 55, 56, 66, 133, 135, 205
Penang, 185, 194
*Peppermint Candy* (*Bakha Satang*, 1999), 60
Peranakan Chinese representation, 185–99
   overview, 8, 185–7, 196–7
   early figurations, deracination and cultural dilution, 187–91
   global figurations and *nyonya*-style aesthetics, 192–6
   performance, and temporal aesthetics, 209–10
Perry, Anthony (aka Anthony Wong), 157
Perry, Imani, 227
Phelan, Peggy, 210
phenomenology, 67
Philippines, 8, 201, 204, 210–13, 215n

Picturehouse cinemas, 221
Pink Space Sexuality Research Centre, 17, 19, 20
'planned films', 127–8
pleasure, cinema of, 15–16, 20–3, 26
Po Chih Leong, 160
  *He Lives by Night*, 155
polyamory, 25
present tense, 200, 201, 206, 207, 210
prostitution, 74, 81, 157
psychoanalytic approach, 1–2

Qiong Yao (aka Chen Che)
  overview, 6
  Firebird Picture Company, 94
  Superstar (Hong Kong) Motion Picture Company, 94, 96
  'Three Flowers', 93–4
  *Up to Rainbow*, 103n
  Xu Jinglei on, 73
Qiong Yao films
  overview, 6
  agency and subjectivity of female protagonists, 93–104
  *Last Night Light*, 102
  *Love in Spring*, 93–4
  *The Marigolds*, 94, 97–8
  *Wells Up in My Heart*, 94, 97, 98
  *The Wild Goose on the Wing*, 94, 98–100
Qi, Xianggu, 194
Queer East, 216, 222, 226, 232
queer feminist politics
  film exhibition, 225, 226
  He Xiaopei and China, 14–20, 22, 23–7

*Rainstorm in Chinatown* (1956), 190, 198n
Ranjit Movietone, xv
Rao, Rahul, 210
*Rat* newspaper, 58
Rawnsley, M., 101
reception contexts, 228
'Reclaim the Frame', 225
*The Red Brigade of Women (Hongse Niangzi Jun*, 1961), 169
Reynaud, Bérénice M., 170
Richie, Donald, 87, 139–40
Riley, Denise, 1
romantic comedy
  Hong Kong, 29, 33, 39–40, 43, 47–8
  South Korea, 59
romantic drama (Japan), 84, 91, 93, 100
Rosen, Marjorie, 1

*Rurouni Kenshin* franchise (2012–21), 79, 91
Russell, Catherine, 142

*Sacrificed Youth (Qingchun Ji*, 1986), 68, 169–70
St Pierre, Elizabeth, 185–6
Sakamoto, Junji, 89
Sang Joon Lee, 209
San Hu, 49n
Schaffer, K., 179
Scorpio Films, 153, 160–1, 163
Scotland, 225
Scotland Loves Anime, 216, 222, 232
screenplays, 126, 127, 131
screenwriters, 7, 124–37
Seno, Shireen, *Nervous Translation*, 200, 201–4, 207, 210–13
Seoul International Women's Film Festival, 61
*Sepet* (2004), 201
sexism, 218, 222–3, 224
sexual harassment, 222, 224
sexuality
  China, queer feminism and He Xiaopei, 18–22, 25, 26
  female gaze, 72
  Qiong Yao films and Taiwan, 98, 100, 101
  South Korean cinema, 57
  Xu Jinglei's *Letter from an Unknown Woman*, 72, 74
sexual violence, 59
shadow economies, 217
Shamoon, Deborah, 85
Shaw Brothers, 153, 156–8, 160, 164
'Shaw Sisters' film season, 164
she-economy, 66
Shimozawa, Kan, 86
Shinmura Izuru, 146
*Shirkers* (2018), 201
Shochiku Studio, 48
*Shomin Eiga/Shoshimin Eiga* (salaryman/salarywoman) genre, 48
Siao, Josephine, 40, 42
*Sight and Sound* (magazine), 224
silent film, 3, 139, 191
*The Silent Wife* (1965), 95
Singapore, 8, 185, 187–95, 200, 204
Singer, Ben, 129
*Sisterhood is Powerful* (anthology), 58
'sixth generation' directors, 167
Smith, Michael, 4
So Jing-man, 164
Song X., 179

Song Yoon-he, 126
Sonoda Sae, 111, 112, *112*
Son Yeon-ji, 137n
Sori, Fumihiko
  *Ichi*, 79, 83
  *Ping Pong*, 83
  *Vexille*, 83
soundscapes, 177, 203, 207
Southeast Asian women's filmmaking
  overview, 5, 8, 200–1
  rethinking the region through temporal performances, 207–13
  thick time, 201–7
  feminist analysis, 200–15
Southeast Asia Treaty Organisation, 211
South Korean cinema
  overview, 124–31
  *Crush and Blush* and *The Truth Beneath*, 131–6
  female screenwriter-directors in the South Korean film industry, 7, 124–37
  Korea and South Korea terminology, 137n
  South Korean womanhood and millennial trauma in *Microhabitat*, 6, 50–65
space, and temporal aesthetics, 209
Spanish cinema, 219
'specialised' film, 219, 221
Staiger, Janet, 172
stars
  creative labour overview, xv, 7
  male stars, 80, 90
  Qiong Yao films, 100
  Takamine Hideko and Matsuyama Zenzō, 138–41, 143, 146, 151
  *Zatoichi* and gender representations, 79–81, 84–7, 90, 91
star text, 141, 146, 151
Stonewall Uprising, 18
'Straits Chinese', 187–9, 193, 194, 196
Straits Settlements, 185, 187, 194
Strathaus, Stephanie, 226–7
streaming platforms, 127, 134–5, 136
*Street Angel* (*Malu Tianshi*, 1937), 169
'strong career woman' figure, 32, 33
subjectivity
  overview, xiv–xv
  Haneda Sumiko, 111, 113–18, 121
  He Xiaopei, 24
  Qiong Yao films, 94, 101
  and voice-over, 68
Sugimoto, Tetta, 82
Sugimura Haruko, 150
Sugino, Corrine Mitsuye, 196
suicide, 76, 77, 177

Suizenji, Kiyoko, 87
Sundance film festival, 168
Superstar (Hong Kong) Motion Picture Company, 94, 96, 101, 102
*Sworn Sisters* (1954), 38, 39

Tachibana, Daigoro, 88
*tai tai wan sui* ('long live the wife' films), 49n
Taiwan
  Angie Chen commercials, 160
  'new wave', 102
  Qiong Yao films, 6–7, 93–6, 100, 102, 104n
Taiwan Film Festival Edinburgh, 216, 232
Taka, Guadalcanal, 88
Takamine Hideko, 138–52
  overview, xv, 7
  autobiographical essays, 138–9, 141, 145
  and Matsuyama Zenzō, 139, 141, 142–51, *147*
  *The Bridge Between*, 147, 148–9
  *Burari Bura-bura Monogatari*, 147, 149
  *Carmen Comes Home*, 142
  *Dark the Mountain Snow*, 147, 149–50
  *Happiness of Us Alone*, 143, 147, 148
  *Lightning*, 142
  *Twenty-Four Eyes*, 138, 142, 143, 149
  *A Wanderer's Notebook*, 142
Takano Etsuko, 119
Takarada Akira, 142
Take 3, 160
*The Tale of Zatoichi* (1962), 86
Tam, Patrick, 156
Tan, E. K., 190
Tang Baoyun, 100
Tang, Stephy, 33
Tanizaki Jun'ichirō, 145
Tartan, 'Asia Extreme', 217
Tasker, Y., 171
teenage girl figures, 115–16
television screenwriting, 125, 127, 129, 133–6
temporal aesthetics
  clock time, 205, 206, 207, 215n
  feminist analysis overview, 200, 201
  rethinking through temporal performances, 207–13
  thick time, 201–7
Teoh, Karen, 185, 187, 189, 192, 195, 196–7
Thailand, 204
*That Day, On the Beach* (1983), 102
thick time, 201–7
Third Window Films, 222

*13 Assassins* (2010), 79, 91
*Three Females* (1960), 45–6
*Three Flowers of the Factory* (1967), 43
*Three Love Affairs* (1963), 43
three obediences, 95, 103n
Tian Zhuangzhuang, 167
time *see* temporal aesthetics
TIWFF *see* Tokyo International Women's Film Festival
Toda Hikaru, 220
To, Johnnie, 33
tokenism, 218
Tokieda Toshie, *Town Politics: Mothers Who Study*, 109
Tokyo Broadcasting System (TBS), 83
Tokyo International Women's Film Festival (TIWFF), 119
Torel, Adam, 222
transient events, 218, 225, 226, 227, 228
Trice, Jasmine Nadua, 200, 201, 209, 212
Truong, Thanh-Dam, xiv
Tsang, Eric, 156
Tsang Tsui-shan, Jessey, 227
  *The Lady Improper*, 220
Tseng-Putterman, Mark, 196
Tsing, Anna Lowenhaupt, 208
*Twenty-Four Eyes* (1954), 138, 142, 143, 149
*Two City Girls* (1963), 46–7

Udine Far East Film Festival, 164
UK-China Film Collab, 216, 233
Umehara Ryūzaburō, 145
Union Film, 39
universities
  education of women, 51, 128
  film societies, 221
University of California Los Angeles (UCLA) film school, 153, 154, 155
UNWCW (United Nations World Conference on Women), 17–18
*Up to Rainbow* (1977), 103n

Veg, Sebastian, 172
Vélez-Serna, Maria, 218, 225, 227, 228
vertical narration, 70, 71
Vietnam, 211
*The Villainess* (2017), 61
Visible Secrets: Hong Kong's Women Filmmakers project, 220–1
Vision Taiwan, 216
visual pleasure, 15–16, 26, 67, 72–3
¡VIVA! festival, 219
Voci, Paola, 24
voice-over narration, 68–71, 73, 76, 115–17
voyeurism, 71, 72, 100, 156

Waddell, Calum, 84
Wai Kar-fai, 33
Waititi, Taika, *Boy*, 213
Walker, Rachel Loewen, 206–7
Wang Lingzhen, 3, 16, 68, 171, 172
Wang Mochou, 100
Wang Yin, 93–4
  *Love in Spring*, 93–4
*The Way We Are* (2008), 39
'weepie' films, 42
Wei, Louisa S., 171
The Weinstein Company, 224
Wei, S. Louisa, *Havana Divas*, 220
*Wells Up in My Heart* (1982), 94, 97, 98
Wertmüller, Lina, 201, 227
WFPP *see* Women Film Pioneers Project
White, Patricia, 3, 16
*The Wild Goose on the Wing* (1978), 94, 98–100
Willis, Andy, 218, 220, 221, 222, 225–6, 230n
*The Witch* (2018), 61
'woman's film' *see* 'women's films'
women
  as a category, 1
  education of, 51, 128
  womanhood, 31–4, 36, 52, 53, 56–8, 60, 63
  women's labour, 48
  women's movement, 96
  women's rights, 17, 206
women directors *see* female directors
Women Film Pioneers Project (WFPP), xiii, 3, 4
women in East Asian cinema
  Angie Chen and Hong Kong film, 153–65
  Celebrating Women in Global Cinema and disruptive programming, 216–30
  female agency and subjectivity in Qiong Yao films, 93–104
  female gaze in Xu Jinglei's *Letter from an Unknown Woman*, 66–78
  female labour in Hong Kong cinema, 29–49
  female screenwriter-directors in the South Korean film industry, 124–37
  female stars and gender representations in *Zatoichi* franchise, 79–92
  feminist analysis of Southeast Asian women's filmmaking, 200–15
  gender representations, creative labour and global histories overview, 1–10
  Haneda Sumiko, authorship and gender perspective, 107–23

He Xiaopei's home video aesthetics and queer feminist politics, 13–28
Ning Ying, authorship and editing, 166–81
*nyonya* figure and Peranakan Chinese representation, 185–99
South Korean womanhood and millennial trauma in *Microhabitat*, 50–65
Takamine Hideko and Matsuyama Zenzō collaboration, 138–52
Women in Film Korea, 59
'Women, Organise!' exhibition, HOME, 219, 227
'women's cinema' *see* 'women's films'
women screenwriter-directors, in South Korean film industry, 7, 124–37
'women's films'
  Chinese film, 168–9
  defining, 114
  generic features, 29–30
  Haneda Sumiko, authorship and gender perspective, 107, 114, 118–21
  Hong Kong cinema, 33
  Kaplan on, 97
  Ning Ying, authorship and editing, 166, 172, 180
  Qiong Yao films and Taiwan, 94, 97, 102
  South Korea and *Microhabitat*, 60
  women's cinema and the politics of pleasure, 15–16
  women's film festivals, 119
  'women's film history', 3
Wong, Anthony (was Anthony Perry), 157
Wong Kar-wai, *The Grandmaster*, 222
Wong, Liza, 32
Wong Tim Lam, 49n
Wong Yan-kwai, Yank, 161, 163
world cinema, 1, 26, 48, 130, 213
Wroot, J., *The Paths of Zatoichi*, 91
Wu, A. X., 172

Xie Fei, 168
Xu Jinglei
  overview, 6, 66–8
  empowering death, 75–7
  female gaze and visual pleasure, 72–3
  feminist character, 73–5
  gazing and feeling(s), 69–71
  voice-over and image maker, 68–9
  *Letter from an Unknown Woman*, 66–78

*yakuza*, 81, 82, 86, 87, 88, 89
Yamagishi, Kikumi, 89
Yang, Edward, *That Day, On the Beach*, 102
Yank Wong Yan-kwai, 161
Yau, Kinnia, 5
Yecies, B. M., 52
Yeh, Emilie Yueh-yu, 198n
Yen, Donnie, 85
Yeoh, Michelle, 193, 195
Yeung, Miriam, 33
Yim Soon-rye, *Little Forest*, 125
Yip, Cecilia, 158
Yogyakarta Festival Film Dokumenter (FFD), 161
Yoshino Keiji, 108, 109, 110, 111
Young Feminist Activism, xvi
Yuan Qiongqiong, 'A place of one's own', 104n
Yuan Yuan, 13, 19, 25
Yukisada, Isao, 83
Yun Suk-yeol, 52

*Zatoichi* franchise, 79–92
  overview, 6, 79–81, 90–1
  female stars and gender representations in *Zatoichi* franchise, 79–92
  films and TV series, 79, 86–7, 90
  *Ichi* within the *Zatoichi* franchise, 81–4
  star power and gender stereotypes, 84–90
  *Ichi* (2008), 79–80, 81–4, 90
  *The Tale of Zatoichi* (1962), 86
  *Zatoichi* (1989), 90
  *Zatoichi* (Kitano 2003), 79, 81, 84, 87–9, 90
  *Zatoichi Challenged* (1967), 87
  *Zatoichi's Cane Sword* (1967), 87
  *Zatoichi: The Last* (2010), 89, 90
Zhang Nuanxin, 68, 167, 169–70
  *The Drive to Win*, 68
  *Sacrificed Youth*, 68, 169–70
Zhang Xi, 21, 22
Zhang Yang, *Shower*, 170
Zhang Yimou, 166, 167
Zhang Yuan, 167
Zhen Zhen, 100
Zhang Ziyi, 85
Zweig, Stefan, *Letter from an unknown woman*, 6, 66, 74, 75–6

EU representative:
Easy Access System Europe
Mustamäe tee 50, 10621 Tallinn, Estonia
Gpsr.requests@easproject.com

www.ingramcontent.com/pod-product-compliance
Lightning Source LLC
Chambersburg PA
CBHW070323240426
43671CB00013BA/2344